Prayers for the Future of Mankind

*Compiled by
Ivor Solomons*

WOLFE

G
11
16

To my parents, Louis and Stella Solomons
who let me happen, and this happened,
with love
To Montse, Bob, Chris and Mitch,
and to my brother and sister, Michael and Lynda
without all of whom things would have been different

First published 1975 by
Wolfe Publishing Limited
10 Earlham Street, London WC2H 9LP

© 1975 Wolfe Publishing Limited

SBN 7234 0659 6

Set by Composing Operations Limited, Tonbridge, Kent

Printed by The Garden City Press Limited
Letchworth, Hertfordshire

099663

[signature]

June 1978
Chester

*Prayers
for the Future
of Mankind*

Contents

Acknowledgements

We would like to thank:

James Clarke & Co. Ltd. for reproduction from *The Kingdom of God*, Council of Clergy and Ministers for Common Ownership (1946).

Fontana Paperbacks; London and Association Press (National Council of YMCA) New York for reproduction of *You been around a long time* from *Treat Me Cool, Lord* by Carl Burke.

The Society of Heshaim for reproduction from the *Sephardi Prayer Book*, translation by D. A. Sola.

Bahá'i Publishing Trust for reproduction from their revised *Bahá'i Prayers: a Selection* (1951).

Museum of the University of Pennsylvania for reproduction of *Sumerian Exorcism* from *Selected Sumerian and Babylonian Texts* by Henry Frederick Lutz (1919).

S.C.M. Press Ltd., London, for reproduction of *Empty Tombs* from *A Kind of Praying* by Rex Chapman. (Published in the USA by the Westminster Press, Philadelphia.)

The Christian Community Press for reproduction of *I am bending my knee* from *Sun Dances, Prayers from the Gaelic*, translated by Alexander Carmichael.

Routledge & Kegan Paul Ltd., for reproduction of the *New Year Service of the Orthodox Synagogue*.

Union of Liberal and Progressive Synagogues for reproduction from *The Gate of Repentance*.

The Fellowship of Reconciliation for reproduction from *When We Call* (1945).

7

John Murray Ltd., for reproduction of *Santideva (circa 750) Bochicarayavatara* from *The Path of Life,* translated by Lionel David Barnett (1911).

B.T. Batsford Ltd., for reproduction from *Prayers for Today,* edited by John Elphinstone-Fyffe (1958).

N.M. Tripathi Private Ltd., India, for reproduction from *Zoroastrian Credo, The Life and Teachings of Zoroaster* by Mrs. Gool K. S. Shavaksha.

The Society for Promoting Christian Knowledge for reproduction from *The Splendour of God,* 7th edition (revised), by Bishop Woods.

Methodist Publishing House for reproduction from *A Preacher's Prayer Book,* compiled by Clement Pugsley (1959).

A.R. Mowbray & Co. Ltd., for reproduction from *A Prayer Manual* by Frederick B. MacNutt (1951).

Introduction

In an age which is witnessing ever-insistent demands for unity among those of different faiths, it is appropriate that this unique collection should be made available.

It brings together, for the first time, prayers for man's future from a wide range of sources: from established religions of the East and West, from little-known faiths of all continents, and from individuals, all looking beyond their own present griefs to a future filled with hope and light.

The reader will find included in this collection some material—anecdotal, meditational, hymnal—which may at first sight not appear to be prayers at all. But those of us accustomed to the ritual of Western religions should remember that to the faithful of other continents such forms of supplication are as meaningful as the Lord's Prayer is for us.

There are prayers for oneself, as a microcosm of the whole of humanity, as well as prayers for the well-being of others, prayers for freedom and equality (two concepts even today more honoured in the breach than the observance), prayers for unity among nations and unity among religions, prayers for those who suffer, and prayers for guidance.

This unique collection of prayers can form the basis of organised religious gatherings, or can be used simply as inspirational material by the individual. Certainly it provides a valuable introduction to the beliefs and way of life of the whole of mankind, and time and again makes it clear that under the skin we are all the same.

Although the situations described in these prayers may sometimes sound outlandish, the human responses they evoke are most certainly not.

In its own small way this volume may help towards the unity of mankind, and show us how to pray with one voice for the future of all of us.

The author would like to thank those individuals and organisations who have so readily given advice and help in the difficult work of preparing this volume. It would take too much space to give all of them the individual mention they deserve, but I should like to offer my thanks to the staff of the British Library for their unfailing help.

Every effort has been made to check the copyright of the material included in the book, but if, for some reason, there has been an oversight, the publishers would be grateful if this could be brought to their attention.

1. For All People

DISPEL PRIDE OF RACE

Almighty God, Who hast created and bound together in kinship and labour all the peoples of the world; deliver us, we beseech Thee, from all false pride of race, break down and utterly destroy the dominion of the many by the few, and in truth and deed unite us to Thyself; through Jesus Christ our Lord. Amen.

The Kingdom of God: Council of Clergy and Ministers for Common Ownership (1946)

THE WAY OF FELLOWSHIP

Lord, Who hast taught us that we do not live by bread alone, and yet dost bid us pray for daily needs, restore among us, we pray Thee, the true conception of our life on earth, that in the production of Thy riches, and due use thereof, our bodies may be satisfied, the way of fellowship made sure, and our unity with Thee declared; Who with the Father and the Holy Spirit art God for ever and ever. Amen.

The Kingdom of God: Council of Clergy and Ministers for Common Ownership (1946)

DEAL KINDLY WITH US

Thou art the Lord our God
In heaven and on earth,
And in the highest heaven of heavens.
Verily thou art the first
And thou art the last
And beside thee there is no God.

11

O gather them that hope for thee from the four corners of
the earth.

Let all the inhabitants of the world perceive and know
That thou art God,
Thou alone,
Over all the kingdoms of the earth.

Thou hast made the heavens and the earth,
The sea and all that is therein;
And which among all the works of thy hands,
Whether among those above
Or among those beneath,
Can say unto thee,
What doest thou?

Our Father who art in heaven,
Deal kindly with us for the sake of thy great name
By which we are called.

*Authorized Daily Prayer Book: translation by
Rev. S. Singer, Singer's Prayer-Book Publication Committee* ©

UNIVERSAL PRAYER

Children of God, high privilege have we,
For whom, throughout the world, all fellow-saints
Exalt to heaven their prayers continually:
Not lonely kneel we, nor unpitied faints
Our heart; nor unaccompanied our low plaints
Ascend: a mighty chain of sympathy
Binds Christian men together, and acquaints
Their souls with love and thoughtful charity.
O joy! that we, who pray for all, by all
Commended are to God in daily prayer:
Yea, now, as in time past, and yet again
Through time to come, that Church which shall not fall,
From night to morn breathes forth upon the air
Meek intercession for the sons of men!

Aubrey Thomas de Vere (1814–1902)

THE GREATNESS OF GOD

What God out of His Mercy bestows on mankind there is none that can withhold: What He doth withhold, there is none can grant apart from Him: He is Exalted in Power, full of Wisdom.

The Koran

BLESS ALL THY PEOPLE

We most earnestly beseech thee, O thou lover of mankind, to bless all thy people, the flocks of thy fold. Send down into our hearts the peace of heaven, and grant us also the peace of this life. Give life to the souls of all of us, and let no deadly sin prevail against us, or any of thy people. Deliver all who are in trouble, for thou art our God, who settest the captives free; who givest hope to the hopeless and help to the helpless; who liftest up the fallen; and who art the haven of the shipwrecked. Give thy pity, pardon and refreshment to every Christian soul, whether in affliction or error. Preserve us in our pilgrimage through this life from hurt and danger, and grant that we may end our lives as Christians, well-pleasing to thee and free from sin, and that we may have our portion and lot with all thy saints: for the sake of Jesus Christ, our Lord and Saviour. Amen.

Liturgy of St. Mark

GOD'S PEOPLE

Whatever ye are given here is but a convenience of this life: But that which is with God is better and more lasting: It is for those who believe and put their trust in the Lord: Those who avoid the greater crimes and shameful deeds, and when they are angry even then forgiven; Those who hearken to their Lord, and establish regular prayer; who conduct their affairs by mutual consultation; Who spend out of what we bestow on them for sustenance; and those who, when an oppressive wrong is inflicted on them, are not cowed down but help and defend themselves.

The Koran

13

MERCY AND GRACE

O Lord Jesu Christ, Son of the Living God, we pray Thee to set Thy Passion, Cross, and Death between Thy judgement and our souls, now and in the hour of our death. Vouchsafe to grant mercy and grace to the living, rest to the dead, to Thy Holy Church peace and concord, and to us sinners everlasting life and glory, Who with the Father and the Holy Ghost livest and reignest God, world without end. Amen.

Prayers in Use at Cuddesdon College (1904)

OPEN THE DEAF EARS

O Lord Jesu Christ, the Great Shepherd of the sheep, Who seekest those that are gone astray, bindest up those that are broken, and healest those that are sick; bless, we beseech thee, the efforts which thy servants [are about to] make to convert souls unto Thee. Loosen the tongues of those who [shall] speak in Thy Name; open the deaf ears of the wanderers that they may hear the words which belong unto salvation, and grant that those whom Thou dost raise to newness of life may, through Thy grace, persevere unto the end; of Thy mercy, O our God, Who art blessed, and livest and reignest for ever and ever. Amen.

Prayers in Use at Cuddesdon College (1904)

PRAYER FOR THE LIVING AND THE DEAD

Lord, whose tender mercies are open to all, who desirest that no man should perish but that all men should be saved, and didst therefore suffer death for mankind, and hast instituted this sacrament: save us thy servants who trust in thee, my God. Remember the assembly of thy faithful, who are thine from the beginning.

Save thy people, Lord, bless thy chosen race; be their shepherd, evermore in thy arms upholding them. Help thy servants, I beseech thee, whom thou hast ransomed with thy precious Blood. Send them aid, Lord, from thy holy place and watch over them from Sion. Have mercy upon my parents, brethren, friends, and benefactors, and . . . Grant them a share in the merits of thy precious Blood shed for our redemption, so

14

that they may have grace to serve and please thee in this world, and at the end come to the glory of eternal life, there to enjoy thy presence for ever.

The Manual of Catholic Prayer

INTO UNION

O Lord, let Thy perpetual providence guide and direct the conduct of hospitals, that doctors, students, and nurses alike, together with the patients committed to their care, may be brought through contact with the mystery of suffering into union with Thee, where alone it is solved; through Jesus Christ our Lord. Amen.

Sursum Corda

FOR THE PEOPLE

O Almighty God, King of the universe, and Hope of all the world; by the might of Thine Eternal Sovereignty grant, we beseech Thee, that government of the people, by the people, for the people, may be established over all the earth; through Jesus Christ our Lord. Amen.

The Kingdom of God: Council of Clergy and Ministers for Common Ownership (1946)

CHILDREN OF AFFLICTION

O Father of all, we humbly beseech Thee to show Thy mercy to the whole world. Let the Gospel of Thy Son run and be glorified throughout the earth. Let it be known by those who as yet know it not, let it be obeyed by all who profess and call themselves Christians. Continue Thy loving kindness, O Lord, to this Nation to which we belong, and increase in us true religion . . . Endue with Thy best gifts all who minister, that they may earnestly feed Thy flock. Visit in compassion all the children of affliction, relieve their necessities, and lighten their burdens, giving them patience and submission to Thy holy will, and in due time deliver them from all their troubles. Into Thy hand we commend all Thy people everywhere. Hear us, O Lord, we humbly beseech Thee, for the sake of Christ Jesus our Lord. Amen.

L. Tuttiett (mid-19th century)

PURGED FROM ALL ERROR

O blessed Jesu, Who art the confidence of all the ends of the earth, may Thy truth and peace be spread among all people; more especially we pray for the Catholic (Universal) Church, that it may be purged from all error, and be reunited as at the beginning, in one faith and love. We humbly beseech Thee so to dispose the hearts of all kings, princes, and governors of this world, that by Thy inspiration may rule in righteousness, and labour for the well-being of the people committed to them. Prosper and bless all who are striving to do Thy will, that, having faithfully ministered before Thee, they may receive the recompense of Thy reward; Who, with the Father and Holy Ghost, livest and reignest, One God, world without end. Amen.

Thomas Thellison Carter (1808–1901)

PERPETUAL PRAISING

O Lord, unto Whom all glory and honour do appertain, replenish us with spiritual joy. Grant that all idolatry and superstition being put away, the whole world may be so enlightened with the light of Thy Holy Word, that every man may give himself up to a perpetual praising of Thy holy Name, and may give unto Thee most hearty thanks for all the benefits which we continually receive at Thy Fatherly hand; through Jesus Christ Thy Son. So be it.

Scottish Psalter (1595)

DEFEND AND COMFORT THEM

O God, almighty and merciful, let Thy Fatherly kindness be upon all whom Thou hast made. Hear the prayers of all that call upon Thee; open the eyes of them that never pray for themselves; pity the sighs of such as are in misery; deal mercifully with them that are in darkness; increase the number and graces of such as fear and serve Thee daily. Preserve this land from the misfortunes of war; this Church from all wild and dangerous errors; this people from forgetting Thee their Lord and Benefactor. Be gracious to all those countries that are made desolate by the sword, famine, pestilence, or persecution.

16

Bless all persons and places to which Thy providence has made us debtors; all who have been instrumental to our good by their assistance, advice, example, or writings, and make us in our turn useful to others. Let none of those that desire our prayers want Thy mercy, but defend and comfort and conduct them through to their life's end; for the sake of Jesus Christ our Lord. Amen.

Bishop Thomas Wilson (1663–1755)

INCREASE OUR FAITH

God the Father of our Lord Jesus Christ, increase us in faith and truth and gentleness, and grant us part and lot among His saints.

St. Polycarp (69–155)

STABILITY AND PEACE

O Lord, we pray for the universal Church, for all sections of Thy Church throughout the world, for their truth, unity, and stability, that love may abound, and truth flourish in them all. We pray for all Thy ministering servants that they may rightly divide the Word of Truth, that they may walk circumspectly; that teaching others they may themselves learn both the way and the truth. We pray for the people, that they make not themselves over-wise, but be persuaded by reason, and yield to the authority of their superiors. We pray for the Kingdoms of the World, their stability and peace; for our own Nation, Kingdom and Empire, that they may abide in prosperity and happiness, and be delivered from all peril and disaster. For the Queen, O Lord, save her; O Lord, give her prosperity, compass her with the shield of truth and glory, speak good things unto her, in behalf of Thy Church and people. Unto all men everywhere give Thy grace and Thy blessing; through Jesus Christ. Amen.

Bishop Lancelot Andrewes (1555–1626)

TO SHINE IN PIETY

O heavenly Father, we bend the knee before Thee on behalf of all Kings, Princes and Governors of this world, beseeching Thee to grant unto them by Thy inspiration, to rule in righteousness, to rejoice in peace, to shine in piety, and to labour for the well-being of the people committed unto them, so that, by the rectitude of the government, all faithful people may live without disturbance in the knowledge of Thee, and labour without hindrance to Thy glory. Amen.

Mozarabic Liturgy

LOVE FOR THE FALLEN

O Christ, our God, remember Thy strong and Thy weak ones, great and small, men and women, for good. Remember the righteous who worship Thee by faith, and bestow on them the blessing of those who not having seen, believed. Remember and bless all who worship Thee by prayer, and reveal Thy gracious Presence unto them. Remember any overthrown through frailty, raise them up and perfect Thy strength in thier weakness. Remember the bereaved in their anguish, and make their latter end better than their beginning. Furnish the fallen with love, and accept their love. Grant to sufferers faith, and reward their faith. Remember the despised, the overlooked, the misunderstood, reserving mercy for them in the day of Thy justice. Remember munificent hands to refill them, and generous hearts to spiritualize them. Remember us all, O God, for good; for the sake of Thy Holy Name. Amen.

Christina Georgina Rossetti (1830–1894)

FROM CLIME TO CLIME

O Lord, be merciful to us and bless us. As Thou hast made our Nation mighty in this world, and a ruler over other Nations, so make it a source of wisdom and truth, of order and sanctity, to all who come under its influence. Let Thy Light pass from clime to clime and enlighten us all. Let Thy Truth be our truth. Let Thy Truth be widely known upon the earth, and distant Nations glorify Thy Name. Unite us all, as Thy children, in Thy common blessing, while we celebrate Thee, the

18

Divine Creator and sole Governor, revering Thy Name and obeying Thy laws. Let the knowledge of Thy Righteousness redound to general goodwill and charity unfeigned rein in all our hearts. The Lord bless us and keep us, the Lord cause His face to shine upon us and give us His peace; through Jesus Christ our Lord. Amen.

Francis William Newman (1805–1897)

THAT OUR FRUIT MAY ABOUND

May God the Father, and the Eternal High Priest Jesus Christ, build us up in faith and truth and love, and grant to us our portion among the saints with all those who believe in our Lord Jesus Christ. We pray for all saints, for kings and rulers, for the enemies of the Cross of Christ, and for ourselves we pray that our fruit may abound and we may be made perfect in Christ Jesus our Lord. Amen.

St. Polycarp (69–155)

EVER CLOSER

O Lord God, Who by Thy Providence hast ordered various ranks among men, draw them ever closer together by Thy Holy Spirit. Teach us to know that all differences of class are done away with in Christ. Take from us and from our countrymen all jealousy and discontent. Unite us one to another by a common zeal for Thy cause, and enable us by Thy grace to offer unto Thee the manifold fruits of our service; through Jesus Christ our Lord. Amen.

Bishop Brooke Foss Westcott (1825–1901)

HEAL THE DIVISIONS

O Lord, to Thy merciful providence we commend the wants of all mankind. Cause the light of Thy glorious Gospel to shine throughout the world. Bless Thy whole Church, heal the divisions of it, and grant to it the blessings of truth, unity, and peace. Bless our country, defend our Queen and all in authority; give faith and diligence to the clergy; hear the cry of the poor and needy: bless the members, absent and present, of this household, be gracious to all our relations and friends, and

19

grant, O Lord, that we may all, at length, find rest and peace with Thy saints in Thine eternal kingdom; through Jesus Christ our Lord. Amen.

William Edward Scudamore (1813–1881)

THY HAND UPON THEM

Look in mercy and loving-kindness upon all our families and friends, and all who have been kind to us, all who have asked for our prayers, and all for whom we ought to pray. Let Thy Holy Spirit ever be with them to keep them from all evil, and to guide them to all that is good for their souls and bodies. Look down, most merciful Lord, on all or any who may have done us wrong or spoken evil against us. Turn their hearts, and have mercy upon them and us.

Have mercy, O Lord God, upon all who are in trouble or misery, either of mind or body. Let Thy grace and mercy be upon them to keep them from falling from Thee. Look with pity, O Lord, upon all who are sick or in pain. Teach them to feel Thy hand upon them and to turn to Thee. Restore them to health, when it shall please Thee and be best for them; for the sake of Jesus Christ, Who suffered for all. Amen.

The Narrow Way (1869)

THY TRUE RELIGION

Let Thy mercy, O God, extend to the whole race of mankind. Bring all nations to the knowledge and belief of Thy true religion; and to those who profess it already, give Thy heavenly grace, that they may strive to adorn their holy profession, by a suitable life and confession. Be merciful and gracious to this our beloved land, endue all orders and degrees of men amongst us, and especially our governors, in Church and State, with those graces and virtues which may enable them to discharge their several trusts, in such a manner as will be most for Thine honour and glory, and for the peace and prosperity of this land and nation; through Jesus Christ our Lord, Who liveth with Thee, and the Holy Spirit, ever one God, world without end. Amen.

Fitz-Henry Hele (19th century)

20

THE BROTHERHOOD OF MEN

Almighty God, the Father of mankind, Who hast commanded us to make intercession for all men, hear us while we pray, we beseech Thee. Bless the whole family of mankind from one end of the earth to the other, and give light to those who sit in darkness and in the shadow of death. Bless our Queen and all the members of the Royal Family, and rule their hearts in Thy faith, fear, and love. Bless all classes of our people that the brotherhood of men, which Thy Son came to establish, may exist among us. Purify and exalt the domestic life of our people and deepen their sense of the worth and sacredness of home. We beseech Thee, O Lord our God, to hear us on behalf of all men everywhere; for we ask all in the Name of Jesus Christ our Lord. Amen.

John Hunter (19th century)

THY HOLY ARM

O Lord, make bare Thy Holy Arm in the eyes of all the nations, that all the ends of the world may see Thy salvation; show forth Thy righteousness openly in the sight of the heathen, that the Kingdom of Thy Christ may be established over all mankind; hasten the coming of the end when He shall deliver up the Kingdom unto Thee, and having put down all rule, and authority, and power, and put all things under His feet, He Himself shall be subject unto Thee, and with Thee in the Unity of the Holy Ghost, Three persons in one God, shall be our All in All for ever and ever. Amen.

Isaiah 52:10; Psalms 98:1; 1 Corinthians 15
(8th century B.C.–1st century A.D., adapted)

SUCCOUR THE POOR AND NEEDY

O God, the God of the spirits of all flesh, we humbly beseech Thee to accept our intercessions on behalf of all men. We pray for Thy universal Church, that it may be guided by Thy Holy Spirit in the way of truth and peace. O Lord, save our Queen. Bless Thy servants the clergy and ministers, and grant that they may shine as lights in the world, and adorn the doctrine of God our Saviour in all things. We commend, O Lord, to Thy

21

Fatherly goodness, our relations, friends, and neighbours, and all who desire, or ought to be specially remembered in our prayers. Succour the poor and needy, bind up the broken-hearted, have mercy on the sick and dying, and help us, by Thy Grace, to live nearer to Thee day by day; through Jesus Christ our Lord. Amen.

H. Stobart (19th century)

OUR RELATIONS AND FRIENDS

Bless, O Lord, we beseech Thee, all our relations and friends. Have mercy on all who are sick, comfort all who are in pain, anxiety or sorrow. Awake all who are careless about eternal things. Bless the children, and keep them in innocency of life. Bless all who are young and in health, that they may give the days of their strength to Thee. Comfort the aged and infirm, that Thy peace may rest upon them. Bless this our family and household, that we may all seek to help and not to hinder one another in the fear and love of Thy Holy Name; through Jesus Christ our Lord. Amen.

A. F. Thornhill (19th century)

MERCY ON ALL MEN

O God, we pray Thee to have mercy upon all men. Bless Thy holy Church throughout the world. Bless that portion of it to which we belong. Bless all Thy ministering servants. Bless, we beseech Thee, our King and all in authority under him. We pray also for our own relations, all the absent members of our respective families, our friends and benefactors. We beseech Thee to hear us on behalf of the poor, the sick, and the distressed; to each and all, grant, O Lord, that which Thou knowest to be best; through Jesus Christ our Lord. Amen.

H. Stobart (19th century)

THAT WHICH IS BEST

Have mercy, we beseech Thee, O Lord, on all mankind. Make Thy way known upon the earth, Thy saving health among all nations. Bring into Thy fold Thine ancient people Israel. Bless, guide, and govern by Thy Spirit Thy whole

Church, heal its divisions, cleanse it from all corruptions, and make it fruitful unto all good works. Have mercy on the people of this land, and pour forth largely Thy blessing on all the colonies and dependencies of it. Bless our King and Government, the Parliament of our Nation, and the Councils of our Church, and grant that all laws made by them may work for righteousness and peace. Bless this place in which we live with a spirit of charity and godliness. Bless our own household and all its absent members. Bless all who are near and dear to us wheresoever they are. Bless the poor and afflicted, the sorrowing and perplexed. To each and all of us grant that which Thou knowest to be best; through Jesus Christ our Lord. Amen.

Anon.

SPREAD THY KINGDOM

O Lord, our most gracious redeemer and king, dwell and reign within us, take possession of us by thy Spirit, and reign where thou hast the right to reign, and spread thy kingdom throughout all the world; through Jesus Christ our Lord.

Father John of the Russian Church (1829–1909)

THE HEARTS OF ALL MEN

O heavenly Father, send into our hearts and into the hearts of all men everywhere the spirit of our Lord Jesus Christ.

John Oxenham (1829–1888)

FORWARD IN TRANQUILLITY

Almighty God, from whom all thoughts of truth and peace proceed; kindle, we pray thee, in the hearts of all men the true love of peace; and guide with thy pure and peaceable wisdom those who take counsel for the nations of the earth; that in tranquillity thy Kingdom may go forward, till the earth be filled with the knowledge of thy love: through Jesus Christ our Lord. Amen.

Bishop Francis Paget (1851–1911)

THE BOND OF PEACE

O God, the Creator and Preserver of all mankind, we humbly beseech thee for all sorts and conditions of men; that thou wouldst be pleased to make thy ways known unto them, thy saving health unto all nations. More especially we pray for the good estate of the Catholick Church; that it may be so guided and governed by thy good spirit, that all who profess and call themselves Christians may be led into the way of truth, and hold the faith in unity of spirit, in the bond of peace, and in righteousness of life. Finally, we commend to thy fatherly goodness all those, who are in any way afflicted or distressed, in mind, body, or estate; that it may please thee to comfort and relieve them, according to their several necessities, giving them patience under their sufferings, and a happy issue out of all their afflictions. And this we beg for Jesus Christ his sake. Amen.

Bishop Peter Gunning (1614–1684)

WELL-PLEASING IN THY SIGHT

O strong Lord God, Who wilt judge all mankind, grant to the exalted humility, to the desolate thankfulness, to the happy sympathy with sorrow; that so earthly eminence may become a stepping-stone to heavenly heights, and loneliness may introduce to the full communion of saints, and joy blossoming in time may bear eternal fruit. Be we high or low, prosperous or depressed, wheresoever, whatsoever we may be, make us and ever more keep us well-pleasing in Thy sight; through Jesus Christ our Lord.

Christina Georgina Rossetti (1830–1894)

SAVE THY PEOPLE

O Lord, Who blessest them that bless Thee and hallowest them that put their trust in Thee, save Thy people and bless Thine inheritance; guard the fullness of Thy Church; hallow them that love the beauty of Thine house; lift them up in glory and reward them by Thy divine power and forsake us not whose hope is in Thee. Give Thy peace to Thy world, to Thy Churches, to priests, to the forces, and to all Thy people; for

24

every good gift and every perfect gift is from above and cometh down from Thee, the Father of lights: and to Thee do we give glory, thanksgiving, and worship, father, son, and Holy Spirit, now and for ever and ever.

Liturgy of St. Chrysostom (345–407)

PRAISE THEE MORE FERVENTLY

Glory be to Thee, O Jesus, my Lord and my God, for thus feeding my soul with Thy most blessed Body and Blood. O let Thy heavenly food transfuse new life and new vigour into my soul, and into the souls of all that communicate with me, that our faith may increase; that we may all grow more humble and contrite for our sins, that we may all love Thee, and serve Thee, and delight in Thee, and praise Thee more fervently, more incessantly, than ever we have done heretofore.

Bishop Thomas Ken (1637–1711)

THE TRUE BREAD

O Lord Jesus Christ, Who hast taught us that man does not live by bread alone; feed us, we humbly beseech Thee, with the true bread that cometh down from heaven, even Thyself, O Blessed Saviour; Who livest and reignest, with the Father and the Holy Spirit, one God, world without end.

Bishop John Dowden (1840–1910)

CONTRITION AND MEEKNESS

We confess unto Thee, O heavenly Father, as Thy children and Thy people, our hardness, and indifference, and impenitence; our grievous failures in Thy faith and in pure and holy living; our trust in riches, and our misuse of them, our confidence in self, whereby we daily multiply our own temptations. We confess our timorousness as Thy Church and witness before the world, and the sin and bitterness that every man knoweth in his heart. Give us all contrition and meekness of heart, O Father; grace to amend our sinful life, and the holy comfort of Thy Spirit to overcome and heal all our evils; through Jesus Christ our Lord.

Archbishop Edward White Benson (1816–1897)

25

EMBRACE OUR FRIENDS IN THEE

O God, Who of Thy great love to man didst reconcile earth to heaven through Thine only begotten Son: grant that we who by the darkness of our sins are turned aside from brotherly love, may be filled with His Spirit shed abroad within us, and embrace our friends in Thee and our enemies for Thy sake; through Jesus Christ our Lord.

Mozarabic Liturgy

BLESS ALL THY SERVANTS

O God, Who didst manifest Thy only begotten Son to the Gentiles, and hast commanded Thy Church to preach the Gospel to every creature, bless all Thy servants who are labouring for Thee in distant lands. Have compassion upon the heathen and upon all who know Thee not. Lead them by Thy Holy Spirit to Him Who is the Light of the World, that walking in the light they may at length attain to the light of everlasting life; through Jesus Christ our Lord. Amen.

Robert Nelson (1656–1715)

IN QUIET FREEDOM

Mercifully receive, O Lord, the prayers of Thy people, that all adversities and errors may be destroyed, and they may serve Thee in quiet freedom, and give Thy peace in our times; through Jesus Christ our Lord. Amen.

Leonine Sacramentary

THE LIGHT OF TRUTH

Thou Maker of mankind,
From whom our spirits came,
Illuminate each darken'd mind,
With more than reason's flame.

O that the light of truth
May enter ev'ry heart!
Bestow thy blessing on our youth,
To them thy grace impart.

So will they choose the way
Thy servants recommend;
Nor from the paths of virtue stray,
Till mortal life shall end.

What might a Nation be,
Instructed by thy laws!
How useful would each subject be!
How serve his country's cause!

God of our fathers! guide
Our youth in wisdom's ways;
Thus may they in thy love abide,
And prosper all their days!

Hymns Original and Select: John Bulmer (1835)

CHILDREN OF THE LIGHT

O Lord our God, Who hast bidden the light to shine out of darkness, Who hast again awakened us to praise Thy goodness and ask for Thy grace: accept now, in Thy endless mercy, the sacrifice of our worship and thanksgiving, and grant unto us all such requests as may be wholesome for us. Make us to be children of the light and of the day, and heirs to Thy everlasting inheritance. Remember, O Lord, according to the multitude of Thy mercies, Thy whole Church: all who join with us in prayer; all our brethren by land or sea, or wherever they may be in Thy vast Kingdom, who stand in need of Thy grace and succour. Pour out upon them the riches of Thy mercy, so that we, redeemed in soul and body, and steadfast in faith, may ever praise Thy wonderful and holy name. Amen.

Eastern Church

FOR THE SICK AND WEARY

Watch Thou, dear Lord, with those who wake, or watch, or weep tonight, and give Thine angels charge over those who sleep.

Tend Thy sick ones, O Lord Christ; rest Thy weary ones; bless Thy dying ones; soothe Thy suffering ones; shield Thy joyous ones; and all for Thy Love's sake.

St. Augustine (354–430)

27

TEN THOUSAND TONGUES

O when shall men, with joyful voice,
    In ev'ry land thy name adore,
    In thy salvation, Lord, rejoice,
And spread thy praise from shore to shore?

Let nations bow before thy throne,
    With holy fear, and sacred joy;
    Since thou art God, and thou alone,
Whose praise should all the earth employ.

Thy gracious pow'r, without our aid,
    Made us of clay, and form'd us men;
And when, like wand'ring sheep we stray'd,
    Didst bring us to thy fold again.

We are thy people, we are thy care,
    Our souls and all our mortal frame:
    What lasting honours shall we rear,
    Almighty Maker, to thy name?

Within thy house, with cheerful songs,
    To Thee our thankful songs we raise:
Let earth, with her ten thousand tongues,
    Confess thy works, and sing thy ways.

Hymns Original and Select: John Bulmer (1835)

A PRAYER FOR ALL CONDITIONS OF MEN

O God, the Creator and Preserver of all mankind, we humbly beseech thee for all sorts and conditions of men; that thou wouldest be pleased to make thy ways known to them, thy saving health to all nations. More especially, we pray for the good estate of the Catholic Church; that it may be so guided and governed by thy good Spirit, that all who profess and call themselves Christians may be led into the way of truth, and hold the faith in unity of spirit, in the bond of peace, and in righteousness of life. Finally, we commend to thy fatherly goodness all those who are in any way afflicted or distressed in mind, body, or estate; that it may please thee to comfort and relieve them, according to their several necessities, giving them patience under their sufferings, and a happy issue out of all their afflictions. And this we beg for Jesus Christ his sake. Amen.

Horae Sacrae: Introduction by John Chandler (1854)

CHRIST IS IN ALL

You have put on the new nature,
which is being renewed in knowledge
after the image of its creator.
Here there cannot be Greek and Jew,
circumcised and uncircumcised,
barbarian, Scythian, slave, free man,
but Christ is all, and in all.
Put on then, as God's chosen ones,
holy and beloved,
compassion, kindness, lowliness,
meekness, and patience.

Colossians 3:10–12 (RSV)

WORTHY OF FREEDOM

God of all nations,
We pray thee for all the people of thy earth;
for those who are consumed in mutual hatred and bitterness;
for those who make war upon their neighbours;
for those who tyrannously oppress;
for those who groan under cruelty and subjection.
We beseech thee to teach mankind to live together in peace:
no man exploiting the weak,
no man hating the strong,
each race working out its own destiny, unfettered, self-respecting, fearless.
Teach us to be worthy of freedom,
free from social wrong,
free from individual oppression and contempt,
pure of heart and hand,
despising none, defrauding none,
giving to all men—in all dealings of life—
the honour we owe to those who are thy children,

29

whatever their colour, their race or their caste.
And now may the blessing of the Lord
rest and remain upon all his people
in every land, of every tongue. Amen.

Prayers for Use in an Indian College:
John S. Hoyland (1830–1894)

BROUGHT TO WORSHIP THEE

O God of all the nations of the earth, remember the multitudes of the heathens, who, though created in Thine image, have not known Thee, nor the dying of Thy Son their Saviour Jesus Christ; and grant that by the prayers of Thy Holy Church they may be brought from all ignorance and unbelief, and brought to worship Thee; through Him whom Thou hast sent to be the Resurrection and the Life of all men, the same Thy Son Jesus Christ our Lord.

St. Francis Xavier (1506–1552)

CLOSE TO THEE

Most High God, our loving Father, we humbly beseech Thee for all those near and dear to us, those for whom we are bound to pray, and those for whom no one prays. Grant them pardon for their sins, perfect their work, grant them their hearts' desires, and keep them close to Thee.

Anon.

FROM SHORE TO SHORE

God bless our native land: may thy protecting hand still guard our shore. May peace her power extend, foe be transformed to friend, and Britain's rights depend on war no more.

Nor on this land alone: but be God's mercies known from shore to shore! And may the nations see that men should brothers be, and form one family the wide world o'er.

W. E. Hickson (1803–1870)

BOND OF PERFECTNESS

O God, Father of the forsaken, the help of the weak, the supplier of the needy; who teachest us that love towards the race of man is the bond of perfectness, and the imitation of Thy blessed Self; open and touch our hearts, that we may see and do, both for this world and that which is to come, the things which belong to our peace.

Anthony Ashley Cooper, 7th Earl of Shaftesbury (1801–1885)

JOY IN EACH OTHER

O God, our heavenly Father, who hast commanded us to love one another as Thy children, and has ordained the highest friendship in the bond of Thy Spirit, we beseech Thee to maintain and preserve us always in the same bond, to Thy glory, and our mutual comfort, with all those to whom we are bound by any special tie, either of nature or of choice; that we may be perfected together in that love which is from above, and which never faileth when all other things shall fail.

Send down the dew of Thy heavenly grace upon us, that we may have joy in each other that passeth not away; and having lived together in love here, according to Thy commandment, may live for ever together with them, being made one in Thee, in Thy glorious kingdom hereafter, through Jesus Christ, our Lord.

George Hickes (1642–1715)

SPIRIT OF LOVE

Pour on us, O Lord, the spirit of love and brotherly-kindness; so that, sprinkled by the dew of Thy benediction, we may be made glad by Thy glory and grace; through Christ our Lord.

Sarum Breviary

SECURITY IN PERFECT LOVE

Eternal God, in whose perfect kingdom no sword is drawn but the sword of righteousness, and no strength known but the strength of love; so guide and inspire, we pray thee, the work of

31

all who seek thy kingdom at home and abroad, that all peoples may seek and find their security, not in force of arms but in the perfect love that casteth out fear and in the fellowship revealed to us by Jesus Christ our Lord.

Anon.

FULL OF BOUNTY

Praise be to God and peace, and peace be on his servants. Lo, the Lord is full of bounty for mankind. Therefore put thy trust in God.

The Koran 27

HELP ONE ANOTHER

God, Ruler of all, may we be all one in co-operation with righteous men throughout the whole world. May we be one with them and may they be one with us. May we all benefit one another and help one another.

Zoroastrian Scriptures

FAMILY OF GOD

All thy creatures, O God, form Thy family, and he is the best loved of Thee who loveth best Thy creatures. O Lord, Lord of my life and of everything in the universe, I affirm that all human beings are brothers unto one another, so may we respect Thy ways and be affectionate to the Family of God.

Muslim

SAVE US FROM INDIFFERENCE

Teach us, O Holy Spirit, to offer the fellowship of the Church of Christ to the world. Save us from indifference to the way in which others are forced to live, and enable us to seek better conditions for the housing and home life of the community. Let us never deny our neighbours what we enjoy ourselves; so may we seek for all, in education, complete development of personality in love and truth and equipment for life. Help us to do our part to end economic injustice and poverty, and to secure a wider diffusion of the fruits of industry. Show us how to make money the servant, not the master, of communal life. Let us strive to secure adequate leisure for others with the facility and knowledge to use it wisely. Give us grace so to live before men, that by word and example we shall do much to eradicate the evil of drink and gambling and impurity from the world. Give us courage to denounce the commercial exploitation of human weakness. Enable us to work peace in all relations of people, social and international; through Jesus Christ our Lord. Amen.

From: The Proclamation of the Order of Christian Citizenship: A Preacher's Prayer Book

ENLIGHTEN OUR MINDS

O God of love and power,
Creator of all things and all men:
We see Thy handiwork revealed
in the vast dome of heaven,
And in the tiny atom;
We learn the secrets of Thy power—
But are ignorant of Thy love.
Enlighten the minds of men:
That in wisdom, love, and courage
We may use Thy gifts of power
To Thy glory
And the good of all mankind;
Through Jesus Christ our Lord. Amen.

Norman J. Bull: A Preacher's Prayer Book

THE DARKENED SOULS

O Thou God of infinite mercy and compassion, in whose hands are the hearts of the sons of men, look, we beseech Thee, graciously upon the darkened souls of the multitude that know not Thee. Enlighten them with the saving knowledge of the truth. Let the beams of Thy Gospel break forth upon them, and bring them to a sound belief in Thee, God manifest in the flesh. Bring in the fulness of the Gentiles; gather together the outcasts of Israel, and make Thy Name known over all the earth. Grant this, through Jesus Christ. Amen.

Bishop Joseph Hall (1574–1656)

LIVE AT PEACE

O Father, who hast declared thy love to men
by the birth of the Holy Child at Bethlehem:
Help us to welcome him with gladness
and to make room for him in our common days;
so that we may live at peace with one another
and in goodwill with all thy family.

Anon.

HOME TO THY FLOCK

O merciful God, who hast made all men, and hatest nothing
that thou hast made, nor wouldest will the death of a sinner,
but rather that he should be converted and live: Have mercy
upon all (who know thee not)* and take from them all
ignorance, hardness of heart, and contempt of thy Word; and
so fetch them home, blessed Lord, to thy flock, that they may
be saved among the remnant of the true Israelites, and be made
one fold under one shepherd, Jesus Christ, our Lord, who
liveth and reigneth with thee and the Holy Spirit, one God,
world without end.

English Reformers

*Jews, Turks, infidels and heretics.

THE HOPE OF THE WORLDS

Thou art the eternal One, in whom all order is centred; Lord
of all things visible and invisible; Prince of mankind; Protector
of the universe!
From thee doth intellect descend upon the rulers of the
earth!
Thou dost embrace all things!
Thou art the Infinite and Incomprehensible, who standest
alone, ruler of the eternal fountains of light!
The ordainer of all good things!
Who givest inspiration and guidance unto all!
From thee cometh light!
Merciful One, exalted above all defects, descend into our
intellects, and purge us of every ill!
Turn our sorrow into joy!

To thee do we cling!
From thee all things seek their light!
Thou art the hope of the worlds!
Thou art the helper of mankind, one and all!

Saboean Litany: attributed to Enoch

A HOUSE FOR ALL

Thus saith the Lord of the strangers that join themselves to the Lord, to minister unto him, and to love the name of the Lord, to be his servants: Them will I bring to my Holy Mountain, and make them joyful in my house of prayer: their offering shall be accepted upon mine altar: for mine house shall be called an House of Prayer for all Peoples.

Isaiah: 56:6, 7

MAY ALL BE SAVED

As the first martyr prayed to Thee for his murderers, O Lord, so we fall before Thee and pray; forgive all who hate and maltreat us and let not one of them perish because of us, but may all be saved by Thy grace, O God the all-bountiful.

Eastern Church

INTERCESSION

Intercession is the best arbitrator of all differences, the best promoter of true friendship, the best cure and preservative against all unkind tempers, all angry and haughty passions.

William Law (1686–1761)

HEIRS OF PEACE

O God, Who art the unsearchable abyss of peace, the ineffable sea of love, the fountain of blessings who sendest peace to those that receive it; open to us this day, the sea of Thy love, and water us with the plenteous streams from the riches of Thy grace, and from the deep springs of Thy loving kindness. Make us children of quietness, and heirs of peace. Enkindle in us the fire of Thy love; sow in us Thy fear; strengthen our weakness by Thy power; bind us closely to Thee and to each other in one firm and indissoluble bond of unity. Amen.

Syrian Clementine Liturgy

MAKE THYSELF KNOWN

Look upon the face of Thy children, and in the abundance of Thy compassion, find a propitiation for the sins of the world, and by the tender mercies of Him Who is from everlasting, and by the strong crying of mankind out of perplexity, make Thyself known to us as our Saviour. Amen.

Rowland Williams (1817–1870)

THE DESIRE OF ALL NATIONS SHALL COME

Come, Thou long-expected Jesus,
Born to set Thy people free,
From our fears and sins release us,
Let us find our rest in Thee.
Israel's strength and Consolation,
Hope of all the earth Thou art,
Dear desire of every nation,
Joy of every longing heart.

Born Thy people to deliver,
Born a Child, and yet a King,
Born to reign in us for ever,
Now Thy gracious kingdom bring.
By Thine own Eternal Spirit
Rule in all our hearts alone;
By Thine all sufficient merit
Raise us to Thy glorious Throne.

Hymns of the Church of God: selected by F. V. Mather (1866)

FRIENDS OF ALL

One more a new day lies before us, our Father. As we go out among men to do our work, touching the hands and lives of our fellows, make us, we pray Thee, friends of all the world. Save us from blighting the fresh flower of any heart by the flare of sudden anger or secret hate. May we not bruise the rightful self-respect of any by contempt or malice. Help us to cheer the suffering of our sympathy, to freshen the drooping of our hopefulness, and to strengthen in all the wholesome sense of worth and the joy of life. Save us from the deadly poison of class-pride. Grant that we may look all men in the face with the eyes of a brother. If any one needs us, make us ready to yield our help ungrudgingly, unless higher duties claim us, and may we rejoice that we have it in us to be helpful to our fellow-men.

Prayers of the Social Awakening:
Walter Rauschenbusch (1861–1918)

THE WORD

It sounds along the ages,
Soul answering to soul;
It kindles on the pages
Of every Bible scroll;
The psalmists heard and sang it,
From martyr-lips it broke,
And prophet tongues outrang it
Till sleeping nations woke.

From Sinai's cliffs it echoed,
It breathed from Buddha's tree,
It charmed in Athens' market,
It gladdened Galilee;
The hammer-stroke of Luther,
The pilgrim's sea-side prayer,
The oracles of Concord,
One holy Word declare.

It dates each new ideal,
Itself it knows not time;
Man's laws but catch the music
Of its eternal chime.
It calls—and lo, new justice!
It speaks—and lo, new truth!
In ever nobler stature
And unexhausted youth.

W. C. Gannett

37

MAKE US WHOLE

Come, Holy Spirit, God and Lord!
Be all thy graces now outpoured
On the believer's mind and soul,
To strengthen, save, and make us whole.
Lord, by the brightness of Thy light,
Thou in the faith dost men unite
Of every land and every tongue:
This to Thy praise, O Lord, be sung.
Alleluia! Alleluia!

Thou strong Defence, Thou Holy Light,
Teach us to know our God aright,
And call Him Father from the heart;
The Word of life and truth impart,
That we may love not doctrines strange,
Nor e'er to other teachers range,
But Jesus for our Master own.
And put our trust in Him alone.
Alleluia! Alleluia!

Thou sacred Ardor, Comfort sweet,
Help us to wait with ready feet
And willing heart at Thy command,
Nor trial fright us from Thy band.
Lord, make us ready with Thy powers:
Strengthen the flesh in weaker hours,
That as good warriors we may force
Through life and death to Thee our course!
Alleluia! Alleluia!

Martin Luther (1483–1546)

PROTECT THY CHURCH

Almighty God, eternal Father of our Lord Jesus Christ, Maker and Sustainer of all things, have mercy upon us, for the sake of thy Son Jesus Christ. We beseech Thee to purify, guide and strengthen us with thy Holy Spirit. Protect and defend thy church and the governments which shelter it.

We give thanks to thee, almighty God, for revealing thyself to us, for sending thy Son Jesus Christ, that he might become a

38

sacrifice, that through him we might be forgiven and receive eternal life. We give thanks to thee, O God, for making us a recipient of thy great favour through the gospel and the sacraments, and for preserving thy Word and thy holy church. O that we might truly declare thy goodness and blessings! Inflame us, we earnestly beseech thee, with thy Holy Spirit, that thanksgiving may shine forth in our lives.

Unto thee, O Jesus Christ, Son of God, who conquered death, to thee we offer thanks for thy intercession with the eternal Father for all mankind. Enlighten our hearts, we beseech thee, that we may be more fully aware of thy favour towards us and forever worship thee with true thanksgiving. Amen.

Melanchthon, Philipp (1497–1560)

HOPE, FAITH AND LOVE

Three living lessons I would write—
Three words as with a burning pen,
In traces of eternal light
Upon the hearts of men.

Have Hope. Though clouds environ now
And Gladness hides her face in scorn,
Put thou the shadow from thy brow—
No night but hath its morn.

Have Faith. Where'er the bark is driven—
The calm's disport, the tempest's mirth—
Know this—God rules the host of Heaven.
The inhabitants of earth.

Have Love. Not love for one alone,
But man as man thy brother call,
And scatter like the circling sun
Thy charities on all.

Thus 'grave these lessons on thy soul
Faith, Hope, and Love—and thou shalt find
Strength when life's surges rudest roll,
Light when thou else were blind.

Johann Christoph Friedrich von Schiller (1759–1805)

THE CHURCH UNIVERSAL

One holy Church of God appears
Through every age and race,
Unwasted by the lapse of years,
Unchanged by changing place.

From oldest time, on farthest shores,
Beneath the pine or palm,
One Unseen Presence she adores,
With silence or with psalm.

Her priests are all God's faithful sons
To serve the world raised up;
The pure in heart her baptized ones,
Love her communion cup.

The Truth is her prophetic gift,
The soul her sacred page,
And feet on mercy's errand swift
Do make her pilgrimage.

O living Church, thine errand speed;
Fulfil thy task sublime;
With bread of life earth's hunger feed;
Redeem the evil time!

Samuel Wadsworth Longfellow (1807–1892)

PRAYER FOR ALL MANKIND

O God, almighty and merciful, let Thy fatherly kindness be upon all that Thou hast made.

Have mercy upon all Jews, Turks, Infidels, and Heretics; and grant that none may deprive themselves of that happiness which Jesus Christ has purchased by His death.

Bless the pious endeavours of all those that strive to propagate the gospel of Christ; and may its saving truths be received in all the world.

Preserve the Church in the midst of the dangers that surround it; purge it from all corruptions, and heal its divisions, that all Christian people may unite and love as becomes the disciples of Christ.

Grant that all bishops and pastors may be careful to observe

40

the sacred rights committed to their trust:—

That godly discipline may be restored and countenanced;

That Christians may not content themselves with bare shadows of religion and piety; but endeavour after that holiness without which no man can see the Lord;

That such as are in authority may govern with truth and justice; and that those whose duty it is to obey, may do so for conscience' sake.

Let all that sincerely seek the truth, be led into it by Thy Holy Spirit; and to all such as are destitute of necessary instruction, vouchsafe a greater measure of Thy grace.

Support and comfort all that labour under trials and afflictions, all that suffer wrongfully; and by Thy mighty grace succour all those that are tempted.

Give unto all sinners a true sense of their unhappy state, and grace and strength to break their bonds.

Visit, with Thy fatherly comforts, all such as are now in their last sickness, that they may omit nothing that is necessary to make their peace with Thee.

Be gracious to all those countries that are made desolate by the sword, famine, pestilence or persecution.

And sanctify the miseries of this life, to the everlasting benefit of all those that suffer. Preserve this land from the miseries of war; this Church from persecution, and from all wild and dangerous errors; and this people from forgetting Thee, their Lord and Benefactor.

Avert the judgments which we have justly deserved; and mercifully prevent the ruin that threatens us; and grant that we may be ever prepared for what Thy providence shall bring forth.

Bless all persons and places to which Thy providence has made me a debtor; all who have been instrumental to my good, by their assistance, advice, example, or writings; and make me in my turn useful to others.

Let none of those who cannot pray for themselves, and desire my prayers, want Thy mercy; but defend, and comfort, and defend them through this dangerous world, that we may meet in paradise, to praise our God for ever and ever. Amen.

Enlighten the minds, and pardon the sin, of all that err through simplicity.

41

Let the wickedness of the wicked come to an end, but guide Thou the just.

Relieve and comfort all that are troubled in mind or conscience; all that are in danger of falling into despair; all that are in prison, in slavery, or under persecution for a righteous cause; all that are in any distress whatever, that all may improve under their sufferings.

Have mercy upon and reclaim all that are engaged in sinful courses, in youthful lusts, in unchristian quarrels, and in unrighteous lawsuits.

Direct all that are in doubt, all that seek the truth.

O God, the Creator and Redeemer of all, have mercy upon all, have mercy upon all whom Thou hast made and redeemed. Amen.

Sacra Privata: Bishop T. Wilson (1663–1755)

MERCY TO INFIDELS AND BELIEVERS

(For the whole state of Christ's church upon earth, proper to be said at the times of *Jubilees* or other indulgences.)

O Eternal Father of our Lord Jesus Christ, Creator of all things, visible and invisible, Source of all our good; infinitely good in thyself, and infinitely gracious, bountiful and good to us: Behold we thy poor servants, the work of thy hands, redeemed by the blood of thy only Son, come, in answer to his summons by his Viceregent, to present ourselves, as humble petitioners, before the throne of thy mercy: we come all in a body, at this time, even all thy people upon earth: and we come in communion with all thy church in heaven, hoping to be assisted by their prayers and merits; and with Jesus Christ at our head, our High Priest and Mediator, in whose precious blood we put all our trust. We prostrate ourselves here before thee, and we most humbly beseech thee to sanctify thy most holy name, by sanctifying and exalting thy holy catholic church throughout the whole world. O eternal king, who hast sent thy only Son down from thy throne above, into this earth of ours, to establish a kingdom, here amongst us, from whence we might hereafter be translated to thy eternal kingdom; look down we beseech thee, upon this kingdom of thy Son, and propagate it among all nations, and through all hearts.

Sanctify it in all truth; maintain it in peace, unity, and holiness. Give to it Saints for its rulers, its chief pastor, and all its other prelates. Enlighten them all with heavenly wisdom, and make them all men according to thy own heart. Give thy grace and blessing to all the Clergy; and send amongst them that heavenly fire, which thy Son came to cast on the earth, and which he so earnestly desired should be enkindled. Assist and protect all apostolic missionaries, that they may zealously and effectually promote thy glory, and the salvations of souls redeemed by the blood of thy Son. Sanctify all religious men and women of all orders: give them the grace to serve thee with all perfection, according to the spirit of their institute, and to shine like lights to the rest of the faithful. Have mercy on all Christian princes; grant them those lights and graces that are necessary for the perfect discharge of their duty to thee and to their subjects; that they may be true servants to thee the King of Kings, true fathers to their people; and nursing fathers to thy church. Have mercy on all magistrates and men in power; that they may all fear thee, love thee, and serve thee; and ever remember that they are thy deputies, and ministers of thy justice. Have mercy on thy people throughout the world; and give thy blessing to thy inheritance; remember thy congregation, which thou hast possessed from the beginning; and give that grace to all thy children here upon earth, that they may do thy holy will in all things, even as the blessed do in heaven.

Extend thy mercy also to all poor infidels, that sit in darkness and in the shadow of death: to all those nations that know not thee, and that have not yet received the faith and law of thy Son their Saviour: to all Pagans, Mahometans; and Jews. Remember O Lord, that all these poor souls are made after thy own image and likeness, and redeemed by the blood of thy Son: O let not satan any longer exercise his tyranny over these thy creatures, to the great dishonour of thy name. Let not the precious blood of thy Son be shed for them in vain. Send among them zealous preachers and apostolic labourers, endued with the like graces and gifts as thy apostles were, and bless them with the like success, for the glory of thy name: that all these poor souls may be brought to know thee, love thee, and serve thee here in thy church, and bless thee hereafter for all eternity.

Look down also with an eye of pity and compassion on all those deluded souls, who, under the name of Christians, have gone away from the paths of truth and unity, and from the one fold of the one shepherd, thy only Son Jesus Christ, into the by-paths of error and schism. O bring them back to thee and thy church. Dispel their darkness by thy heavenly light, take off the veil from before their eyes, with which the common enemy has blindfolded them: let them see how they have been misled by misapprehensions and misrepresentations. Remove the prejudices of their education: take away from them the spirit of obstinacy, pride, and self-conceit. Give them an humble and docile heart. Give them a strong desire of finding out thy truth, and a strong grace to enable them to embrace it, in spite of all the opposition of the world, the flesh, and the devil. For why should these poor souls perish, for which Christ died? Why should satan any longer possess these souls, which by their baptism were dedicated to thee, to be thy eternal temple?

O Father of lights, and God of all truth, purge the whole world from all errors, abuses, corruptions and vices. Beat down the standard of satan: and set up everywhere the standard of Christ: Abolish the reign of sin, and establish the kingdom of grace in all hearts. Let humility triumph over pride and ambition: Charity over hatred, envy, and malice: Purity and temperance over lust and excess: Meekness over passion: And disinterestedness and poverty of spirit over covetousness and love of this perishable world. Let the Gospel of Jesus Christ, both in its belief and practice, prevail throughout all the universe.

Grant to us thy peace, O Lord, in the days of our mortality, even that peace which thy Son bequeathed as a legacy to his disciples: a perpetual peace with one another; and a perpetual peace with ourselves. Grant that all Christian princes and states may love, cherish, and maintain an inviolable peace among themselves. Give them a right sense of the dreadful evils that attend on wars. Give them an everlasting horror of all that bloodshed, of the devastations and ruin of so many territories; of the innumerable sacrileges; and the eternal loss of so many thousand souls, as are the dismal consequences of war. Turn their hearts to another kind of warfare; teach them to fight for a heavenly kingdom.

Remove, O Lord, thy wrath, which we have reason to

apprehend actually hanging over our heads for our sins. Deliver all Christian people from the dreadful evil of mortal sin: make all sinners sensible of their misery; give them the grace of a sincere conversion to thee, and a truly penitential spirit; and discharge them from all their bonds. Preserve all Christendom; and in particular this nation, from all the evils that threaten impenitent sinners, such as plagues, famines, earthquakes, fires, inundations, mortality of cattle, sudden and unprovided death, and thy many other judgements here, and eternal damnation hereafter. Comfort all that are under any affliction, sickness, or violence of pain: support all that are under temptation: reconcile all that are at variance: deliver all that are in slavery or captivity; defend all that are in danger: grant a relief to all in their respective necessities: give a happy passage to all that are in their agony. Grant thy blessing to all our friends and benefactors, and to all those for whom we are particularly bound to pray; and have mercy on all our enemies. Give eternal rest to all the faithful departed; and bring us all to everlasting life, through Jesus Christ thy Son. Amen.

*Meditations and Other Devotions for the
Use of the Faithful for the Time of the
Jubilee, Anno MDCCLXXVI*

GRACE TO ALL

O Blessed Lord, who hast appointed divers orders and conditions of men, be pleased to bestow upon them all such grace as may be needful for them in their several stations, and under their respective circumstances of life.

Give grace to those who are rich, not to hoard up their wealth as a treasure, nor trust in it, nor rejoice in it, rather than in Thee, the Giver of it; but to make due provision for themselves and those whom they are bound to support; to enjoy the means with which Thou hast blessed them, with prudence, moderation, and thankfulness; and at the same time to endeavour to do good with them; and to set their affections on things above.

Give grace to all who are dependent upon their labour, to endeavour to gain an honest livelihood; to provide for themselves and their families; and to acquire the means of doing good; without having a love of money.

Give grace to all who are poor, to endeavour to be patient, submissive, and contented with their lot; to put their trust in Thee, wait on Thee, and stay on Thee; and to look forward to the inheritance of the saints in light.

Have mercy upon the afflicted in mind, body, or circumstances, and give them relief according to their several necessities.

Succour, protect and provide for the old and the young; the sick and the infirm; the widow and the fatherless; the stranger, the prisoner, the captive, and the oppressed; the helpless, the desolate, and the destitute.

Strengthen, support and comfort the labouring poor, and all who are in need.

Let Thy grace be with all who are engaged in visiting the poor and the sick.

Give health and strength, skill and integrity, kindness and piety to the members of the medical profession, and others who are engaged in or about the removal or alleviation of maladies in mind or body. And pour down Thy blessing upon all hospitals, infirmaries, and other institutions for the mitigation of suffering and distress.

Vouchsafe to us an abundant supply of the produce of the earth; preserve from disease and multiply the cattle and other creatures which minister to our necessities; and grant us national prosperity in all other temporal respects, although our iniquities are great, and we are undeserving of the least of all Thy mercies.

Give strength, valour, and endurance, and a devout and merciful spirit to all who are in arms in the service of their country, by land or by sea. At the same time, grant unto us the blessings of peace; and hasten that happy period when wars shall cease in all the earth.

Let Thy fatherly care be over all who are in danger, by land or by water; especially over those whose lives are spent on the mighty ocean.

Give every needful grace to all who are entrusted with the education of the young; and grant that they may be impressed with the paramount importance of instilling into them the saving truths of Thy Holy Word, and bringing them up in the nurture and admonition of the Lord.

Give grace to those who conduct the public press, or by their writings or publications have any influence upon the opinions or conduct of others, that they may promote peace and happiness, truth and justice, religion and piety in the world.

And dispose all who are engaged in any kind of business or employment, to be honest, faithful, upright, and conscience in all their dealings; ever mindful of Thee, and of the uncertainty of life, and the certainty of judgement to come.

Mercifully grant these petitions, O God, for Christ our Saviour's sake.

Prayers: Josiah W. Smith (c. 1880)

A PRAYER FOR ALL MANKIND

'O God, who hast made of one blood all nations of men for to dwell on all the face of the earth, and hast determined the times before appointed, and the bounds of their habitation,' hear my prayer and supplication which I offer before Thee in behalf of all mankind. Hear them, O God, in behalf of the many thousands of Thy creatures who have gone astray from Thee, who have 'forsaken Thee, the fountain of living waters, and have hewed them out of cisterns, that can hold no water.' Hear them in behalf of a 'world which lieth in wickedness,' that it may not continue for ever in a state of estrangement from Thee—but that Thou mayest mercifully interfere in its behalf to bring it back to Thyself, to remove from it the evils under which it has so long groaned, and to rescue it from the domination of that cruel enemy who is the 'god of this world—the prince of the power of the air—the spirit that now worketh in the children of disobedience.'

O merciful Father! look, I beseech Thee, with compassion upon all the nations of the earth. Look especially with the eyes of pity upon those which 'walk in darkness.' For, O God the Lord, notwithstanding the light of Thy glorious gospel hath so long shined in the world, yet many 'are the people which sit in darkness,' and in 'the land of the shadow of death'; many are the 'dark places of the earth which are full of the habitations of cruelty'; many are the nations which are sunk in superstition, whose 'land also is full of idols,' and who 'worship the work of their own hands'; and large indeed is the portion of Thy world, who are ignorant of Thee, 'the only true God, and Jesus Christ whom Thou hast sent.' Enlighten then, O God, I beseech Thee, the dark corners of the earth. Let the light of Thy truth be everywhere diffused, and everywhere accompanied with that 'power from on high,' which only can make it effectual, that the people which 'dwell in darkness' may 'see a great light'; that the 'habitations of cruelty' may become the abodes of joy and love; that the nations which are sunk in superstition, 'for the fear of the Lord, and for the glory of His Majesty, when He shall arise to shake terribly the earth, may cast away their idols of silver, which they have made each one for himself to worship, to the moles and to the bats'; and that this earth, which has so long been estranged from Thee, which is the 'habitation of devils, the hold of every foul spirit, and a cage of every unclean and hateful bird,' may be filled with righteousness, and become as one great temple, in which, 'from the rising of the sun even unto the going down of the same, Thy name shall be great among the Gentiles; and in every place incense shall be offered unto Thy name, and a pure offering.'

O God, I beseech Thee hasten the time when wars shall cease unto the ends of the earth; when 'nation shall not lift up a sword against nation, neither shall they learn war any more'; but when 'they shall beat their swords into ploughshares, and their spears into pruning-hooks; and they shall sit every man under his vine, and under his fig-tree, and none shall make them afraid, for the mouth of the Lord of hosts hath spoken it.'

'Hasten, O God, the time when men shall dwell together in love, when the wolf also shall dwell with the lamb, and the leopard shall lie down with the kid, and the fatling together; and a little child shall lead them; and the cow and the bear shall feed, their young ones shall lie down together, and the lion shall eat straw like the ox; and the sucking child shall play on the hole of the asp, and the weaned child shall put his hand on the cockatrice's den. They shall not hurt nor destroy in all Thy holy mountain; for the earth shall be full of the knowledge of the Lord, as the waters cover the sea.' Hasten, O God, the time when oppression, cruelty and injustice of every kind shall cease among men; when a king shall 'reign in righteousness, and princes shall rule in judgement'; and when 'He whose right it is,' shall take to Himself His 'great power'; and when there shall be 'great voices in heaven, saying, The kingdoms of the world are become the kingdoms of our Lord, and of his Christ, and He shall reign for every and ever.'

Finally, 'O merciful God, who hast made all men, and hatest nothing that thou hast made, nor wouldest the death of a sinner, but rather that he should be converted, and live; have mercy, I beseech Thee, upon all Jews, Turks, Infidels, and Hereticks, and take from them all ignorance, hardness of heart, and contempt of Thy word; and so fetch them home, blessed Lord, to Thy flock, that they may be saved among the remnant of the true Israelites and may be made one fold under one shepherd, Jesus Christ our Lord, who liveth and reigneth with Thee and the Holy Spirit, one God, world without end.' Amen.

Prayers in Retirement: Joseph Elisha Freeman (1866)

ALL OF ONE BLOOD

For we are all of one blood. And charity, that more excellent way, is a tender affection for the whole creation of God.

To promote the kingdom of God, is to increase and hasten one's own happiness.

That man is born to trouble, I see wherever I turn my eyes. I know what pain is by experience; and though I was never in want, yet, from the complaint of others, I see it is grievous, and fit are those things to be laid before the throne of grace.

And since many have desired my prayers, and others have been my benefactors, and do constantly pray for me, I should not neglect to pray for them.

There are also many who cannot, and many who forget to pray for themselves, for whom charity should oblige one to pray.

And I should by no means forget the place of my birth, education, and preferment, that I may be some way useful to them, at least desire that God will accept my prayers for them.

O God, almighty and merciful, let thy fatherly kindness be upon all whom Thou hast made. Hear the prayers of all that call upon Thee; open the eyes of them that never pray for themselves: pity the sighs of such that are in misery: deal mercifully with them that are in darkness, and increase the number and the graces of such as fear and serve Thee daily. Preserve this land from the misfortunes of war; this Church from all wild and dangerous errors; this people from forgetting Thee, their Lord and Benefactor. Be gracious to all those countries that are made desolate by the sword, famine, pestilence, or persecution. Bless all persons and places to which Thy providence has made me a debtor; all who have been instrumental to my good by their assistance, advice, example, or writings. And make me in my turn useful to others. Let none of those that desire my prayers want Thy mercy, but defend, and comfort, and conduct them through.

'Noon Meditation' from Sacra Privata:
Bishop T. Wilson (1663–1755)

AN ACT OF INTERCESSION

O Lord, on whom the eyes of all do wait, remember every creature of thine for good, and visit the whole world with thy mercy.

O thou preserver and lover of men, think graciously upon mankind; and as thou hast concluded all under sin and unbelief, so let thy pity and pardon extend to all.

O thou, who for this end didst both die, and rise, and revive, that thou mightest be the Lord both of the dead and the living; since, whether we live, or whether we die, still are we thine, O Lord; let thy mercy be ever upon us, both in life and in death.

O thou helper of the helpless, our seasonable refuge in the time of trouble, remember all that lie under any sort of extremity, and call upon thee for succour and protection.

O thou, who art the God of grace and truth, establish and strengthen in thy truth them that stand; restore the weak, and raise up them that fall, through heresies and sins.

Thou, who art the wholesome defence and strength of thine anointed, think upon the congregation which thou hast purchased and redeemed of old; and let the multitude of them that believe be of one heart and of one soul.

Thou, Lord, who walkest in the midst of the golden candlesticks, remove not, we pray thee, our candlestick out of its place; but set in order the things which are wanting among us, and strengthen those which remain and are ready to die.

Send forth, we pray thee, O Lord of the harvest, labourers in all points fitted by thy grace to do the work of that harvest.

Thou, who art the portion of them that wait at thine altar, grant that thy clergy may always be enabled rightly to divide, and uprightly to walk in, the word of thy truth; and let thy people always be ready, with meek heart and due reverence, to receive the same at their mouths.

O thou great King over all the earth, strengthen and support the several governing powers, as being thine own ordinance, though man's convenience and contrivance. Scatter the nations that delight in blood, and command wars to cease in all the world.

O God, on whom the isles do wait, and in whose arm they trust, defend this island, and every part thereof, from all calamity, danger, and death.

O Lord of lords, and holy Ruler of princes, be watchful over those whom thou hast deputed to rule thy world here below, and more especially over our gracious queen; assist and prosper all her righteous undertakings, and inspire her with noble and good designs for the advantage of thy Church, and of all thy people committed to her charge. Bless her with firm and honourable peace, that under her we may lead quiet lives in all godliness and honesty.

Thou, who distributest among men different degrees of power severally as thou wilt, grant that all persons of eminence and authority may be as eminent for virtue, and sincere regard for thy true religion. Fill all our counsellors with godly wisdom; let our nobles do much in behalf of, but nothing against, the truth. Guide thou our judges and magistrates in the administration of justice to all persons, and in all causes, without preferring one before another, or doing anything by partiality.

O Lord of hosts, and God of battles, strengthen, protect and prosper all Christian forces engaged against the enemies of our most holy faith.

Give all our people grace to live in subjection to the higher powers, not only for wrath, but also for conscience' sake.

Bless our husbandmen with fruitful seasons; our fleets with favourable winds; our merchants with successful voyages; our tradesmen with a spirit of honesty and contentment; our artificers, even to the meanest, even to the poorest among us, with grace to follow their respective labours diligently and patiently, for fair and reasonable profit, and in humble dependence upon thy blessing.

Furthermore, in regard thou art the God not of us only, but of our posterity, extend, we pray thee, thy blessing to our

51

children; that our sons and daughters may grow up as young plants, and with their age and stature may increase in wisdom and virtue, and in favour with God and man.

Thou, who hast commanded a due care of our relations, and abhorrest those who are void of natural affection, be favourable to my kindred, whether by blood or alliance; preserve among us all peace, friendship and tenderness, and make us evermore ready to seek and rejoice in another's good.

O thou, who requirest us to love them that love us, pour out thy blessings great and manifold upon all my friends and benefactors, all who have done or wish me well, many perhaps unknown to me; preserve them, O Lord, and keep them alive, that they may be blessed upon the earth, and deliver them not into the will of their enemies.

O thou, who hast pronounced that man worse than an infidel who is regardless of his own household, behold with thy favour every person belonging to this family; yea, let thy peace rest upon this whole house, and the Son of peace ever dwell in it.

O thou, who hast declared that our brotherly love must far exceed that of publicans and sinners, grant me never to be wanting in kindness and civil respect to all who live peaceably and quietly in my neighbourhood, but cheerful, and in making suitable returns of love to all that love me. My own friends, my father's friends, and the children of both our friends, never let me ungratefully despise, neglect, or forsake.

O thou, who hast directed us to overcome evil with good, and hast expressly commanded our prayers for them that persecute us and despitefully use us, pardon and bless all that speak evil of me, all that have hated me with or without a cause; some of them, perhaps, even for my good will, for speaking distasteful truth, or doing necessary justice; but whatever the occasion or the offence may have been, which, if given on my part, I entreat thee and them to forgive, have the same mercy, O Lord, on all my enemies as on myself, and bring them, I beseech thee, to thy heavenly kingdom, as I hope and pray thou wilt at length bring me.

Soften and convert those hardened foolish hearts, who, through ignorance and prejudice, contemn thy word and ordinances, who deride thy holy religion, and wilfully forbear and refuse to pray; give them a sorrowful sense of this evil heart of unbelief, and preserve others from the infection of such pestilent examples. And for a more effectual check to such daring and dangerous wickedness, assist and prosper all that are employed in any laudable undertaking, whereby the glory of thy name, the increase of thy Church, and the good of mankind, may be promoted and secured: particularly be pleased to reward a hundredfold all who bountifully contribute of their substance to works of piety and charity.

Once more, therefore, I entreat thee to look down, gracious Lord, on all ages and conditions of men—sucklings and infants, children and young people, middle-aged and declining, old and bed-rid, the hungry and thirsty, the naked and sick, prisoners and strangers, those that have no settled dwelling while they live, and those who are destitute of friends to bury them when they die; all of superannuated understanding, or discontented or disturbed minds; all who labour under any temptation to destroy themselves, who are vexed with evil spirits, or driven to despair of thy mercy; the distressed in body or soul, the timorous or faint-hearted, the criminals and condemned to die, the orphans and widows, travellers by land or by water, women labouring with child, captives and slaves, in chains, in the mines or in the galleys; all that wander about in caves or deserts, and all that lie expiring in the agonies of death.

Do thou, Lord, save both man and beast; for excellent is thy mercy, O God; and the children of men shall put their trust under the shadow of thy wings.

The Lord bless and keep us; the Lord make his face to shine upon us, and be gracious unto us; the Lord lift up the light of his countenance upon us, and give us peace.

Bishop Lancelot Andrewes (1555–1626)

YOU BEEN AROUND A LONG TIME

God, you been around a long time,
Even before hill and
Trees and stuff like that.
You just always been God.

You make and bust men
And tell them where to go.
A thousand years is nothing to you.

You can take care of the bad guys
Just like they never was,
Or didn't last even a day.

We can get hurt if you get mad
And we just can't hide anything from you.
We know you check us out real good-like.

So, even if we get to join the Golden Ages
You still know us
And even that just ain't much time with you.
And they is gone too.

So, God, teach us to wise up
And get groovie.

Then, God, help us to hope you have pity on us—
And we will know your love is around in the morning.

Help us to get happy real soon.
And let everything go pretty good,
From now to forever.

By a 'delinquent' teenager, from
Treat me Cool, Lord, by Carl Burke

2. *Prayers for the Future*

GROUNDED IN PERFECT FAITH

O Holy Lord, Father Almighty, everlasting God, carry onward in all Thy Priests the gifts of Thy grace; and mercifully bestow by Thy Spirit what human frailty cannot attain, that they who attend at the sacred altars may be both grounded in perfect faith, and conspicuous by the brightness of their souls. Amen.

Leonine Sacramentary

TRUTH, UNITY AND CONCORD

Almighty and everlasting God, we beseech Thee to inspire continually the Universal Church with the spirit of truth, unity, and concord, that all they that do confess Thy holy Name may agree in the truth of Thy holy Word, and live in unity and godly love; for Jesus Christ's sake, our only Mediator and Advocate. Amen.

Prayers in Use at Cuddesdon College (1904)

GUARD THIS YEAR

O Lord, our God! bless us for this year;
As also every kind of it's produce for our benefit:
And bestow dew and rain for a blessing
Upon the face of the earth:
And water the surface of the earth;
And satisfy the world with thy goodness.

Replenish our hands with thy blessings,
And with the rich gifts of thy hands.
Protect and guard this year from all manner of evil,

And from every form of calamity and destruction:

Cause our hope therein to be good,
So that it may end peacefully.

Sephardi Prayer Book: translation by
D. A. de Sola, Society of Heshaim ©

AS THE WATERS COVER THE SEA

O God, we pray for Thy Church which is set today amid the perplexities of a changing order, and is face to face with new tasks: fill us afresh with the Spirit of Pentecost; help us to bear witness boldly to the coming of Thy kingdom; and hasten the time when the knowledge of Thyself shall fill the earth as the waters cover the sea.

Anon.

THE WAYS OF MUTUAL HELP

O Thou in Whose hand are the hearts of Thy creatures, shed abroad Thy peace upon the world. By the might of Thy Holy Spirit quench the pride, and anger, and greediness which cause man to strive against man, and people against people. Lead all nations in the ways of mutual help and goodwill, and hasten the time when the earth shall confess Thee indeed for its Saviour and King, and no evil deeds of man shall defile Thy glorious creation, through Jesus Christ our Lord. Amen.

Anon.

AN ARMOUR OF FAITH

We give Thee thanks, O Lord, holy Father, almighty everlasting God, Who not for any merit of ours, out of the condescension of Thy mercy only, hast vouchsafed to feed us sinners, Thy unworthy servants, with the precious Body and Blood of Thy Son our Lord Jesus Christ. And we humbly entreat Thy boundless mercy, almighty and merciful Lord, that this Holy Communion may not bring guilt upon us to condemnation, but may be unto us for pardon and salvation. Let it be to us an armour of faith and a shield of good resolution. Let it be to us a riddance of all vices, an extermination of all evil desires and lusts, and an increase of love and patience, of humility and obedience, and of all virtues; a sure defence against the wiles of our enemies, visible or invisible; a perfect quietening of all sinful impulses. fleshly or spiritual; a firm adherence to Thee, the one true God, and a blessed consummation of our end. And we pray to Thee that Thou wouldest vouchsafe to bring us sinners to that ineffable feast, where Thou, with Thy Son and the Holy Spirit, art to Thy saints true light, abundant fulfilment, and everlasting joy, and perfect happiness; through the same Jesus Christ our Lord.

St. Thomas Aquinas (1225–1274)

PARTAKERS OF JOY

O God, Who hast brought us near to an innumerable company of angels and to the spirits of just men made perfect; grant us in our pilgrimage on earth to continue in their fellowship, and in our heavenly country to become partakers of their joy; through Jesus Christ our Lord.

William Bright (1824–1901)

SEND US THY BLESSING

Almighty God, Lord of heaven and earth, in Whom we live and move and have our being; Who doest good unto all men, making Thy sun to rise on the evil and the good, and sending rain on the just and the unjust; favourably behold us Thy servants, who call upon Thy Name, and send us Thy blessing from heaven, in giving us fruitful seasons, and filling our hearts with food and gladness; that both our hearts and mouths may be continually filled with Thy praise, giving thanks to Thee in Thy holy Church, through Jesus Christ our Lord.

Bishop John Cosin (1594–1672)

THAT BLESSED REST

Grant, Almighty God, that, since the dullness and harshness of our flesh is so great that it is needful for us in various ways to be afflicted, we may patiently bear Thy chastisement, and under a deep feeling of sorrow flee to Thy mercy displayed to us in Christ; and that not depending upon the earthly blessings of

57

this perishable life, but relying only upon Thy Word, we may go forward in the course of our calling; until at length we be gathered to that blessed rest which is laid up for us in heaven; through Jesus Christ our Lord.

John Calvin (1509–1564)

THE THINGS ETERNAL

May God Almighty direct our days in His peace, and grant us the gifts of His blessing; may He deliver us in all our troubles, and establish our minds in the tranquillity of His peace; may He so guide us through things temporal that we finally lose not the things eternal.

Gregorian Sacramentary

THY WORD IS AN ANCHOR

O God, Who never forsakest those that hope in Thee: grant that we may ever keep that hope which Thou hast given us by Thy Word as an anchor to our souls, to preserve us sure and steadfast, unshaken and secure in all the storms of life; through Jesus Christ our Lord.

Anon.

THE BEAUTY OF THY GLANCE

O Christ, a light transcendent
Shines in Thy countenance,
And none can tell the sweetness,
The beauty of Thy glance.

In This may Thy poor servants
Their joy eternal find;
Thou calledst them, O rest them,
Thou lover of mankind.

St. John Damascene (700–754)

EVERLASTING KINGDOM

I will extol Thee, my God, O King; and I will bless Thy Name for ever and ever. Every day I will bless Thee; and I will praise Thy name for ever and ever. I will speak of the glorious honour of Thy majesty, and of Thy wondrous works. All Thy works shall praise Thee, O Lord; and Thy saints shall bless Thee. They shall speak of the glory of Thy Kingdom and talk of Thy power; to make known to the sons of men his mighty acts, and the glorious majesty of his kingdom. Thy kingdom is an everlasting Kingdom, and Thy dominion endureth throughout all generations.

Psalm 145; 1–2, 5, 10–13

THE FUTURE WORLD

All sin comes from the mouth that speaks untruth and from the heart that denies the future world.

Buddhist Scriptures

HE WILL LEAD

Let us praise the Lord of all, who is the Maker of heaven and earth. He was the guide of our fathers through the ages; and He will lead mankind unto the time when the knowledge of Him and obedience to His laws shall fill the hearts of all men. He is our God, there is none else.

Jewish Prayer Book

PARDONING, WE ARE PARDONED

Merciful God, to Thee we commend ourselves and all those who need Thy help and correction. Where there is hatred, give love; where there is injury, pardon; where there is doubt, faith; where there is despair, hope; where there is sadness, joy; where there is darkness, light. Grant that we may not seek so much to be consoled, as to console; to be understood, as to understand; to be loved, as to love; for in giving we receive, in pardoning we are pardoned, and dying we are born into eternal life.

St. Francis of Assisi (1182–1226)

MAY EVIL FLY AWAY

Beneficent God, may cheerfulness, joy and goodness arrive to men; may disease, misery, selfishness and all such evil fly away. May the good be powerful. May the evil-minded be powerless and may they repent of their evil deeds. May our thoughts, words and actions be on the line of righteousness. We pray for the good of the life of all living creatures which Thou hast created. May the faith which worships one omniscient God spread and continue in the wide world. May the thoughts, words and actions of us all be truthful and righteous, so that, in the end, all mankind may be benefitted in this world and in the other world.

Zoroastrian Scriptures

LAND OF JUSTICE

O God, grant us a vision of our land, fair as she might be; a land of justice, where none shall prey on others; a land of plenty, where vice and poverty shall cease to fester; a land of brotherhood, where all success shall be founded on service, and honour shall be given to nobleness alone; a land of peace, where order shall not rest on force, but on the love of all for the land, the great mother of the common life and weal. Hear Thou, O Lord, the silent prayer of all our hearts, as we pledge out time and strength and thought to speed the day of her coming beauty and righteousness.

Prayers of the Social Awakening:
Walter Rauschenbusch (1861–1918)

HOPE FEEDS US

Behold, hope feeds us, nurses us, strengthens us, and comforts us in this toilsome life. In our hope itself we sing. Amen.

St. Augustine (354–430)

TO WALK WITHOUT STUMBLING

O thou, who art the true son of the world, ever rising, and never going down; who, by thy most wholesome appearing and sight dost nourish and gladden all things in heaven and earth; we beseech thee mercifully to shine into our hearts, that the night and darkness of sin, and the mists of error on every side, being driven away by the brightness of thy shining within our hearts, we may all our life walk without stumbling, as in the daytime, and, being pure and clean from the works of darkness, may abound in all good works which thou hast prepared for us to walk in.

Erasmus (1466–1536)

WITH FAITHFUL HEARTS

O Thou, who art ever the same, grant us so to pass through the coming year with faithful hearts, that we may be able to please Thy loving eyes: through Jesus Christ our Lord. Amen.

Mozarabic Liturgy (before 700 A.D.*)*

THAT THY FLOCK MAY PROSPER

Graciously cast Thy light, O Lord, upon Thy Church, that Thy flock may everywhere go on and prosper, and its pastors, by Thy governance, may become acceptable to Thy Name; through Jesus Christ our Lord. Amen.

Gregorian Sacramentary

I WILL POUR OUT MY SPIRIT

And it shall come to pass afterward, that I will
pour out my spirit on all flesh;
your sons and your daughters shall prophesy,
your old men shall dream dreams,
and your young men shall see visions.
Even upon the menservants and maidservants
in those days, I will pour out my spirit.

Joel 2: 28–29

COME AS THE WIND

O Holy Ghost,
come to us, and among us;
come as the wind, and cleanse us;
come as the fire, and burn;
come as the dew, and refresh:
convict, convert, and consecrate
many hearts and lives
to our great good
and thy greater glory,
and this we ask for Jesus Christ's sake.

Anon.

A GREAT HIGHWAY

In that day there will be a great highway to Assyria, and the
Assyrian will come into Egypt, and the Egyptian into Assyria,
and the Egyptians will worship with the Assyrians. In that day
Israel will be the third with Egypt and Assyria, a blessing in the
midst of the earth, whom the Lord of hosts has blessed, saying,
Blessed be Egypt my people, and Assyria the work of my
hands, and Israel my heritage.

Isaiah 19: 23–25

REST IN THEE

O Lord, thou hast made us for thyself,
and our hearts shall find no rest,
until they find their rest in thee.

St. Augustine (354–430)

FILLED WITH THY GRACE

Grant thy servants, O God, to be set on fire with thy spirit,
strengthened by thy power, illumined by thy splendour, filled
with thy grace, and to go forward with thy aid.

Gallican Sacramentary (4th century)

THROUGH THE STORMS

May the sacred feast of Thy table, O Lord, always strengthen and renew us, guide and protect our weakness amid the storms of the world, and bring us into the haven of everlasting salvation; through Jesus Christ our Lord.

Leonine Sacramentary (5th century)

BORN AGAIN

Almighty and everlasting God, so lead us into the fellowship of heavenly joys that, born again in the Holy Spirit, we may enter into Thy Kingdom; and that the simple sheep may come hither, whither the noble Shepherd has gone before.

Gregorian Sacramentary (9th century)

INTO THE FUTURE

God! by whose will created
The time and man are mated,
Give us such chiefs again,
Give us such kings of men
Who shout no narrow creed,
And do no little deed,
But to their work impart
A grace-touch'd human heart.

Primate William Alexander (1824–1911)

THE LORD WILL COME

The Lord will come! the earth shall quake,
The hills their fixed seats forsake;
And withering from the vault of night,
The stars withdraw their feeble light.

The Lord will come! but not the same
As once in lowly form He came,
A silent Lamb to slaughter led,
The bruised, the suffering, and the dead.

The Lord will come! a dreadful form,
With wreath of flame and robe of storm,

63

On cherub wings, and wings of wind,
Appointed Judge of human kind.

Can this be He who wont to stray
A pilgrim on the world's highway,
By power oppressed, and mocked by pride,
The Nazarene, the crucified?

Go, tyrants! to the rocks complain;
Go, seek the mountain's cleft in vain;
But faith, victorious o'er the tomb,
Shall sing for joy, 'The Lord is come!'

Hymns of the Church of God:
selected by F. V. Mather (1866)

COMMON OBEDIENCE

O Lord Jesus Christ, we pray Thee to pour Thy Spirit upon the students of all nations; that they may consecrate themselves to Thy service, and may come to love and understand one another through their common obedience to Thee.

Anon.

HIDE NOT THE RIGHT ROAD

God said, O Sásán! thou art my friend; hide not the right road.
There is no one who seeketh me and findeth me not;
All know me according to the capacity of their understanding.
Instead of sensible words, men are answered with weapons of
war.
O Sásán! evils await thee. Thou art my prophet:
If mankind follow thee not, for them it is evil, not for thee.
The good will come in thy path.
Lay not affliction to heart; God will give it an end.

The Desátir, or Regulations (Persian)

REALISATION OF TRUTH

O God, whose revelation never faileth and who showest a new aspect of Thy eternal truth to each generation; Grant unto us to see the truth as Thou dost set is before us in this our day and strive for its realisation among our fellows; through Jesus Christ our Lord.

Anon.

SPARKS OF HOPE

Among the haunts and dwellings of mankind,
Men lived together even as spirits do.
None fawned, none trembled, none with eager fear
Gazed on another's eye of cold command.

None wrought his lips in truth-entangling lines
Which smiled the lie his tongue disdained to speak;
None with firm sneer trod out in his own heart
The sparks of hope, the holy fire of love.

Man had grown gentle, just and passionless,
Master of fate, a king over himself,
And women passed, frank, beautiful and kind;
Speaking the wisdom once they could not think.

To forgive wrongs darker than death or night,
To love and bear; to hope—this is to be
Good, great and happy, beautiful and free;
This is alone Life, Joy, and Victory.

Percy Bysshe Shelley (1792–1822)

PURGE OUT OUR DROSS

O God the Holy Ghost who art Light
unto Thine elect,
Evermore enlighten us.
Thou who art the Fire of Love,
Evermore enkindle us.
Thou who art Lord and Giver of Life,
Evermore live in us.
Thou who bestowest sevenfold grace,

Evermore replenish us.
As the wind is Thy symbol,
So forward our goings.
As the dove,
So launch us heavenwards.
As water,
So purify our spirits.
As a cloud,
So abate our temptations.
As dew,
So revive our languor.
As fire,
So purge out our dross.

Christina Georgina Rossetti (1830–1894)

FOR EMPLOYERS

We invoke Thy grace and wisdom, O Lord, upon all men of good will who employ and control the labour of men. Amid the numberless irritations and anxieties of their position, help them to keep a quiet and patient temper, and to rule firmly and wisely, without harshness and anger. Since they hold power over the bread, the safety and the hopes of the workers, may they wield their powers justly and with love, as older brothers and leaders in the great fellowship of labour. Suffer not the heavenly light of compassion for the weak and the old to be quenched in their hearts. When they are tempted to follow the ruthless ways of others, and to sacrifice human health and life for profit, do Thou strengthen their will in the hour of need, and bring to naught the counsels of the heartless. Save them from repressing their workers into sullen submission and helpless fear. May they not sin against the Christ by using the bodies and souls of men as mere tools to make things, forgetting the human hearts and longings of these their brothers.

Raise up among us employers who shall be makers of men as well as of goods. Give us masters of industry who will use their higher ability and knowledge in lifting the workers to increasing independence and vigour, and who will train their helpers for the larger responsibilities of the coming age. Give us men of faith who will see beyond the strife of the present and catch a vision of a nobler organisation of our work, when all will still follow the leadership of the ablest, not in fear but by the glad will of all, and when none shall be master and none shall be man, but all shall stand side by side in a strong and righteous brotherhood of work.

Prayers of the Social Awakening:
Walter Rauschenbusch (1861–1918)

FOR THOSE WHO COME AFTER US

O God, we pray Thee for those who come after us, for our children, and the children of our friends, and for all the young lives that are marching up from the gates of birth, pure and eager, with the morning sunshine on their faces. We remember with a pang that these will live in the world we are making for them. We are wasting the resources of the earth in our headlong greed, and they will suffer want. We are building sunless houses and joyless cities for our profit, and they must dwell therein. We are making the burden heavy and the pace of work pitiless, and they will fall wan and sobbing by the wayside. We are poisoning the air of our land by our lies and our uncleanness, and they will breathe it.

O God, Thou knowest how we have cried out in agony when the sins of our fathers have been visited upon us, and how we have struggled vainly against the inexorable fate that coursed in our blood or bound us in a prison-house of life. Save us from maiming the innocent ones who come after us by the added cruelty of our sins. Help us to break the ancient force of evil by a holy and steadfast will and to endow our children with purer blood and nobler thoughts. Grant us grace to leave the earth fairer than we left it; to build upon it cities of God in which the cry of needless pain shall cease; and to put the yoke of Christ upon our business life that it may serve and not destroy. Lift the veil of the future and show us the generation to come as it will be if blighted by our guilt, that our lust may be cooled and we may walk in the fear of the Eternal. Grant us a vision of the far-off years as they may be if redeemed by the sons of God, that we may take heart and do battle for Thy children and ours.

Prayers of the Social Awakening:
Walter Rauschenbusch (1861–1918)

WE BUILD FOR EVER

The ideal of self-denial for the sake of posterity, of practising present economy for the sake of debtors yet unborn, of planting forests that our descendants may live under their shade, or of raising cities for future nations to inhabit, never, I suppose, efficiently takes place among publicly recognized motives of exertion. Yet these are not the less our duties; nor is it our part fitly sustained upon the earth, unless the range of our intended and deliberate usefulness includes not only the companions but the successors of our pilgrimage. God has lent us the earth for our life; it is a great entail. It belongs as much to those who are to come after us, and whose names are already written in the book of creation, as to us; and we have no right, by anything that we do or neglect, to involve them in unnecessary penalties, or deprive them of benefits which it was in our power to bequeath. And this the more, because it is one of the appointed conditions of the labour of men that, in proportion to the time between the seed-sowing and the harvest, is the fulness of the fruit; and that generally, therefore, the farther off we place our aim, and the less we desire ourselves to be the witnesses of what we have laboured for, the more wide and rich will be the measure of our success. Men cannot benefit those that are with them as they can benefit those that come after them. Nor is there, indeed, any present loss, in such respect for futurity. Every human action gains in honour, in grace, in all true magnificence, by its regard to things that are to come. It is the far sight, the quiet and confident patience, that, above all other attributes, separate man from man, and near him to his Maker; and there is no action nor art, whose majesty we may not measure by this test. Therefore, when we build, let us think that we build for ever. Let it not be fore present delight, nor for present use, alone; let it be such work as our descendants will thank us for, and let us think, as we lay stone on stone, that a time is to come when those stones will be held sacred because our hands have touched them, and that men will say as they look upon the labour and wrought substance of them, 'See! this our fathers did for us.'

The Seven Lamps of Architecture:
John Ruskin (1819–1900)

PURIFY THE WORLD

O Lord Jesus, Son of God the Father, Who hast redeemed us by Thy blood, the fountain of peace, and source of pure love, grant, we beseech Thee, that God may be exalted in this new age, that He may be the First and the Last, the Beginning and the end of our thoughts, plans and actions. Let the love of God be spread abroad in all hearts, kindling the fire of true religion. May the Church of God be filled with the one spirit, united, and uniting men in the one Body, able with great power to give its witness and draw the world to Thee. Fill all men and women with the ardour of true service, that they may not look to their own things but to the things of others and live by Thy example, Who didst not please Thyself but came, not to be ministered to, but to minister, and went about doing good. Draw, attract, arouse, constrain all men in all nations to come unto Thee and be saved and grant them in Thy light to see light.

Bind together all classes and professions in the State, teaching each and all to do loyally and honourably the work that Thou hast assigned, that they may regard themselves as members of one great family, working together for the good of all and growing into unity of affection.

Purify the world till it becomes Thy Kingdom, knowing no King but Thee, obeying no law but Thy law, and moving with the consent of every will in the accomplishment of Thy will, to the glory of Thy great Name. Amen.

Form of Prayer for India, adapted

JOY, HEALTH AND SALVATION

We render unto Thee our thanksgiving, O Lord our God, Father of our Lord and Saviour Jesus Christ, by all means, at all times, in all places. For that Thou hast sheltered, assisted, supported, and led us on through the time past of our life, and brought us to this hour. And we pray and beseech Thee, O God and loving Lord, grant us to pass this day, this year, and all the time of our life without sin, with all joy, health, and salvation. But all fear, all envy, all temptations, all the working of Satan, do Thou drive away, O God, from us, and from Thy Holy Church. Supply us with things good and profitable. Whereinsoever we have sinned against Thee, in word, deed, or thought,

69

be Thou pleased in Thy love and goodness to forgive, and forsake us not, O God, who hope in Thee, neither lead us into temptation, but deliver us from the evil one and from his works; by the grace and compassion of Thine only begotten Son, Jesus Christ. Amen.

Liturgy of St. Mark

OF THE FLEETING LIFE OF MAN

Now, if we consider attentively the fleeting [literally: floating] nature of the life of man, it is but an evanescent thing; the beginning, the middle and the end of this existence is a period like the twinkling of an eye. At present, there is no endowment with a human body which attains its ten thousand years. A lifetime soon passes away, and who is there now who retains his form for a hundred years! Whether I am first or another is first, whether it be today or tomorrow, we know not—they who are behind and they who go before are thicker than the drops by the roots and the dew on the top of the herbage.

And thus in the morning our body shows a ruddy countenance—in the evening it is whitened bones. If there comes a variable wind, in a moment [our] two eyes close; if one breath is cut off, our ruddy countenance changes away, and loses the adornment of the peach and the plum. Then, although relatives of every degree assemble, and there is mourning and lamentation, yet it is of no avail, and there is nothing to be done but to send out the remains on the waste, and turn them into the smoke of midnight, till only some whitened bones remain. Alas! it is vain to speak of it.

Wherefore, there being no distinction between old and young in this fragile condition of humanity, let each one, speedily laying to heart the first importance of the life to come, place profound reliance on Amida Buddha, and call Him to remembrance.

With much respect.

The Gobunsho or Ofumi of Rennyo Shonin:
(a series of letters) Rennyo Shonin (Ken-jyu) (1415–1499)

70

PRAYER FOR A REVIVAL

Saviour, visit thy plantation,
Grant us, Lord, a gracious rain!
All will come to desolation,
Unless thou return again:
Keep no longer at a distance,
Shine upon us from on high;
Lest, for want of thine assistance,
Every plant should droop and die.

Surely once thy garden flourished,
Every part looked gay and green;
Then thy word our spirits nourished,
Happy seasons we have seen!
But a drought has since succeeded,
And a sad decline we see;
Lord, thy help is greatly needed,
Help can only come from thee.

Where are those we counted leaders,
Filled with zeal, and love, and truth—
Old professors, tall as cedars,
Bright examples to our youth?
Some, in whom we once delighted,
We shall meet no more below;
Some, alas! we fear are blighted,
Scarce a single leaf they show.

Younger plants—the sight how pleasant
Covered thick with blossoms stood:
But they cause us grief at present,
Frosts have nipped them in the bud!
Dearest Saviour, hasten hither,
Thou canst make them bloom again:
Oh, permit them not to wither,
Let not all our hopes be vain!

Let our mutual love be fervent,
Make us prevalent in prayers;
Let each one esteemed thy servant
Shun the world's bewitching snares;
Break the tempter's fatal power;

71

Turn the stony heart to flesh;
And begin, from this good hour,
To revive thy work afresh.

John Newton (1725–1807)

THE LONGING

From out this dim and gloomy hollow,
Where hang the cold clouds heavily,
Could I but gain the clew to follow,
How blessed would the journey be!
Aloft I see a fair dominion,
Through time and change all vernal still;
But where the power and what the pinion
To gain that ever-blooming hill?

Afar I hear the music ringing—
The lulling sounds of heaven's repose,
And the light gales are downward bringing
The sweets of flowers the mountain knows.
I see the fruits all golden glowing,
Beckon the glossy leaves between,
And o'er the blooms that there are blowing
Nor blight nor winter's wrath hath been,

To suns that shine forever, yonder,
O'er fields that fade not, sweet to flee;
The very winds that there may wander,
How healing must their breathing be!
But lo, between us rolls a river,
O'er which the wrathful tempest raves!
I feel the soul within me shiver
To gaze upon the gloomy waves.
A rocking boat mine eyes discover,
But, woe is me, the pilot fails!
In, boldly in, undaunted over!
And trust the life that swells the sails!
Thou must believe, and thou must venture,
In fearless faith thy safety dwells;

By miracles alone men enter
The glorious land of miracles!

*Johann Christoph Friedrich von Schiller (1759–1805),
translated by Sir Edward Bulwer Lytton (1803–1873)*

FILL THE SOULS OF ALL

Magnified be Thy name, O my God, for that Thou hast manifested the Day which is the King of Days, the Day which Thou didst announce unto Thy chosen Ones and Thy Prophets in Thy most excellent Tablets, the Day whereon Thou didst shed the splendour of the glory of all Thy names upon all created things. Great is his blessedness whosoever hath set himself towards Thee, and entered Thy presence, and caught the accents of Thy voice.

I beseech Thee, O my Lord, by the name of Him round Whom circleth in adoration the kingdom of Thy names, that Thou wilt graciously assist them that are dear to Thee to glorify Thy word among Thy servants, and to shed abroad Thy praise among Thy creatures, so that the ecstasies of Thy revelation may fill the souls of all the dwellers of Thine earth.

Since Thou hast guided them, O my Lord, unto the living waters of Thy grace, grant, by Thy bounty, that they may not be kept back from Thee; and since Thou hast summoned them to the habitation of Thy throne, drive them out out of Thy presence, through Thy loving-kindness. Send down upon them what shall wholly detach them from aught else except Thee, and make them able to soar in the atmosphere of Thy nearness, in such wise that neither the ascendancy of the oppressor nor the suggestions of them that have disbelieved in Thy most august and most mighty Self shall be capable of keeping them back from Thee.

*Bahá'í Prayers: a selection (1951),
Bahá'í Publishing Trust ©*

3. *Give Us Virtue*

THREE KINDS OF SILENCE

There are three kinds of silence; the first is of words, the second of desires, and the third of thoughts. The first is perfect; the second is more perfect; and the third is most perfect. In the first, that of words, virtue is acquired. In the second, namely, of desires, quietness is attained. In the third, of thoughts, internal recollection is gained. By not speaking, not desiring, and not thinking, one arrives at the true and perfect mystical silence, where God speaks with the soul, communicates himself to it, and in the abyss of its own depth teaches it the most perfect and exalted wisdom.

Michael de Molinos (1640– 1697)

TRUTH, JUDGEMENT, PEACE

By three things the world is preserved:
By truth,
By judgement,
And by peace.

Authorized Daily Prayer Book: translation by Rev. S. Singer, Singer's Prayer-Book Publication Committee

THY GOOD SPIRIT

Almighty Everliving Father, Who hast promised unto Thy faithful people life by Thine Incarnate Son, even as He liveth by thee; grant unto us all, and especially to those whom Thy Providence hath in anywise entrusted with the treasure of Thy holy doctrine amongst us, Thy good Spirit, always so to believe and understand, to feel and firmly hold, to speak and to think, concerning the mystery of the Communion of the Body and Blood of Thy dear Son, as shall be well pleasing to Thee, and profitable to our souls; through the same our Lord Jesus Christ, Who liveth and reigneth with Thee in the unity of the same Spirit one God, world without end. Amen.

John Keble (1792–1866)

THE TRUE COURAGE

Take from us, O God, all pride and vanity, all boasting and forwardness, and give us the true courage that shows itself by gentleness; the true wisdom that shows itself by simplicity; and the true power that shows itself by modesty; through Jesus Christ our Lord.

Charles Kingsley (1819–1875)

EVIL GO FORTH

Walking the streets, attacking dwellings, penetrating bolts,
Evil man, whose face is evil,
Whose mouth is evil, whose tongue is evil,
Evil spell, sorcery, witchcraft,
Enchantment, evil deed
Go forth from the house!
By heaven mayest thou be exorcised!
By earth mayest thou be exorcised!
Unto the man, the son of his god,
Mayest thou not approach!
Mayest thou go off!
Mayest thou not sit in his seat!
Mayest thou not lie on his bed!
Mayest thou not rise over his fence!
Mayest thou not enter into his chamber!
Mayest thou be exorcised by heaven and earth!
Mayest thou depart!

Sumerian exorcism, from: Selected Sumerian and Babylonian Texts, Henry Frederick Lutz (1919)

A CLEARER PROSPECT

Behold, O Lord God, our strivings after a truer and more abiding order. Give us visions that bring back a lost glory to the earth, and dreams that foreshadow the better order which Thou hast prepared for us. Scatter every excuse of frailty and unworthiness: consecrate us all with a heavenly mission: open to us a clearer prospect of our work. Give us strength according to our day gladly to welcome and gratefully to fulfil it; through Jesus Christ our Lord.

Bishop Brooke Foss Westcott (1825–1901)

PRAYER ABOVE ALL THINGS

Give unto us, O God, the girdle, the helmet, the breastplate, the shield, the sandals, the sword—above all things, prayer. Grant unto us the power and opportunity of well-doing, that before the day of our departure may come, we may have wrought at least somewhat, whose good fruit may remain; that we may behold Thy Presence in righteousness, and be satisfied with Thy glory; for Christ's sake. Amen.

Bishop Lancelot Andrewes (1555–1626)

USING THY GIFTS

Lord, grant us grace, to make Thy goodness our trust: shutting our hearts against pride, our mouths against evil words, our ears against foul knowledge, and using Thy gifts to the promotion of Thy glory and of man's salvation; for His blessed sake, in Whom we have all and are full and abound, Jesus Christ.

Christina Georgina Rossetti (1830–1894)

RETURN BLESSING FOR CURSING

We would further entreat Thee to plant in our hearts gentleness and patience, a meek and long-suffering spirit. Endow us, we beseech Thee, with such charity, that we may be enabled to return blessing for cursing, good for evil, kind words for harsh reproaches. Thus living all our days with meekness and loving-kindness, keeping peace with all men, and loving our neighbours as ourselves, and Thee, Lord Jesus, more than ourselves, we may at last enter with them into the regions of everlasting love, where Thou livest, who lovest all men, and wouldest not that any perish, but that all men should turn to Thee and be saved; for Thy name's sake. Amen.

Fielding Ould (19th century)

THAT WE MAY PERSEVERE

O blessed Lord, we beseech Thee to pour down upon us such grace as may not only cleanse this life of ours, but beautify it a little, if it be Thy will, before we go hence and are no more seen. Grant that we may love Thee with all our heart, and soul, and strength and our neighbour as ourselves, and that we may persevere unto the end; through Jesus Christ our Lord. Amen.

James Skinner (19th century)

SHOW US THE WAY

May we, O God, keep ourselves modest, faithful, and valiant. Show us the way and keep us in it.

Epictetus (1st century)

GIFTS OF VIRTUE

In word, in act, be justice in our view:
Nor ever any thoughtless course pursue:
And this good truth bear always in our mind
That once to die is destined for mankind.
And while wealth fails one lasting joy to give,
The gifts of virtue shall for ever live.

Pythagoras (580–500 B.C.)

LAW OF PIETY

May we truly follow the excellent Law of Piety—in many good deeds, compassion, liberality, truthfulness and purity.

Asoka (3rd century B.C.)

GOODNESS AND PURITY

Love the saints of every faith;
Put away thy pride;
Remember, the essence of religion
Is meekness and sympathy,
Not fine clothes,
Not the Yogi's garb and ashes,
Not the blowing of the horn,
Not the shaven head,
Not long prayers,
Not recitations and torturings,
Not the ascetic way,
But a life of goodness and purity,
Amid the world's temptations.

Guru Nanak (1469–1538)

TEACH US CONTROL

Teach us, O Blessed One, control of speech, control of thought, control of action. Help us to keep these roads of action clear and so find the Way made known by Thee to the wise in heart.

Buddhist Scriptures

VIRTUE

When righteousness declines and evil is strong I rise up in every age, taking visible form, and moving a man amongst men, succouring the good, thrusting the evil back, and setting virtue on her seat again.

Hindu Scriptures (Bhagavad Gita)

FREE FROM HATRED

A man is not wise because he has much to say. The wise man is he who is patient, fearless and free from hatred.

A man is not wise because he knows many verses. He who knows little of the law, but lives it himself, is called righteous.

Pali Buddhist Scriptures (Dhammapada)

THE BEST

The best soldier is not warlike; the best fighter is never angry; the best conqueror takes no part in war.

Tao Te Ching: Lao Tse (604–517 B.C.*)*

THE DEEDS OF MERCY

We do pray for mercy
And that same prayer doth teach us all to render
The deeds of mercy.

The Merchant of Venice:
William Shakespeare (1564–1616)

THY NEARER LIGHT

O God, who leadest us through seasons of life to be partakers of Thine eternity, the shadows of our evening hasten on. Quicken us betimes, and spare us that sad word: 'The harvest is past, the summer ended, and we are not saved.' Anew we dedicate ourselves to Thee. We would ask nothing, reserve nothing for ourselves, save only leave to go whither Thou mayest guide, to live not far from Thee, to die into Thy nearer light. Content to accept the reproach of truth, we would take upon us the yoke of Christ, whom it behoved to suffer ere He entered into His glory. We ask it in the Name and for the sake of the same Jesus Christ our Lord. Amen.

James Martineau (1805–1900)

THE FAITHFULNESS OF LEARNERS

In times of doubts and questionings, when our belief is perplexed by new learning, new teaching, new thought, when our faith is strained by creeds, by doctrine, by mysteries beyond our understanding, give us the faithfulness of learners and the courage of believers in Thee: give us boldness to examine, and faith to trust all truth: patience and insight to master all difficulties; stability to hold fast our traditions with enlightened interpretations, to admit all truth made known to us, and in times of trouble to grasp new knowledge and combine it loyally and honestly with the old. Save us and help us, we

79

humbly beseech Thee, O Lord. Amen.

Bishop Ridding (1828–1904)

HIS HOLY STEPS

O God, whose most dearly beloved Son was, by Thy mighty power, exalted into the heavens, that He might prepare a place in Thy Kingdom of glory for them that truly love Thee, so lead and uphold us, O merciful Lord, that we may both follow the most holy steps of His life on earth, and may enter with Him hereafter into Thy everlasting rest; that where He is, we may be also; through the merits of the same Jesus Christ our Lord. Amen.

William Edward Scudamore (1813–1881)

GIVE WITHOUT PAY

And preach as you go, saying, 'The kingdom of heaven is at hand.' Heal the sick, raise the dead, cleanse lepers, cast out demons. You received without pay, give without pay.

Matthew 10: 7–8, RSV

WHATEVER IS TRUE

Finally, brethren, whatever is true, whatever is honourable, whatever is just, whatever is pure, whatever is lovely, whatever is gracious, if there is any excellence, if there is anything worthy of praise, think about these things.

Philippians 4: 8

FORGIVE ALL OUR SINS

We call to mind, O God, before Thy throne of grace, all those whom Thou has given to be near and dear to us, and all for whom we are especially bound to pray; beseeching Thee to remember them all for good, and to fulfil, as may be expedient for them, all their desires and wants. We commend to Thee any who may have wronged us, whether by word or deed, beseeching Thee to forgive them and us all our sins, and to bring us to Thy heavenly kingdom; through Jesus Christ our Lord. Amen.

Bishop Hamilton (1808–1869)

LET OUR LIGHT SHINE

O Lord, who hast given us Thy summer sun to gladden us with his light and to ripen the fruits of the earth for our support, and who biddest him to set when his work is done, that he may rise again tomorrow; give Thy blessing to us Thy servants, that the lesson of the works of Thy hand may be learnt by us Thy living works, and that we may run our course like the sun which is now gone from us.

Let us rise early and go late to rest, being ever busy and zealous in doing Thy will. Let our light shine before men, that they may glorify Thee, our Heavenly Father. Let us do good all our days, and be useful to and comfort others. And let us finish our course in faith, that we too may rise again to a course which shall never end.

Thomas Arnold (1795–1842)

JOYS AND SUFFERINGS

Lord Jesus, take away the veil from our eyes, that we may contemplate the beauty of thy ideals. Grant to us thy power, to the end that we may be faithful partakers of the joys and the sufferings of thy Kingdom.

Epaminondas M. do Amaral

PITY FOR THE WICKED

A Durwaish, in his prayer, said, 'O God! show pity towards the wicked, for on the good thou hast already bestowed mercy by having created them virtuous.'

The Gulistan: Sadi of Shiraz (1184–1291)

PATIENCE

An African mendicant at Aleppo, in the quarter occupied by the dealers in linen cloths, was saying, 'O wealthy sirs! if there had been justice amongst you, and we had possessed contentment, there would have been an end of beggary in the world.' O contentment! make me rich; for without thee there is no wealth. Lókman made a choice of patience in retirement.

Whosoever hath not patience, neither doth he possess philosophy.

The Gulistan: Sadi of Shiraz (1184–1291)

INVESTIGATION

Things have their root and their completion. It cannot be that when the root is neglected, what springs from it will be well ordered.

The ancients, who wished to illustrate illustrious virtue throughout the empire, began, said Confucius, with investigation. Things being investigated, knowledge became complete. Knowledge being complete, their thoughts were sincere. Their thoughts being sincere, their hearts were then rectified. Their hearts being rectified, their persons were cultivated. Their persons cultivated, their families were regulated. Their families being regulated, their states were rightly governed. Their states being rightly governed, the whole empire was made tranquil and happy.

The Great Learning: Confucius (551–479 B.C.)

THE POISONOUS ROOT

Patience and resignation is the one road;
Buddha has declared no better path exists:
The disciple who is angry or impatient
Cannot really be called a saint.
Destroy anger and there will be rest;
Destroy anger and there will be peace:
Anger is the poisonous root
Which overthrows the growth of virtue.
Without complaint, without envy;
Continuing the practice of the precepts;
Knowing the way to moderate appetite;
Ever joyous without any weight of care
Fixed and ever advancing in virtue:
This is the doctrine of the enlightened.

Buddhist Scriptures (Catena)

RESTRAIN ONESELF FROM EVIL

In aid of the proceedings that are among men, wisdom is good; in seeking renown, liberality is good; in the advancement of justice, devotedness is good; in the speaking of explanations, truth is good; in the progress of business, energy is good; in the attainment of benefit therefrom, thankfulness is good; in keeping oneself unblemished, the discreet speaking which is in truth is good; in keeping back misfortune, employment is good; before an assembly, eloquent discourse is good; for peace of mind, friendship is good; with an associate in one's own deeds, the giving of advantage is good; among the superior, mildness and humility are good; among the inferior, instruction and civility are good; in bodily health, moderate health and keeping the body at work are good; among dependants and servants, good behaviour and dignity are good; for having little grief in one's self, contentment is good; for not coming to dishonour, knowledge of oneself is good; and in every place and time, to restrain oneself from evil, and to be diligent in the performance of good deeds are good. Occupation, and preserving pure language, are above everything.

Parsi Scriptures (Mainyo-i-Khard)

HUMANITY AND JUSTICE

All men have in themselves the feelings of mercy and pity, of shame and hatred of vice. It is for each one by culture to let these feelings grow or to let them wither. They are part of the organisation of men, as much as the limbs or senses, and may be trained as well. The mountain Nicon-chau naturally brings forth beautiful trees. Even when the trunks are cut down, young shoots will constantly rise up. If cattle are allowed to feed there, the mountain looks bare: shall we say then that bareness is natural to the mountain? So the lower passions are let loose to eat down the nobler growths of reverence and love in the heart of man: shall we therefore say that there are no such feelings in his heart at all? Under the quiet peaceful airs of morning and evening the shoots tend to grow again. Humanity is the heart of man; justice is the path of man. To know heaven is to develop the principle of our higher nature.

Mencius (or Meng-tse, 372–289? B.C.)

THE SAME IN HEART AND LIFE

Buddha said, 'There are difficult things in the world—Being poor, to be charitable; being rich and great, to be religious; to escape destiny; to repress lust and banish desire; to see an agreeable object and not seek to obtain it; to be strong without being rash; to bear insult without anger; to move in the world (to touch things) without setting the heart on it; to investigate the matter to the very bottom; not to condemn the ignorant; thoroughly to extirpate self-esteem; to be good, and at the same time to be learned and clever; to see the hidden principle in the profession of religion; to attain one's end without exultation; to save men by converting them; to be the same in heart and life; to avoid controversy.'

Buddhist Scriptures

TO THOSE WHO DO YOU EVIL

It is the determination of the spotless not to give sorrows to others, although they could obtain by it the right powers which confer greatness.

It is the determination of the spotless not to do evil in return to those who have done evil to them.

If a man inflict suffering, even on those who without cause hate him, it will in the end give him irremovable sorrow.

The punishment of those who have done you evil, is to put them to shame by showing great kindness to them.

What benefit has he derived from his knowledge who does not endeavour to keep off pain from another as much as from himself?

Why does a man inflict on others that which were grievous to himself?

If a man in the morning seek sorrow for another, in the evening sorrow will visit him unsought.

Hindu Scriptures (Cural II)

GIVE UP EVIL THOUGHTS

Without purity of mind, to what end is the worship of God? Why say, 'I will go to Benares'? Why long for the sacred wells? How shall the true Benares be attained by the evil-doer?

Though we roam the wilds, sanctity is not in them; nor is it in the sky; nor on the earth at the confluence of holy streams. Make thy body pure and thou shalt behold the King.

The devout man by the gradual progress of his soul shall attain his desire. He who is converted into pure mind knows the great secret.

Convert thy body into a temple, and restrain thyself; give up evil thoughts, and see God with thy internal eye. When we know him we shall know ourselves.

Hindu Scriptures (Vemana)

TO ACCOMPLISH PERFECTLY

God of all goodness, grant us to desire ardently, to seek wisely, to know surely, and to accomplish perfectly Thy holy will, for the glory of Thy name.

St. Thomas Aquinas (1227–1274)

A HOLY NATION

Yet O for his sake who sits now by thee
All crown'd with victory,
So guide us through this Darkness, that we may
Be more and more in love with day;

Settle, and fix our hearts, that we may move
In order, peace, and love,
And taught obedience by the whole Creation,
Become an humble, holy nation.

Give to thy spouse her perfect, and pure dress,
Beauty and holiness,
And so repair those Rents, that men may see
And say, Where God is, all agree.

Henry Vaughan (1622–1695)

CLEARLY, DEARLY, NEARLY

O most merciful Redeemer, Friend, and Brother,
May we know Thee more clearly,
Love Thee more dearly,
Follow Thee more nearly:
For ever and ever. Amen.

St. Richard of Chichester (1197–1253)

TO PACIFY ANGER

O Lord Jesus Christ, give us a measure of Thy spirit that we may be enabled to obey Thy teaching to pacify anger, to take part in pity, to moderate desire, to increase love, to put away sorrow, to cast away vainglory, not to be vindictive, not to fear death, ever entrusting our spirit to immortal God, who with Thee and the Holy Ghost liveth and reigneth world without end.

St. Apollonius (flourished 133–185), adapted

WITH A PURE HEART

O God, the Father of our Saviour Jesus Christ, Whose name is great, Whose nature is blissful, Whose goodness is inexhaustible, God and Ruler of all things, Who are blessed forever; before Whom stand thousands and thousands, and ten thousand times ten thousand, the hosts of holy angels and archangels;

Sanctify, O Lord, our souls and bodies and spirits, search our consciences, and cast out of us every evil thought, every base desire, all envy and pride, all wrath and anger, and all that is contrary to Thy holy will. And grant us, O Lord, Lover of men, with a pure heart and contrite soul to call upon Thee, our holy God and Father who art in heaven. Amen.

The Syrian Rite

BRING US NEARER THEE

Before Thy throne, O God, we kneel;
Give us a conscience quick to feel,
A ready mind to understand

The meaning of Thy chastening hand;
Whate'er the pain and shame may be,
Bring us, O Father, nearer Thee.
Search out our hearts and make us true,
Wishful to give to all their due;
For love of pleasure, lust of gold,
From sins which make the heart grow cold,
Wean us and train us with Thy rod;
Teach us to know our faults, O God.

Bishop W. B. Carpenter (1841–1918)

TO PRACTISE VIRTUE

Let us pray that we may learn what we are and what we ought to be. By this means, we shall not only learn the number and the evil effects of our peculiar faults, but we shall also learn to what virtues we are called, and the way to practise them. The rays of that pure and heavenly light that visits the humble soul will beam on us; and we shall feel and understand that everything is possible to those who put their whole trust in God.

François de Salignac de la Mothe Fénélon (1651–1715)

THEM THAT LOVE GOD

We know that all things work for the good of them that love God.

Romans 8: 28

SHOW US THE WAY

Endue our soul with the righteousness of a holy faith, living and working by charity. Show us the way we should walk in; teach us to do whatsoever pleaseth thee: quicken our souls in the paths of life, and so continue the conduct of Thy spirit to us, that it may never leave us. Amen.

Bishop Jeremy Taylor (1613–1667)

THREE PRECIOUS THINGS

I have three precious things which I hold fast and prize.
The first is gentleness; the second is frugality;
The third is humility, which keeps me from putting myself
before others.
Be gentle, and you can be bold; be frugal, and you can be
liberal;
Avoid putting yourself before others, and you can become a
leader of men.
Gentleness brings victory to him who attacks, and safety to
him who defends.
Those whom Heaven would save, it fences round with
gentleness.
The greatest conquerors are those who overcome their
enemies without strife.

Tao Te Ching: Lao Tse (604–517 B.C.)

LIVE HAPPILY

Let us live happily, then, though we call nothing our own!
We shall become like the bright gods who feed on happiness.
Let us live happily, free from ailments among the ailing!
Let us dwell free from afflictions, among men who are sick
at heart.
Let us live happily, free from care among the busy.
Let us dwell free from yearning among the men who are
anxious.
Let us live happily, not hating those who hate us.
Let us live free from hatred among men who hate.
For never does hatred cease by hatred, hatred ceases by love,
this is always its nature.
Let us, therefore, overcome anger by kindness, evil by good,
falsehood by truth.
Let us speak the truth; yield not to anger; give when asked,
even from the little that we have.
By these things shall we enter the presence of the gods.

Pali Buddhist Scriptures (Dhammapada)

PEACE IN SILENCE

Go placidly amid the noise and haste, and remember what peace there may be in silence. As far as possible without surrender be on good terms with all persons. Speak your truth quietly and clearly; and listen to others, even the dull and ignorant; they too have their story. Avoid loud and aggressive persons, they are vexatious to the spirit. If you compare yourself with others you may become vain and bitter; for always there will be greater and lesser persons than yourselves. Enjoy your achievements as well as your plans. Keep interested in your own career, however humble; it is a real possession in the changing fortunes of time. Exercise caution in your business affairs; for the world is full of trickery. But let this not blind you to what virtue there is; many persons strive for high ideals and everywhere life is full of heroism. Be yourself. Especially do not feign affection. Neither be cynical about love; for in the face of all aridity and disenchantment it is perennial as the grass. Take kindly the counsel of the years, gracefully surrendering the things of youth. Nurture strength of spirit to shield you in sudden misfortune. But do not distress yourself with imaginings. Many fears are born of fatigue and loneliness. Beyond a wholesome discipline, be gentle with yourself. You are a child of the universe, no less than the trees and the stars; you have a right to be here. And whether or not it is clear to you, no doubt the universe is unfolding as it should. Therefore be at peace with God whatever you conceive him to be, and whatever your labours and aspirations, in the noisy confusion of life, keep peace with your soul. With all its sham, drudgery and broken dreams, it is still a beautiful world. Be careful. Strive to be happy.

Found in Old St. Paul's Church, Baltimore, dated 1692

AGAINST THE SERVANTS OF MAMMON

We cry to Thee for justice, O Lord, for our soul is weary with the iniquity of greed. Behold the servants of Mammon, who defy Thee and drain their fellow men for gain; who grind down the strength of the workers by merciful toil and fling them aside when they are mangled and worn; who rack-rent the poor and make dear the space and air which Thou hast made free; who paralyse the hand of justice by corruption and blind the eyes of the people by lies; who nullify by their craft the merciful laws which nobler men have devised for the protection of the weak; who have made us ashamed of our dear country by their defilements and have turned our holy freedom into a hollow name; who have brought upon Thy Church the contempt of men and have cloaked their extortion with the gospel of Thy Christ.

For the oppression of the poor and the sighing of the needy now do Thou arise, O Lord; for because Thou art love, and tender as a mother to the weak, therefore Thou art the great hater of iniquity and Thy doom is upon those who grow rich on the poverty of the people.

O God, we are afraid, for the thundercloud of Thy wrath is even now black above us. In the ruins of dead empires we have read how Thou hast trodden the wine-press of Thine anger when the measure of their sin was full. We are sick at heart when we remember that by the greed of those who enslaved a weaker race that curse was fastened upon us all which still lies black and hopeless across our land, though the blood of a nation was spilled to atone. Save our people from being dragged down into vaster guilt and woe by men who have no vision and know no law except their lust. Shake their souls with awe of Thee that they may cease. Help us with clean hands to tear the web which they have woven about us and to turn our people back to Thy law, lest the mark of the beast stand out on the right hand and forehead of our nation and our feet be set on the downward path of darkness from which there is no return for ever.

Prayers of the Social Awakening:
Walter Rauschenbusch (1861–1918)

THE OTHER CHEEK

Of all the portions of the Gospels, the Sermon on the Mount always had for me an exceptional importance. I now read it more frequently than ever. Nowhere does Jesus speak with greater solemnity, nowhere does he propound moral rules more definitely and practically, nor do these rules in any other form awaken more readily an echo in the human heart; nowhere else does he address himself to a larger multitude of the common people. If there are any clear and precise Christian principles, one ought to find them here. I therefore sought the solution of my doubts in Matthew 5, 6, and 7, comprising the Sermon on the Mount. These chapters I read very often, each time with the same emotional ardour, as I came to the verses which exhort the hearer to turn the other cheek, to give up his cloak, to be at peace with all the world, to love his enemies—but each time with the same disappointment. The Divine words were not clear. They exhorted to a renunciation so absolute as to entirely stifle life as I understood it; to renounce everything, therefore, could not, as it seemed to me, be essential to salvation. And the moment this ceased to be an absolute condition, clearness and precision were at an end.

I read not only the Sermon on the Mount: I read all the Gospels and all the theological commentaries on the Gospels. I was not satisfied with the declarations of the theologians that the Sermon on the Mount was only an indication of the degree of perfection to which man should aspire; that men, weighed down by sin, could not reach such an ideal; and that the salvation of humanity was in faith and prayer and grace. I could not admit the truth of these propositions. It seemed to me a strange thing that Jesus should propound rules so clear and admirable, addressed to the understanding of everyone, and still realise man's inability to carry his doctrine into practice.

Then as I read these maxims I was permeated with the joyous assurance that I might that very hour, that very moment, begin to practise them. The burning desire I felt led me to the attempt, but the doctrine of the Church rang in my ears—Man is weak, and to this he cannot attain—my strength soon failed. On every side I heard, 'You must believe and pray'; but my wavering faith impeded prayer. Again I heard, 'You must pray, and God will give you faith; this faith will inspire prayer, which in turn will invoke faith that will inspire more prayer, and so on indefinitely.' Reason and experience alike convinced me that such methods were useless. It seemed to me that the only true way was for me to try to follow the doctrine of Jesus.

And so, after all this fruitless search and careful meditation over all that had been written for and against the divinity of the doctrine of Jesus, after all this doubt and suffering, I came back face to face with the mysterious Gospel message. I could not find the meanings that others found, neither could I discover what I sought. It was only after I had rejected the interpretations of the wise critics and theologians, according to the words of Jesus, 'Except ye become as little children ye shall not enter into the kingdom of heaven' (Matthew 18:3)—it was only then that I suddenly understood what had been so meaningless before. I understood, not through exegetical fantasies or profound and ingenious textual combinations; I understood everything, because I put all commentaries out of my mind. This was the passage that gave the key to the whole—'Ye have heard that it hath been said, An eye for an eye, and a tooth for a tooth: but I say unto you, that ye resist not evil.'

One day the exact and simple meaning of these words came to me; I understood that Jesus meant neither more nor less than what he said. What I saw was nothing new; only the veil that had hidden the truth from me fell away, and the truth was revealed in all its grandeur.

My Religion: Leo Tolstoy (1828–1910)

THE PERFECT GOOD

Buddha was residing at Jetavana. In the night a heavenly being, illuminating Jetavana with his radiance, approached him, saying—'Many gods and men, aspiring after good, have held divers things to be blessings; declare the things that are excellent.' Buddha said—

'To serve the wise, and not the foolish, and to honour those worthy of honour; these are excellencies.

'To dwell in the neighbourhood of the good, to bear the remembrance of good deeds, and to have a soul filled with right desires; these are excellencies.

'To have knowledge of truth, to be instructed in science, to have a disciplined mind, and pleasant speech; these are excellencies.

'To honour father and mother, to provide for wife and child and to follow a blameless vocation; these are excellencies.

'To be charitable, act virtuously, be helpful to relatives, and to lead an innocent life; these are excellencies.

'To be pure, temperate and persevering in good deeds; these are excellencies.

'Humility, reverence, contentment, gratitude, attentiveness to religious instruction; these are excellencies.

'To be gentle, to be patient under reproof, at due seasons to converse with the religious, these are excellencies.

'Self-restraint and chastity, the knowledge of the great principles, and the hope of the eternal repose; these are great excellencies.

'To have a mind unshaken by prosperity or adversity, inaccessible to sorrow, secure and tranquil; these are great excellencies.

'They that do these things are invincible; on every side they walk in safety; they attain the perfect good.'

Ceylon, Pali, Buddhist, Khuddaka,
Pathâ Scriptures (compilation)

MERCY ON ALL THE POOR SONS OF MEN

O Lord God, heavenly Father, we thank Thee for Thy grace that Thou hast sent us Thy Son, and hast appointed Him to be the King of righteousness, and our Saviour and Redeemer, Who should rescue us from the dominion of darkness, and bestow on us righteousness, salvation and blessedness. May He take up His abode among us and within us, and may we ever continue in His kingdom and allegiance. Incline the hearts and will of all princes and peoples to open their gates unto the King of Kings and Lord of Glory; may He enter into their lands, cities and churches, to dwell there, and to rule and govern all things by His Word and spirit. Restrain and check all influences that would close the door against Him and forbid Him to come in, while giving free entrance to false teachers and dreamers. Bring their evil enterprise to nought. But show forth Thy power and mercy on all the poor sons of men who are bound in the fetters of oppression, or the dreariness of unbelief, in idolatry, false doctrine, or utter careless ungodliness; may Christ come to their hearts. Amen.

Riga Prayer Book

EVERYTHING THAT IS GOOD

We worship the pure, the Lord of purity.

We worship the universe of the true spirit, visible, invisible, and all that sustains the welfare of the good creation.

We praise all good thoughts, all good words, all good deeds, which are and will be, and keep pure all that is good.

Thou true happy Being! we strive to think, to speak, to do only what, of all actions, may promote the two lives—the body and the mind.

We beseech the spirit of the earth, by means of these best works [agriculture], to grant us beautiful and fertile fields, for believer and unbeliever, for rich and poor.

We worship the Wise One who formed and furthered the spirit of earth.

We worship him with our bodies and souls.

We worship him as being united with the spirits of pure men and women.

We worship the promotion of all good, all that is very beautiful, shining, immortal, bright, everything that is good.

Anon.

WALK NOT PROUDLY

Verily the Lord is round about mankind.

Man prayeth for evil as he prayeth for good.

Every man's fate hath God fastened about his neck.

Read thy book: thou needst none but thyself to make out an account against thee this day.

For his own good only shall the guided yield to guidance, and to his own loss only shall the erring err; and the heavy-laden shall not be laden with another's load. Not to any shall the gifts of Thy Lord be denied.

Give full measure when you measure, and weigh with just balance.

Follow not that of which though hast no knowledge.

Of knowledge only a little to you is given.

Walk not proudly in the earth.

Speak kindly.

To him who is of kin render his due, also to the poor and to the wayfarer; yet waste not.

If ye do well, to your own behoof will ye do well; and if ye do evil, against yourselves will ye do it.

Guided indeed is he whom God guideth. And he whom God guideth shall have none to mislead him.

Nothing hath been said to thee which hath not been said of old to apostles before thee.

The Koran

THE GREATEST BLESSING

Not to serve the foolish, but to serve the wise;
To honour those worthy of honour—this is the greatest
blessing.

Much insight and education, self-control and pleasant
speech,
And whatever word be well spoken—this is the greatest
blessing.

To live righteously, to give help to kindred,
To follow a peaceful calling—this is the greatest blessing.

To be long-suffering and meek, to abhor and cease from evil,
Not to be weary in well-doing—this is the greatest blessing.

To be gentle, to be patient under reproof,
To be charitable, act virtuously—this is the greatest blessing.

Reverence and humility, contentment and gratitude,
To be pure, to be temperate—this is the greatest blessing.

To dwell in a pleasant land with right desires in the heart,
To bear the remembrance of good deeds—this is the greatest
blessing.

Beneath the stroke of life's changes, the mind that shaketh
not,
Without grief or passion—this is the greatest blessing.

On every side are invincible they who do acts like these,
On every side they walk in safety—and theirs is the greatest
blessing.

Buddhist Scriptures

THE SOUL IS ITS OWN REFUGE

Though permitted to receive presents, let the Brahman avoid
a habit of taking them, since by taking many gifts his divine
light soon fades.

95

By falsehood, the sacrifice becomes vain; by pride, the merit of devotion is lost, and by proclaiming a largess, the fruit of life is destroyed.

Giving no pain to any creature, let a man collect virtue by degrees, as the white ant builds his nest by degrees, that he may acquire a companion to the next world. His virtue alone will adhere to him. With virtue for his guide he will traverse a gloom, how hard to be traversed.

All things have their sense ascertained by speech. In speech they have their basis, and from speech they proceed; consequently, a falsifier of speech falsifies everything.

Alone in some solitary place, let him meditate on the divine nature of the soul; by such meditation he will attain happiness.

Neither by explaining omens and prodigies, nor by skill in astrology and palmistry, nor by casuistry and expositions of holy texts, let the Brahman gain his daily support.

No man who is ignorant of the Supreme Spirit can gather the fruit of mere ceremonial acts.

The soul itself is its own witness; the soul itself is its own refuge: offend not thy conscious soul, the supreme internal witness of men!

Hindu Scriptures (Manu)

ALL ARE UNCERTAIN

When Caundilya, the warrior, saw his son dead, he fainted through in grief: as he lay on the ground his kinsmen sat down by him. A holy man named Capila said to him, 'There is no stability. Youth, beauty, life, collected wealth, dominion, the society of friends, are all uncertain: in this the wise are not deceived. Whither are the lords of the world gone, with their armies, their valour, and their equipage? The earth itself remains to this day a witness of the separation from it. In the transient world, which never affords permanent pleasure, let the wise strengthen devotion and multiply the delights of holiness.'

Caundilya, hearing this, rose up, and said, 'What then have I to do with my vain palace? I will go as a pilgrim into the desert.'

Capila rejoined, 'He who has controlled his own spirit and desires, who has knowledge, piety, and good character, gathers the fruit of a pilgrimage. Even in the sacred forest inflamed passions cause crime; and in the mansion, self-control brings piety to dwell. The virtuous man's home is his desert of devotion. They whose food is only to sustain life, whose voice is only to speak truth, make hardships easy. Thyself art the sacred river—its waters truth; its banks right conduct; its waves benevolence. Here wash thy lips, O son of Pandu! for the interior soul is not purified by holy water! If truth be placed in a balance with a thousand sacrifices of horses, truth will outweigh a thousand sacrifices.

Hindu Scriptures (Hitopadesa)

THE PATH OF VIRTUE

Who shall find out the plainly shown path of virtue, as a clever man finds out the right flower?

Death carries off a man who is carrying flowers, and whose mind is distracted, before he is satiated in his pleasures.

As a bee collects nectar and departs without injuring the flower, its colour or scent, so let the wise man dwell on earth.

Not the failures of others, not their sins of omission and commission, but his own misdeeds and negligences should he take notice of.

Like a beautiful flower, full of colour but without scent, are the fine but fruitless words of him who does not act accordingly.

The fields are damaged by weeds; mankind by hatred. As the Vassiká-plant sheds its withered flowers, men should shed passion and hatred.

As many kinds of wreaths can be made from a heap of flowers, so many good things may be achieved by a mortal if once he is born.

The scent of flowers does not travel against the wind, nor that of sandalwood; but the odour of good people travels even against the wind: a good man pervades every place.

Sandalwood or Tagára, Vassiká, the lotus-flower, have peerless fragrance; but the odour of excellent people rises up as the highest.

As from a heap of rubbish cast on the highway, the lily will grow of sweet perfume and delightful, even so the disciple of the truly enlightened Teacher will shine forth amid those who

97

are like rubbish, those who walk in darkness.

Pali, Dhammapada, Buddhist compilation

SPITTING AT HEAVEN

Buddha said, 'A man who foolishly does me wrong (or regards me as being, or doing, wrong), I will return to him the protection of my ungrudging love; the more evil comes from him, the more good shall go from me; the fragrance of these good actions always rebounding to me, the harm of the slanderer's words returning to him.' There was a foolish man once heard Buddha, whilst preaching, defend this great principle of returning good for evil, and therefore he came and abused Buddha. Buddha was silent, and would not answer him, pitying his mad folly. The man having finished his abuse, Buddha asked him, saying, 'Son, when a man forgets the rules of politeness in making a present to another, the custom is to say, 'Keep your present.' Son, you have now railed at me; I decline to entertain your abuse, and request you to keep it—a source of misery to yourself. For as a sound belongs to the drum, and shadow to the substance, so in the end misery will certainly overtake the evildoer.'

Buddha said, 'A wicked man who reproaches a virtuous man, is like one who looks up and spits at heaven; his spittle soils not heaven, but comes back and defiles his own person.'

Buddhist Scriptures (Catena)

THE SPEED OF VIRTUE

Is virtue far off? I wish to be virtuous, and lo! it is at hand. Virtue runs swifter than the royal postilions.

Is any one able for one day to apply his strength to virtue? I have not seen the case in which his strength would be insufficient.

Even a man's faults may reflect his virtues.

A man should not be concerned that he has no place: he should be concerned to fit himself for one.

Virtue is not left to stand alone. He who practises it will have neighbours.

Let every attainment in what is good be firmly grasped.

The man of perfect virtue is slow of speech; for when a man feels the difficulty of doing, can he be other than cautious and slow in speaking?

The firm, the enduring, the simple, and the modest, are near to virtue.

Let every man consider virtue as what devolves upon himself. He may not yield the performance of it to any teacher.

My friend Chang can do things hard to be done, but yet he is not perfectly virtuous.

The wise man hastens, neither in his studies nor words; he is sometimes, as it were, mute, but when it concerns him to act and practise rectitude, he, as I may say, precipitates all.

The She-King says, 'Heaven created all men, having their duties and the means of performing them. It is the natural and constant disposition of men to love beautiful Virtue.' He who wrote this ode knew right principles.

Analects: Confucius (551–479 B.C.)

THE VIRTUE OF MAN

On hearing of the slander of mankind, taste not its anger.

On hearing of the flattery of mankind, tast not its joy.

On hearing persons talk of man's wickedness, partake not of their pleasure.

On hearing men speak of the virtues of mankind, approve, follow, and rejoice therein.

Rejoice on beholding the virtuous man.

Rejoice on hearing the record of virtuous actions.

Rejoice in the diffusion of correct principles.

Rejoice in the diffusion and doing of good.

On hearing of the wickedness of mankind, let it be to you as thorns penetrating the back.

On hearing of virtuous and benevolent acts, bind them about you as a garland of flowers.

Then the heart will never cease thinking thereon, and the feet never cease walking in the right path.

When man ceases not the exchange of civilities there is nothing he may not possess.

Kang Tsze Chow

THE ABODE OF HOLINESS

This is what should be done by him who is wise in seeking his own good, and gaining a knowledge of the tranquil lot of Nirvána:

Let him be diligent, upright, and conscientious; not vainglorious, but gentle and lowly;

Contented and cheerful; not oppressed with cares; not burdened with riches; tranquil, prudent, free from arrogance and avarice.

Let him not do any mean action, nor incur the reproval of wise men.

Let all creatures be prosperous and happy, let them be of joyful mind; all beings that have life, be they feeble or strong, be they minute or vast:

Seen or unseen, near or afar, born or seeking birth, let all things be joyful.

Let no man deceive another; let none be harsh to any; let none wish ill to his neighbour.

Let the love that fills the mother's heart as she watches over an only child, even such love, animate all.

Let the goodwill that is boundless, immeasurable, impartial, unmixed with enmity, prevail throughout the world—above, below, around.

If a man be of this mind, wherever he moves, and in every moment, the saying is come to pass, 'This place is the abode of holiness.'

Singhalese, Pali, Buddhist, Kuddaka Patha Scriptures (compilation)

VIRTUE NEEDS NO DISPLAY

The poem says, 'That is the right imperial domain where the people have repose.'

Make happy those who are near, and those who are far will come.

The great man will cultivate himself with reverential carefulness, that he may give rest to all the people.

Where rulers love justice, the people respond readily with service.

The path is not far from men. The ode says, 'As we cut axe-handles, we grasp one handle to hew another.' So the wise governor uses what is within man to reform men.

The acts of a wise ruler are for ages a law to the empire; his words are for ages a lesson to the empire.

Chung-Ne handed down the doctrines of the sages as if they were his ancestors. He harmonised with heaven above, and beneath with sea and land. In alternating progress he was as the four seasons.

What needs no display is virtue.

The wise man does not use rewards, and the people are stimulated to virtue; he does not show anger, and the people are awed more than by battle-axes.

Heaven and earth are without doubleness.

The superior man being sincere and reverential, the whole world is conducted to a state of happy tranquillity.

Great energies are traced in great transformations.

The Doctrine of the Mean:
Confucius (551–479 B.C.*)*

FOR THEM THAT HURT US

Help us, O heavenly Father, that according to thy commandment we may love our enemies, and pray for them that have hurt us. Bring to pass, through thy Holy Spirit, that all those unto whom we have done harm may also forgive us. For we grieve and are sorry that at any time we have transgressed Christian love and charity, and have beguiled, deceived, or offended any man by evil example or with too few benefits. We beseech thee, O Lord, through Jesus Christ, to forgive them that ever hurt us in thought, word, or deed.

To thy faithfulness and protection, O dearest Father, we commit all that concerneth us, especially our wives, children, friends, and all such as thou hast put under our governance. Comfort and help thou all those that lie in bonds, and are persecuted for thy Word's sake.

Have mercy upon all that are in prison, poverty, sickness, and heaviness. O bring thou the whole world to the knowledge of thy Holy Word, that they may live according to thy godly will, and throughout all troubles endure and continue still in the Christian faith, Amen.

Otho Wermullerus (16th century)

COURAGE IN DISTRESS

Most high God, our loving Father, infinite in majesty, we humbly beseech Thee for all Thy servants everywhere, that Thou wouldst give us a pure mind, perfect love, sincerity in conduct, purity in heart, strength in action, courage in distress, self-command in character. May our prayers ascend to Thy gracious ears, and Thy loving benediction descend upon us all, that we may in all things be protected under the shadow of Thy wings. Grant us pardon of our sins; perfect our work; accept our prayers; protect us by Thine own Name, O God of Jacob; send us Thy saving help from Thy holy place, and strengthen us out of Zion. Remember all Thy people everywhere, give us all the grace of devotion to Thy will; fulfil our desires with good gifts, and crown us with Thy mercy. When we serve Thee with faithful devotion, pardon our sins and correct us with Fatherly tenderness. Grant that, being delivered from all adversity, and both here and eternally justified, we may praise Thee for ever and ever, saying, Holy, Holy, Holy; through Jesus Christ our Lord and Saviour, Who with Thee and the Holy Ghost, liveth and reigneth, even one God, world without end. Amen.

Gallican Sacramentary (4th century)

THOU ART THE JUSTICE

Incantation. O Shamash, at the foundations of the heavens
thou flamest up.
The look of the brilliant heaven thou hast opened.
The bolt of the heaven thou hast removed.
O Shamash, to the earth thou hast lifted up thy head.
O Shamash, thou hast covered the earth with heavenly
splendour,
When thou lookest upon the land establishest thou light.
The way of the land truly guide thou!
The beasts of the field, the living creatures thou hast created.
To Shamash, like unto a father and mother they listen.
Food they are fed.
O Shamash, the chief of the gods art thou!
He who goes before the Anunaki art thou!
With Anu and Enlil a king of mankind art thou!
Guide thou the law of all the people!

O god of justice in the heaven eternal art thou!
Thou art the justice and the wisdom of the land!
Thou knowest the pious, thou knowest the wicked.
O Shamash, righteousness lifteth up to thee its head.
O Shamash, wickedness like a whip becomes torn through
thee.
O Shamash, the helper of Anu and Enlil art thou.
O Shamash, the exalted judge of heaven and earth art thou.

Hymn to Shamash, the Sun God

NIRVANA

Again, there was a Brahmatchari called Basita, who resumed
the conversation thus: Gotama! Is that which you call Nirvana
a permanent state of Being or not? Yes, Brahmatchari. Basita
replied, Gotama, then we may not say that Nirvana consists in
the absence of sorrow? Yes, Brahmatchari, it may be so
defined. Basita said, Gotama, there are four kinds of condition
in the world which are spoken of as non-existent: the first, that
which is not as yet in being, like the pitcher to be made out of
the clay; secondly, that which, having existed, has been
destroyed, as a broken pitcher; third, that which consists in the
absence of something different from itself, as we say the ox is
not a horse; and, lastly, that which is purely imaginary as the
hair of the tortoise, or the horn of the hare. If, then, by having
got rid of sorrow we have arrived at Nirvana, Nirvana is the
same as 'nothingness,' and may be considered as non-existent;
but, if so, how can you define it as permanence, joy,
personality, and purity?

Buddha said, Illustrious disciple, Nirvana is of this sort, it is
not like the pitcher not yet made out of the clay, nor is it like the
nothingness of the pitcher which has been broken; nor is it like
the horn of the hare, nor the hair of the tortoise, something
purely imaginary. But it may be compared to the nothingness
defined as the absence of something different from itself.
Illustrious disciple, as you say, although the ox has no quality
of the horse in it, you cannot say that the ox does not exist; and
though the horse has no quality of the ox in it, you cannot say
the horse does not exist. Nirvana is just so. In the midst of
sorrow there is no Nirvana, and in Nirvana. So we may justly
define Nirvana as that sort of non-existence which consists in

the absence of something essentially different from itself.

Basita replied: Gotama, if this is the character of Nirvana, viz., that it consists in the absence of something different from itself, then 'I will assume that it consists'—in the absence of permanence, joy, personality, and purity—how then, Gotama, can you say that it consists in the possession of these very qualities?

Buddha said, Illustrious disciple,·what you say as to the absence of something different from itself, as constituting non-existence, must be limited by the consideration that there may be a result following this absence of the one in the other that may be just the opposite to non-existence; for example, take the ailments to which men are subject—fever, flatulence, or cold; for the first, ghee is given as a remedy; for the second, oil; for the third, honey. Let me ask you, illustrious disciple, with respect to the flatulence and the oil: the one does not exist in the other, any more than the horse exists in the ox; this, then, is an instance of the third kind of nothingness or non-existence to which you have referred. And so with reference to the other medicines; the cold does not exist in the honey, nor the honey in the cold. Well, in the same way, there are three moral diseases—covetousness, aversion, delusion; and for these there are three medicines or cures—(1) The perception of impurity; (2) A heart full of love; (3) A knowledge of the nexus of cause and effect. Illustrious disciple, by expelling covetousness, there is produced a non-covetous disposition; by expelling aversion, there is produced a placable disposition; and by expelling delusion, there is produced an intelligent state of mind. Yet the three diseases do not co-exist in the three medicines, nor vice versa. Illustrious youth, because of this non-existence of the one in the other, we come to speak of permanence, joy, personality, and purity, as the result of the eradication of the disease. Basita said, Tathagata speaks of permanence and non-permanence; but what are these? Buddha replied, Illustrious disciple, matter [Rupa] is impermanent; getting free from this there is permanence; and so with respect to all the *skandhas* down to *manas,* getting rid of these there is permanence. Illustrious disciple, whatever male or female follower of mine is able to realise the impermanence of the five *skandhas,* he or she has arrived at the condition of permanence.

Parinirvâna Sutra (Kiouen 34, p. 1)

4. Help Us

EMPTY TOMBS *(Mark 16: 1–8)*

Your tomb, they say, is empty.
Christ is risen, they say.
You are risen indeed, I reply.
Lord, deepen my faith in the new man 'born in a grave'.
Deepen my faith in myself to burst forth from the tomb
within that is so carefully sealed and guarded.
Deepen my faith, optimism, hope in life.
Deepen our faith in each other, so that we, the church, so
carefully sealed and guarded against the Spirit, may burst
open with new life.

A Kind of Praying: Rex Chapman,
S.C.M. Press Ltd., Westminster Press USA ©

CITY OF PEACE

My Lord, make this a City of Peace, and feed its people with
fruits, such of them as believe in God and the Last Day.

The Koran

OUTPOURINGS OF THY GRACE

My God, Whom I worship and adore! I bear witness unto
Thy unity and Thy oneness, and acknowledge Thy gifts, both
in the past and in the present. Thou art the All-Bountiful, the
overflowing showers of Whose mercy have rained down upon
high and low alike, and the splendours of Whose grace have
been shed over both the obedient and the rebellious.

O God of mercy, before Whose door the quintessence of
mercy hath bowed down, and round the sanctuary of Whose
Cause loving-kindness, in its inmost spirit, hath circled, we

beseech Thee, entreating Thine ancient grace, and seeking Thy present favour, that Thou mayest have mercy upon all who are the manifestations of the world of being, and to deny them not the outpourings of Thy grace in Thy days.

All are but poor and needy, and Thou, verily, art the All-Possessing, the All-Subduing, the All-Powerful.

Bahá'í Prayers: a selection (1951),
Bahá'í Publishing Trust ©

LOVE THAT CASTETH OUT FEAR

Eternal God, in whose perfect kingdom no sword is drawn but the sword of righteousness, and no strength but the strength of love: so guide and inspire, we pray Thee, the work of all who seek thy kingdom at home and abroad, that all peoples may seek and find their security, not in force of arms but in the perfect love that casteth out fear and in the fellowship revealed to us by thy Son, Jesus Christ our Lord.

Anon.

BE NEAR THEM

Lord Jesus Christ, be near them to defend them, within them to refresh them, around them to preserve them, before them to guide them, behind them to justify them, above them to bless them; Who liveth and reigneth with the Father and the Holy Ghost, God for evermore. Amen.

10th-Century Prayer

GIVE US GRACE

O God, the God of all righteousness, mercy, and love, give us all grace and strength to conceive and execute whatever may be for Thine honour and the welfare of the needy; that we may become at last, through the merits and intercession of our common Redeemer, a great and happy because a wise and understanding people.

Anthony Ashley Cooper, 7th Earl of Shaftesbury (1801–1885)

TO WORK FOR THY KINGDOM

O Blessed Jesus, Saviour, Who didst agonise for us: God Almighty, Who didst make Thyself weak for the love of us: stir us up to offer to Thee our bodies, our souls, our spirits; and in all we love and all we learn, in all we plan and all we do, to offer ourselves, our labours, our pleasures, our sorrows, to Thee; to work for Thy kingdom, to live as those who are not their own, but bought with Thy Blood, fed with Thy Body. And enable us now, in Thy most Holy Sacrament, to offer to Thee our repentance, our prayers, our praises, living, reasonable, and spiritual sacrifices—Thine from our birth-hour, Thine now, and Thine for ever.

Charles Kingsley (1819–1875)

THY UNSPEAKABLE JOY

O God, the Enlightener of men, Who of all graces givest the most abundant blessing upon heavenly love; we beseech Thee to cleanse us from selfishness, and grant us, for Thy love, so to love our brethren that we may be Thy children upon earth; and thereby, walking in Thy Truth, attain to Thy unspeakable joy, Who art the Giver of life to all who truly love Thee. Grant this prayer, O Lord, for Jesus Christ's sake. Amen.

Rowland Williams (1817–1870)

AS FATHER TO SON

Most blessed and glorious Trinity, Three Persons in one God, teach us to worship and adore that absolute Trinity, that perfect Unity. And that we may adore Thee, that our worship may not be a mockery, make us to know that we are one in Christ, as the Father is one with the Son, and the Son with the Father. Suffer us not to look upon our sectarianism as if it were a destiny. Help us to regard it as a rebellion against Thee. Help us to see all distinctions more clearly in the light of Thy everlasting love. Help us to recognise the truth of every effort to express something of that which passes knowledge. Help us to feel and confess the feebleness of our own efforts. So may Thy holy Name embrace us more and more. So may all creatures in heaven and earth and under the earth at last glorify Thee throughout all ages. Amen.

Frederick Denison Maurice (1805–1872)

OVERCOME EVIL WITH GOOD

O Almighty God, help us to put away all bitterness and wrath, and evil-speaking, with all malice. May we possess our souls in patience, however we are tempted and provoked, and not be overcome with evil, but overcome evil with good. Enable us, O God of patience, to bear one another's burdens, and to forbear one another in love. Oh, teach and help us all to live in peace, and to love in truth, following peace with all men, and walking in love, as Christ loved us, of Whom let us learn such meekness and lowliness of heart, that in Him we may find rest for our souls. Subdue all bitter resentments in our minds, and let the law of kindness be in our tongues, and a meek and quiet spirit in all our lives. Make us so gentle and peaceable that we may be followers of Thee, as dear children, that Thou, the God of peace, mayest dwell with us for everymore; to the honour and glory of Thy great Name. Amen.

Benjamin Jenks (17th century)

CLEAN MIND AND BODY

Lord God Almighty, shaper and ruler of all creatures, we pray thee for thy great mercy to guide us to thy will, to make our minds steadfast, to strengthen us against temptation, to put far from us all unrighteousness. Shield us against our foes, seen and unseen; teach us that we may inwardly love thee before all things with a clean mind and a clean body. For thou art our Maker and our Redeemer, our help and our comfort, our trust and our hope, now and ever.

King Alfred (849–901)

NEVER DECLINE THE PATH

O God, who hast commanded us to be perfect, as thou our Father in heaven art perfect; put into our hearts, we pray thee, a continual desire to obey thy holy will. Teach us day by day what thou wouldst have us do, and give us grace and power to fulfil the same. May we never from love of ease decline the path which thou dost appoint, nor for fear of shame turn away from it; for the sake of Jesus Christ our Lord.

Dean Henry Alford (1810–1871)

TO SEEK WISELY

God of all goodness, grant us to desire ardently, to seek wisely, to know surely, and to accomplish perfectly thy holy will, for the glory of thy name. Amen.

St. Thomas Aquinas (1225–1274)

FEARFUL DOUBT

Help us to free ourselves from fearful doubt, for when we begin to doubt then doubt has no end. Thou hast no voice, O God, Thy form is unseen, yet we can hear Thy words and know Thee near.

Bunjiro (1814–1883)

TO LIVE BY TRUTH

O Christ, thou hast bidden us pray for the coming of Thy Father's Kingdom in which righteousness will be done on earth. We have treasured Thy words, but we have forgotten their meaning, and thy great hope has grown dim in thy church. We bless thee for the inspired souls of all ages who saw afar the shining city of God. As we have mastered nature that we might gain wealth, help us now to master the social relations of mankind that we may gain justice and a world of brothers.

Make us determined to live by truth and not by lies, to found our common life on the eternal foundations of righteousness and love, and no longer to prop the tottering house of wrong by legalised cruelty and force. Help us to make the welfare of all the supreme law of our land, so that our commonwealth may be built strong and secure on the love of all its citizens. Our master, once more we make thy faith our prayer: 'Thy kingdom come, Thy will be done on earth.' Amen.

Prayers of the Social Awakening:
Walter Rauschenbusch (1861–1918)

DEFEND US FROM FEAR

O God, from whom all holy desires, all good counsels, and all that peace which the world cannot give; that both our hearts may be set to obey thy commandments and also that by thee we being defended from the fear of our enemies may pass our time in rest and quietness; through the merits of Jesus Christ our Saviour.

Gelasian Sacramentary

TEACH US WHAT TO DO

O Lord, Jesus Christ, who art the way, the truth and the life, we pray thee suffer us not to stray from thee who art the way, nor to distrust thee who art the truth, nor to rest in any other thing than thee, who art the life. Teach us by thy Holy Spirit what to believe, what to do and wherein to take our rest. For thy name's sake we ask it.

Erasmus (1467–1536)

THE SPIRIT OF WISDOM

O God, by whom the meek are guided in judgement, and light riseth up in darkness for the godly; grant us, in our doubts and uncertainties, the grace to ask what thou wouldst have us to do; that the Spirit of wisdom may save us from false choices, and that in thy light we may see light, and in thy straight path may not stumble; though Jesus Christ our Lord.

William Bright (1821–1901)

LET US SOW LOVE

Lord, make us instruments of thy peace.
Where there is hatred, let us sow love;
where there is injury, pardon;
where there is discord, union;
where there is doubt, faith;
where there is despair, hope;
where there is darkness, light;
where there is sadness, joy;
for thy mercy and for thy truth's sake.

St. Francis of Assisi (1182–1226)

ALWAYS SERVING THEE

Govern all by Thy wisdom, O Lord,
So that our souls may always be serving Thee as Thou dost
will, and not as we may choose.
Do not punish us, we beseech Thee, by granting that which
we wish or ask, if it offend Thy love, which would always
live in us.
Let us ever live to Thy glory. Amen.

St. Teresa (1515–1582)

SANCTIFY OUR SOULS

Sanctify, O Lord, our souls and bodies and spirits, search
our consciences, and cast out every evil thought, every base
desire, all envy and pride, all wrath and anger, and all that is
contrary to Thy holy will. And grant us, O Lord, Lover of men,
with a pure heart and contrite soul, to call upon Thee, our holy
God and Father who art in heaven. Amen.

Liturgy of St. James (2nd century)

KEEP US HUMBLE

O merciful God, fill our hearts, we pray Thee, with the graces
of Thy Holy Spirit, with love, joy, peace, long-suffering,
gentleness, faith, meekness, temperance. Teach us to love those
who hate us, to pray for those who despitefully use us, that we
may be the children of Thee, our Father, who makest the sun to
shine on the evil and on the good, and sendest the rain on the
just and the unjust. In adversity grant us grace to be patient; in
prosperity keep us humble; may we guard the door of our lips;
may we lightly esteem the pleasures of the world, and thirst
after heavenly things; through Jesus Christ our Lord. Amen.

St. Anselm (1033–1109)

PERFECT FAITH

O God, whose ways are all mercy and truth, carry on Thy
gracious work, and bestow by Thy benefits, what human frailty
cannot attain; that they who attend upon the heavenly
mysteries may be grounded in perfect faith, and shine forth

conspicuous by the purity of their souls; through Jesus Christ our Lord. Amen.

Leonine Sacramentary

HAPPINESS THROUGH WISDOM

O God, the God of all righteousness, mercy, and love, give us grace and strength to conceive and execute whatever may be for Thine honour and the welfare of the needy; that we may become at last, through the merits and intercession of our common Redeemer, a great and happy because a wise and understanding people. Amen.

Anthony Ashley Cooper, 7th Earl of Shaftesbury (1801–1885)

MERCY AND GRACE

O Lord Jesus Christ, Son of the living God, set Thine holy passion, Cross and Death between Thy judgement and our souls, both now and in the hour of death. And vouchsafe, we beseech Thee, to grant unto the living mercy and grace, to the dead pardon and rest, to thine holy Church peace and concord, and to us miserable sinners life and joy everlasting; who livest and reignest with the Father and the Holy Ghost, one God, world without end.

Prayer of 1559

THE GIFTS OF HOPE

Bright, O Lord, is the Heavenly Ray; by whose unwonted light, brought us through the Resurrection of Thy Son, the horror of the perpetual night is shattered. We bear witness to the glory of Thy mighty works; for Thou didst make the day of things that pass radiant with a Light which is eternal. Do Thou, therefore, Almighty God, Father of our Lord, receive in Thine unmoved serenity the supplications that rise to heaven from Thy praying people. Strengthen us. Grant us the gifts of hope. To them that make offering give Thou peace, and to them that are dead give the quiet of eternal rest.

Mozarabic Liturgy

HEAVENLY DESIRES

O God who in the burning fire of Thy love wast pleased to pour out the Holy Spirit on Thy disciples: Grant us by the same Spirit to be new lit with heavenly desires and with the power to fulfil them; through Jesus Christ our Lord.

Gelasian Sacramentary (5th century)

ONE EVERLASTING CITY

Merciful and loving Father, We beseech Thee most humbly, even with all our hearts, to pour out upon our enemies with bountiful hand, whatsoever things Thou knowest will do them good.

And chiefly a sound and uncorrupt mind wherethrough they may know Thee and love Thee in true charity and with their whole heart, and love us, Thy children, for Thy sake.

Let not their first hating of us turn to their harm, seeing that we cannot do them good for want of ability.

Lord, we desire their amendment and our own. Separate them not from us by punishing them, but join and knit them to us by Thy favourable dealing with them.

And seeing that we be all ordained to be citizens of one everlasting City, let us begin to enter into that way here already by mutual Love which may bring us right forth thither.

Old English Prayer

THE HOPE OF REVEALED RELIGION

'Tis this hope only can make all Men equally happy, and send the poor, the unfortunate as to the circumstances of this World, and the oppressed, to bed as contented as the greatest Prince. 'Tis this only can make us cheerfully dispense with the Miseries and Hardships of Life, and think of Death with Comfort. . . . It is our Joy, our Comfort and our Life; it carries us beyond Death and secures our eternal Felicity, Justice, and Charity and Peace are the fruits of it here, and Glory hereafter.

A Sermon on the Fall of Man:
Archbishop William King (1650–1729)

BANISH IGNORANCE

Most glorious of immortals, O Zeus of many names, almighty and everlasting, sovereign of nature, directing all in accordance with law, thee it is fitting that all mortals should address . . . Thee all this universe, as it rolls circling round the earth, obeys wheresoever thou dost guide, and gladly owns thy sway. . . .

No work upon earth is wrought apart from thee, Lord, nor through the heavenly sphere, nor upon the sea; save only whatsoever wicked deeds men do in their own foolishness. Nay, thou knowest how to make even the rough smooth, and to bring order out of disorder: and things not friendly are friendly in thy sight. For so hast thou fitted all things together, the good and the evil, that there might be one eternal law over all. . . . Deliver men from fell ignorance. Banish it, father, from their soul, and grant them to obtain wisdom, whereon relying thou rulest all things with justice.

Cleanthes (301–225 B.C.*)*

TO REFUSE THE EVIL

Lord Jesus, everywhere and always inspire us to refuse the evil and choose the good; and, we beseech Thee, give us grace never to judge our neighbours rashly, whilst one by one we ourselves endeavour to learn and perform thy will; for Thine own Name's sake. Amen.

Christina Georgina Rossetti (1830–1894)

TAKE US TO THY CARE

O Lord Jesus Christ, our Watchman and Keeper, take us to thy care; grant that, our bodies sleeping, our minds may watch in thee, and be made merry by some sight of that celestial and heavenly life, wherein thou art the King and Prince, together with the Father and the Holy Spirit, where thy angels and holy souls be most happy citizens. Oh purify our souls, keep clean our bodies, that in both we may please thee, sleeping and waking, for ever. Amen.

Christian Prayers: compiled by the Rev. Henry Bull (1566)

IN THE FOOTPRINTS OF THY SON

God Almighty, Eternal, Righteous and Merciful, give to us poor sinners to do for thy sake all that we know of thy will, and to will always what pleases thee, so that inwardly purified, enlightened and kindled by the fire of the Holy Spirit, we may follow in the footprints of thy well-beloved Son, our Lord Jesus Christ. Amen.

St. Francis of Assisi (1182–1226)

LIGHT INTO OUR SOULS

O Lord, Who hast brought us through the darkness of the night to the light of the morning, and Who by Thy Holy Spirit dost illumine the darkness of ignorance and sin; we beseech Thee, of Thy lovingkindness, to pour Thy Holy Light into our souls; that we may be ever devoted to Thee, by Whose wisdom we were created, by Whose mercy we are redeemed, and by Whose providence we are governed, to the honour and glory of Thy great name. Amen.

Book of Hours

HEAR OUR HUMBLING CRY

O King of mercy, from Thy throne on high
Look down in love, and hear our humbling cry,
Thou art the Bread of heaven, on Thee we feed;
Be near to help our souls in time of need.

Thomas Rawson Birks (1810–1883)

THY PLENTEOUS FOUNTAIN

O God, with Whom is the well of life, and in Whose light we see light; increase in us we beseech Thee, the brightness of divine knowledge, whereby we may be able to reach Thy plenteous fountain; impart to our thirsting souls the draught of life, and restore to our darkened minds the light of heaven. Amen.

Mozarabic Liturgy

SHIELD US WITH THY TRUTH

Praise be Thou, O God, Almighty Ruler, Who dost make the day bright with Thy sunshine, and the night with the beams of heavenly fires!

Listen now to our prayers, and forgive us both our conscious and unconscious transgressions.

Clothe us with the armour of righteousness; shield us with Thy truth; watch over us with Thy power; save us from all calamity; and give us grace to pass all the days of our life blameless, holy, peaceful, free from sin, terror and offence. For with Thee is mercy and plenteous redemption, our Lord and God, and to Thee we bring our thanks and praise. Amen.

Eastern Church

WARM OUR FROZEN HEARTS

O Lord, the Author and Persuader of peace, love and goodwill, soften our hard and steely hearts, warm our frozen and icy hearts, that we may wish well to one another, and may be the true disciples of Jesus Christ. And give us grace even now to begin to show forth that heavenly life, wherein there is no hatred, but peace and love on all hands, one toward another. Amen.

Ludivicus Vives (1492–1540)

SHOW US THE ROAD

Do thou accept us with the children,
O thou, our God, and God of all!
Show us the road that we may reach thy door,
O thou towards whom is the way of all men.

Persian Scriptures (Amir Khusraü)

STAR AND GUIDE

Oh come, Thou refreshment of them that languish and faint. Come, Thou Star and Guide of them that sail in the tempestuous sea of the world; Thou only Haven of the tossed and shipwrecked. Come, Thou Glory and Crown of the living, and only Safeguard of the dying. Come, Holy Spirit, in much

116

mercy, and make me fit to receive Thee.

St. Augustine (354–430)

COME NEAR AND BLESS US

Sun of my soul! Thou Saviour dear,
It is not night if Thou be near;
O may no earth-born cloud arise
To hide Thee from Thy servant's eyes.

Abide with me from morn till eve,
For without Thee I cannot live;
Abide with me when night is nigh,
For without Thee I dare not die.

If some poor wandering child of Thine
Have spurned today the voice divine,
Now, Lord, the gracious work begin;
Let him no more lie down in sin.

Watch by the sick; enrich the poor
With blessings from Thy boundless store;
Be every mourner's sleep tonight,
Like infant's slumbers, pure and light.

Come near and bless us when we wake,
Ere through the world our way we take;
Till, in the ocean of Thy love,
We lose ourselves in Heaven above.

*Hymns of the Church of God:
selected by F. V. Mather (1866)*

BE OUR LIGHT

Sweet Saviour, bless us ere we go,
Thy word into our minds instil,
And make our lukewarm hearts to glow
With lowly love and fervent will.

(Chorus)
Through life's long day, and death's dark night,
O gentle Jesus, be our Light!

The day is done, its hours have run,

117

And Thou hast taken count of all,
The scanty triumphs grace hath won,
The broken vow, the frequent fall.

(Chorus)

For all we love, the poor, the sad,
The sinful unto Thee we call;
O, let Thy mercy make us glad;
Thou art our Saviour and our All.

(Chorus)

All travellers, Lord, by land or sea,
Defend with Thy protecting care;
When in their need they call on Thee,
Hear Thou in highest heaven their prayer.

(Chorus)

Sweet Saviour, bless us; night is come.
Through night and darkness near us be;
Good angels watch about our home,
And we are one day nearer thee.

(Chorus)

Hymns of the Church of God:
selected by F. V. Mather (1866)

THE STUDENT'S PRAYER

Assuredly the Divine clemency suffereth not those who piously and humbly seek the truth to wander in the darkness of ignorance, to fall into the pits of false opinions, and to perish in them. For there is no worse death than the ignorance of truth, no deeper whirlpool than the accepting of false things for true, which is the essential note of error. For out of these, foul and abominable monsters are wont to shape themselves in human thoughts, while loving and following which, as if they were true, turning its back upon the true light, striving to embrace flying shadows and not able to do it, the carnal soul falls ever into the pit of misery. Wherefore we ought continually to pray and to say, 'God, our salvation and redemption, who hast given us nature, grant us also grace.

118

Shew forth Thy light to us, as we grope after Thee, and seek Thee, in the shades of ignorance. Recall us from our errors. Stretch out Thy right hand to us weak ones who cannot, without Thee, attain to Thee. Show Thy very Self to those who seek nothing besides Thee! Break the clouds of vain phantasies which suffer not the eye of the mind to behold Thee after that fashion in which Thou permittest Thyself, the invisible, to be seen of them who seek Thy face, which is their rest, their goal, beyond which they crave for nothing, seeing that there is nought beyond the supreme good that is above all sense.'

The Division of Nature: John Scotus Erigena (800–877)

WE SHOULD PLEASE THEE

O Adorable, Eternal God! Hast Thou made me a free agent? And enable me if I please to offend Thee infinitely? What other end couldst Thou intend by this, but that I might please Thee infinitely? That having the power of pleasing or displeasing, I might be the friend of God! Of all exaltations in all worlds this is the greatest. To make a world for me was much, to command Angels and men to love me was much, to prepare eternal joys for me was more. But to give me a power to displease Thee, or to set a sin before Thy face, which Thou infinitely hatest, to profane eternity, or to defile Thy works, is more stupendous than all these. What other couldst Thou intend by it but that I might infinitely please Thee? And having the power of pleasing or displeasing, might please Thee and myself infinitely, in being pleasing! Hereby thou hast prepared a new fountain and torrent of joys greater than all that went before, seated us in the Throne of God, made us Thy companions, endued us with a power most dreadful to ourselves, that we might live in sublime and incomprehensible blessedness for evermore. For the satisfaction of our goodness is the most sovereign delight of which we are capable. And that by our own actions we should be pleasing to Thee, is the greatest felicity Nature could contain. O Thou who art infinitely delightful to the sons of men make me and the sons of men, infinitely delightful unto Thee. Replenish our actions with amiableness and beauty, that they may be answerable to Thine, and like unto Thine in sweetness and value. That Thou in all Thy works art pleasing to us, we in all our works may be so to Thee; our own actions are pleasing to Thee being an offspring of pleasures sweeter than all.

Thomas Traherne (1637–1674)

QUICKEN OUR DULL HEARTS

Almighty and most merciful Father, Who hast given us grace in times past, and hast mercifully brought us to see the end of another year, grant that we may continue to grow in grace and in the knowledge of Thy dear Son. Lead us forward by Thy Spirit from strength to strength, that we may more perfectly serve Thee, and attain a more lively hope of Thy mercy in Jesus Christ. Quicken our dull hearts, inspire us with warmer affections for Thee, O God, and for Thy heavenly Truth. Stir up the gift that is in us, and pour down from above more abundant gifts of grace, that we may make progress in heavenly things. Increase our faith as Thou dost increase our years, and the longer we are suffered to abide on earth, the better may our service be, the more willing our obedience, the more consistent our daily lives, the more complete our devotion to Thee. Grant this our prayer, O gracious Father, which we humbly offer at the throne of grace, in the name and for the sake of Jesus Christ Thy Son, our Lord and Saviour. Amen.

Tracts for Christian Seasons (19th century)

LOVE TOWARDS GOD

I am bending my knee
In the eye of the Father who created me,
In the eye of the Son who purchased me,
In the eye of the Spirit who cleansed me,
In friendship and affection.
Through Thine own Anointed One, O God,
Bestow upon us fullness in our need,
Love towards God,
The affection of God,
The smile of God,
The wisdom of God,
The grace of God,

The fear of God,
And the will of God,
To do on the world of the Three,
As angels and saints
Do in heaven;
Each shade and light,
Each day and night,
Each time in kindness,
Give Thou us Thy Spirit.

The Sun Dances, Prayers and Blessings from the Gaelic:
translation by Alexander Carmichael,
The Christian Community Press, London

PRAYER OF SUPPLICATION

Lord God almighty, Father of Christ, thy blessed Son, who givest audience to those who call upon thee with right intent, and knowest the prayers even of those who do not speak: we give thee thanks because it has pleased thee to account us worthy to partake of thy holy sacrament which thou hast given to make us fully aware of what we have already learnt, to nourish piety, and to pardon our sins; for the name of thy Christ has been invoked upon us and we have been made one with thee. Thou who hast removed us from fellowship with the wicked, make us one with those who are consecrated to thee; establish us in truth by the coming of the Holy Spirit; make known the things of which we are ignorant, supply what we lack, and confirm what we already know.

Keep thy priests without reproach in thy service, protect our rulers in peace, our magistrates in justice; make the seasons temperate, the harvest abundant; rule the whole world with almighty Providence.

Pacify warlike nations, convert the erring, sanctify the people, guard the honour of maidens, keep the married true to each other, bring children to the fulness of age. Hearten those newly baptised; enlighten those who are receiving instruction in the faith, and make them worthy to become members of the Church; and gather us all together into the kingdom of heaven, in Christ Jesus our Lord, with whom to thee and the Holy Spirit be glory, honour, and adoration for evermore. Amen.

The Manual of Catholic Prayer

121

MEAT TO THE HUNGRY

They that are ensnared and entangled in the extreme penury of things needful for the body cannot set their mind upon thee, O Lord, as they ought to do; but when they be disappointed of the things which they do so mightily desire, their hearts are cast down and quail from excess of grief. Have pity on them, therefore, O merciful Father, and relieve their misery from thine incredible riches, that by thy removing of their urgent necessity, they may rise up to thee in mind. Thou, O Lord, providest enough for all men with thy most liberal and bountiful hand; but whereas thy gifts are, in respect of thy goodness and free favour, made free unto all men, we (through our haughtiness and niggardship and distrust) do make them private and peculiar. Correct thou the things which our iniquity hath put out of order; let thy goodness supply that which our niggardliness hath plucked away. Give thou meat to the hungry and drink to the thirsty; comfort thou the sorrowful; cheer thou the dismayed: strengthen thou the weak: deliver thou them that are prisoners; and give thou hope and courage to them that are out of heart.

Queen Elizabeth's Prayer Book

5. For the Unity of All Individuals

TO THY LIGHT

Nations shall come to thy light and kings to the brightness of thy rising.

Isaiah 60 : 3

THE TRIUMPHANT STRENGTH

Our God and God of our fathers,
Reign over the whole Universe in thy glory,
And in thy splendour be exalted over all the earth.

Shine forth in the majesty of the triumphant strength,
Over all the inhabitants of thy world,
That every form may know that thou hast formed it,
And every creature understand that thou hast created it,
And that all that hath breath in its nostrils may say:

The Lord God of Israel is King
And his dominion ruleth over all.

*New Year Service of the Orthodox Synagogue :
Routledge & Kegan Paul, Ltd.* ©

ALL MEN THY CHILDREN

We pray for all mankind.
Though divided into nations and races,
Yet are all men your children.
Drawing from you their life and being,
Commanded by you to obey your laws . . .

Cause hatred and strife to vanish,

123

That abiding peace may fill the earth,
And all humanity enjoy its blessing.

Gate of Repentance (undated),
Union of Liberal and Progressive Synagogues ©

ALL OF ONE HEART

O God, the Father of our Lord Jesus Christ, our only Saviour, the Prince of Peace; give us grace seriously to lay to heart the great dangers we are in by our unhappy divisions. Take away all hatred and prejudice, and whatsoever may hinder us from godly union and concord; that, as there is but one Body, and one Spirit, and one hope of our calling, one Lord, one faith, one baptism, one God and Father of us all, so we may henceforth be all of one heart, and of one soul, united in one holy bond of truth and peace, of faith and charity, and may with one mind and one mouth glorify Thee; through Jesus Christ our Lord. Amen.

Prayers in Use at Cuddesdon College (1904)

UNDER ONE BANNER

Eternal God, in whose perfect kingdom no sword is drawn but the sword of righteousness, and no strength but the strength of love: We pray thee, so mightily to shed and spread abroad thy Spirit, that all peoples and ranks may be gathered under one banner of the Prince of Peace; as children of one Father, Lord of Love; to whom alone be dominion and glory now and for ever. Amen.

The Splendour of God (1960)

A WORLD MADE ONE

Show unto nations, O Father of all, the way to rise above the causes that divide us and seek in faith a world made one in Thee, that we may keep to paths of justice, peace and freedom; in the might and by the power of Thy Holy Spirit, through Jesus Christ our Lord. Amen.

The Kingdom of God: Council of Clergy and
Ministers for Common Ownership (1946)

DELIVERY FROM SATAN

Enlarge Thy kingdom, O God, and deliver the world from the tyranny of Satan. Hasten the time, which Thy Spirit hath foretold, when all nations whom Thou hast made shall worship Thee and glorify Thy Name. Bless the good endeavours of those who strive to propagate the truth, and prepare the hearts of all men to receive it; to the honour of Thy Name.

Bishop Thomas Wilson (1663–1755)

OUT OF THE WAY OF DEATH

God of all grace, whose arms were outstretched with Christ's on Calvary, call to the nations of the earth to cease from strife, that all may join to fight, not one another, but their common foes of want and ignorance, disease and sin. Lead back humanity out of the way of death into the way of life; and from destruction to the building up of a new world of righteousness and peace, of liberty and joy. End the dark night of lies and cruelty; bring in the dawn of mercy and of truth. Hold up before the people of all lands that Cross in which alone is there salvation, on which forgiving and defenceless died the Lamb of God, who taketh away the sins of the whole world.

When We Call: Fellowship of Reconciliation (1943)

HEALER OF SOULS

O Son of God, our Redeemer, we beseech Thee by the mystery of Thy holy Incarnation, by Thy precious sacrifice, oblation, and satisfaction for the sins of all mankind, by the kindness and love of Thy blessed appearing, by Thy prayers and supplications, by Thy strong crying and tears, by Thy lifting up upon the Cross for us lost and helpless sinners: draw all men unto Thee, O Thou healer of souls.

Oxford Mission to Calcutta

NO LONGER IN DARKNESS

Give unto me, O God, and unto all that have communicated this day in the divine mysteries, a portion of all the good prayers which are made in heaven and earth; the intercession of our Lord, and the supplications of all Thy servants; and unite

125

us in the bands of the common faith and a holy charity; that no interests or partialities, no sects or opinions, may keep us any longer in darkness and division.

Bishop Jeremy Taylor (1613–1667)

NO NARROW WALLS

We beseech Thee, O Lord, to set our feet in a large place, where hearts are made pure by faith in Thee, and faces are turned to the light; where all are one in Thee, and no narrow walls between man and man destroy the unity Thou hast made in the Spirit of Thy Son, Jesus Christ our Lord.

Anon.

LIGHT, COURAGE AND LOVE

May God give us light to guide us, courage to support us, and love to unite us, now and evermore.

Anon.

IN PRAYER TO THEE

O God, Who by Thy Word dost marvellously work out the reconciliation of mankind, grant, we beseech Thee, that by this holy fast we may both be subjected to Thee with all our hearts, and be united to each other in prayer to Thee; through Jesus Christ our Lord. Amen.

Gelasian Sacramentary (5th century)

BROTHERLY CHARITY

Gracious Lord, thou art not the God of confusion or discord, but the God of concord and of peace; unite our hearts and affections in such sort together, that we may as brethren walk in Thy House, in brotherly charity and love, and as members of the body of Christ. Let the oil of sanctification, that is Thy Holy Spirit, inflame us, and the dew of Thy blessing continually fall upon us, that we may obtain life eternal; through the same Jesus Christ Thy Son. So be it.

Scottish Psalter (1595)

THE BOND OF PEACE

O God, Who biddest us dwell with one mind in Thine house, of Thy mercy put away from us all that causeth us to differ, that through Thy bountiful goodness we may keep the Unity of the Spirit in the bond of peace; through Jesus Christ our Lord. Amen.

Canon Edward Bouverie Pusey (1800–1882)

UNITY OF LOVE

O God the Father, Origin of Divinity, Good beyond all that is good, Fair beyond all that is fair, in Whom is calmness, peace and concord; do Thou make up the dissensions which divide us from each other, and bring us back into a unity of love, which may bear some likeness to Thy Divine Nature. And as Thou art above all things, make us one by the unanimity of a good mind, that through the embrace of charity and the bonds of affection, we may be spiritually one, as well in ourselves as in each other; through that peace of Thine which maketh all things peaceful, and through the grace, mercy, and tenderness of Thy Son, Jesus Christ. Amen.

St. Dionysius (181–848)

ALL MEN ARE BROTHERS

Perfect virtue is when you behave to everyone as if you were receiving a great guest. Within the four seas all are brothers.

Confucius (551–479 B.C.)

DELIVERY FROM FEAR

The greatest and mightiest and amplest of all societies is that which is composed of mankind and God, and from Him have descended all creatures that are upon the earth (but especially reasoning beings, since to those alone hath nature given it to have communion and intercourse with God, being linked with Him through reason). Wherefore should such a one name himself a Citizen of the Universe, wherefore not a Son of God? Wherefore shall he fear anything that may come to pass among men? To have God for our mother and father and guardian,

127

shall this not deliver us from griefs and fears?

Epictetus (1st century)

COMMON BE OUR PRAYER

O God,
Let us be united;
Let us speak in harmony;
Let our minds apprehend alike.
Common be our prayer;
Common be the end of our assembly;
Common be our resolution;
Common be our deliberations.
Alike be our feelings;
Unified be our hearts;
Common be our intentions;
Perfect be our unity.

Hindu Scriptures (Rig Veda)

EQUAL IN DIGNITY

O God, it is thy word that mankind is a single nation, so all human beings are born free and equal in dignity and rights, they are endowed with reason and conscience, and should act towards one another in a spirit of brotherhood.

The Koran

THE BANNER OF ONENESS

O Thou kind Lord! Thou hast created all humanity from the same stock. Thou hast decreed that all shall belong to the same household. In Thy Holy Presence they are all Thy servants, and all mankind are sheltered beneath Thy Tabernacle; all have gathered together at Thy Table of Bounty: all are illumined through the light of Thy Providence.

O Thou kind Lord! Unite all. Let the religions agree and make the nations one, so that they may see each other as one family and the whole earth as one home. May they all live together in perfect harmony.

O God! Raise aloft the banner of the oneness of mankind.

Abdu'l-Baha (1884–1921)

MUTUAL LOVE

What wall or fort, strongly built, with well-compacted and large stones, is so impregnable against the assaults of the enemy as the united band of men, joined by mutual love and sealed by oneness of mind?

St. Chrysostom (345–407)

THE SAME CITY

We who have the same City, the same House and Table, and Door, and Root, and Life, and Head, the same Shepherd, and King, and Judge, and Maker and Father, what indulgence can we deserve if we be divided one from another?

St. Chrysostom (345–407)

ALL KNIT TOGETHER

Look up, my soul, and see the innumerable multitude of triumphing spirits.

Behold, the glorious angels fall down before the throne, and prostrate adore him that liveth for ever.

Hark how they fill that spacious temple with their hymns, while night and day they continually sing:

'Holy, holy, holy, Lord God of hosts!

Heaven and earth are full of thy glory—

Hallelujah.'

Behold, the blessed saints lay their crowns at his feet, and on their faces adore him that liveth for ever and ever.

Nor is envy in them if we aspire to song the same bright name which they adore;

Since there is but one family of us both in heaven and earth, under one head, and all are knit together by one Spirit.

John Austin (1613–1669)

ALL THY CHILDREN

We pray for all mankind. Though divided into nations and races, yet are all men your children, drawing from you their life and being, commanded by you to obey your laws. Cause hatred and strife to vanish, that abiding peace may fill the earth, and all humanity enjoy its blessings.

Gate of Repentance (undated), Union of
Liberal and Progressive Synagogues ©

NO SEPARATE ALTARS

Great God, unite our severing ways;
No separate altars may we raise,
But with one tongue now speak thy praise—
With peace that comes of purity

Building the temple yet to be,
To fold our broad humanity.

White flowers of love its walls shall climb,
Soft bells of peace shall ring its chime,
Its days shall all be holy time.

A sweeter song shall then be heard—
The music of the world's accord,
Rejoicing o'er the broken sword:

That song shall swell from shore to shore,
One hope, one faith, one love restore,
One brotherhood for evermore.

John Greenleaf Whittier (1807–1892)

FOR UNITY

O God the Father of our Lord Jesus Christ, our only Saviour, the Prince of Peace, give us grace seriously to lay to heart the great sin and danger of our unhappy divisions. Take away all hatred and prejudice, and whatsoever may hinder us from godly union and concord; that as there is but one Body, and one Spirit, and one Hope of our calling; one Lord, one Faith, one Baptism, one God and Father of us all; so we may henceforth be all of one Heart, and of one Soul, united in one holy bond of Truth and Peace, of Faith and Charity; and may with one mind and one mouth glorify Thee; through Jesus Christ our Lord. Amen.

A Manual Intended to Aid the Pious Christian in the Duty of Family Prayer and Private Devotion: John Frere, Rector of Cottenham (1851)

ACCEPT US WITH THE CHILDREN

Do thou accept us with the children,
O thou, our God and the God of all!
Show us the road that we may reach thy door,
O thou towards whom is the way of all men!
Amen.

Sufi Prayer

GRASS TWISTED TOGETHER

The union of the small and the weak performs great works. By blades of grass twisted together the elephant is tied fast. The birds caught in the fowler's net plied their wings in concert, and bore away the net through the air.

Hindu Scriptures (Hitopadesa)

BANISH DISCORD

Come, O Holy Spirit, replenish the hearts of thy faithful believers, and kindle in them the fire of thy love, thou that through manifold tongues hast gathered together all the nations of the heathen in unity of faith. O take all dissension and discord out of thy holy church, and make us to be of one mind and unfeigned love, without which we cannot please thee. Amen.

William Coverdale (1488–1568)

ONE FAMILY

The narrow-minded ask, 'Is this one of our tribe, or is he a stranger?' But to those who are of a noble disposition, the whole world is but one family.

Panchatantra

131

GOD'S PURPOSE

My spirit has pass'd in compassion and determination
around the whole earth,
I have looked for equals and lovers and found them ready
for me in all lands.
Lo, soul, seest thou not God's purpose from the first?
The earth to be spanned, connected by network,
The races, neighbours, to marry and be given in marriage,
The oceans to be cross'd, the distant brought near,
The lands to be weld together,
Europe to Asia, Africa join'd, and they to the New World,
The lands, geographies, dancing before you holding a
festival garland,
As brides and bridegrooms hand in hand.
Leaves of Grass: Walt Whitman (1819–1892)

SAVE US FROM OURSELVES

O most merciful Father, save us from ourselves, and show us
the pattern of a world made new, wherein Thy will is done and
all men are accepted as brothers; through Jesus Christ our
Lord.

Anon.

A PRAYER FOR ALL MEN AND WOMEN

Save us, defend and keep us in thy fear and love, O thou God
of mercy and grace: Give unto us the light of thy countenance,
pardon our sins, health of our body, sanctification of our
spirits, peace from heaven, and salvation of our souls in the day
of our Lord Jesus. Amen.

A Collection of Offices:
Bishop Jeremy Taylor (1613–1667)

THE ANIMALS' COMPACT

God brought the animals to Gilshádeng, and made them
subject to him, and he divided them into seven classes.
And when seven sages were with the prince, there came seven
kings from the animal kingdom, soliciting redress from the
tyranny of mankind.

The wise camel said, 'O prophet of God! in what consists the superiority of man over us?'

The sage Huristeh said, 'There are many proofs of man's superiority over animals; one of them is speech.'

The camel answered, 'If the object of speech be to make the hearer understand, animals possess it.'

Huristeh said, 'The speech of man alone is intelligible.'

The camel replied, 'Because thou dost not understand the language of animals, dost thou imagine it unintelligible? The inhabitants of the West understand not them of the East.'

Huristeh said, 'You have been ordained for our service.'

The camel answered, 'And you also have been ordained to bring us water and grain and grass.'

The sage had nothing to say in answer.

Then the sage ant came forward, and said, 'O prophet! Wherein consisteth the surpassing excellence of man above animals?'

The sage Shásar hastily answered, 'In the excellence of his shape and upright deportment.'

The ant replied, 'The intelligent do not pride themselves on shape, and yet we are all on a level in regard to the combinations of the members of our body. And even you, when you would praise any beautiful person, describe her as stag-eyed, as having the gait of a partridge, or a peacock's waist; whence it may be understood that the superiority is ours.'

To this Shásar returned no answer.

Next the knowing fox, taking up the speech, said, 'What superiority in arts doth man possess?'

The wise Jemshíd answered 'The superiority of men consisteth in the good dress, and the agreeable food and drink which they have always had.'

The wise fox said, 'In former times your clothes were of wool, and hair, and skins of animals, and still are so. And your sweetest food is supplied by the bee. With animals, all that requireth to be covered is covered naturally.'

Jemshíd replied, 'It ill becometh you to join in this controversy, you who cruelly tear each other to pieces.'

The fox rejoined, 'We have learned this practice from you, for Jilmis slew Tilmis. Moreover ravenous animals live on flesh; but men slay each other without necessity.'

Jemshíd returned no answer.

Next the sagacious spider coming forward said, 'Wherein consisteth the superior excellence of man?'

The sage Simrâsh said, 'Men understand the arts.'

The spider answered, 'Animals exceed men in these: knowest thou not that crawling things and insects build triangular and square houses without wood or brick? Behold my work, how, without loom I weave fine cloth.'

Simrâsh replied, 'Man can write and express his thoughts on paper.'

The spider said, 'Animals do not transfer the secrets of God from a living heart to a lifeless body.'

Simrâsh hung down his head from shame.

The tortoise next advanced saying, 'What proof is there of the superiority of man?'

The sage Shalish-herta said, 'Kings and ministers, and generals and physicians and astronomers afford proof of man's superiority.'

The tortoise said, 'Animals too possess the classes that you have mentioned. Observe the sovereignty of the bee and of the ant in their kind, and attend to the viziership of the fox; and recollect the generalship of the elephant; and the cock is an astronomer, who knoweth right well the time of the day and night.'

Shalish-herta remained silent.

Next the peacock, sailing in, said, What proof is there of man's superior dignity?'

The wise vizier, Vizlûr, said, 'Mankind possesses the faculty of judgment and discrimination.'

The peacock answered, 'If during the darkness of a single night a hundred sheep have young, each knoweth its lamb, and each lamb knoweth its mother, and turns to its mother; and this kind of instinct mankind do not possess.'

Vizlûr then said, 'Men are brave.'

The peacock answered, 'They are not bolder than the lion.'

Vizlûr had nothing to reply.

Next the *hûmâ* advancing said, 'Where is the sage who will afford me proof of man's superiority?'

The sage Mezdam-hertaiendeh said, 'One superiority of man consisteth in knowledge, as by means of it he ascendeth from a low to an exalted station.'

The *hûmâ* replied, 'By knowledge animals distinguish good plants from poison.'

The sage said, 'Knowledge has a root and a branch; you have the branch, but the root consisteth in the sayings of the prophets, which belong to man alone.'

The *hûmâ* said, 'Among animals each tribe hath its customs, and in like manner as among you prophets reveal their prophecies, among us there are counsellors, one of whom is the bee.'

The sage said, 'The heart of man attaineth self-possession, and effecteth an union with the soul, and by means of knowledge is elevated to the glorious nature of the angels.'

The *hûmâ* said, 'We animals likewise become tame.'

The sage replied, 'It is true; yet your perfection consisteth in attaining only a single one of the qualities of man, while man's perfection consisteth in attaining the nature of disembodied spirits.'

The *hûmâ* said, 'True; yet in spite of this, in his putting to death of animals and similar acts, man resembleth the beasts of prey, and not angels.'

The Prophet of the World then said, 'We deem it sinful to kill harmless, but right to slay ravenous, animals. Were all ravenous animals to enter into a compact not to kill harmless animals, we would abstain from slaying them, and hold them dear as ourselves.'

Upon this the wolf made a treaty with the ram, and the lion became the friend of the stag. And no tyranny was left in the world; till man (Dèhak) broke the treaty, and began to kill animals.

In consequence of this, nobody observed the treaty except the harmless animals.

This is the dialogue that passed concerning the grand secret.

The Desátir, or Regulations (Persian)

MANKIND ARE ONE IN SPIRIT

When a deed is done for Freedom,
Through the broad earth's aching breast
Runs a thrill of joy prophetic,
Trembling on from east to west,

135

And the slave, where'er he cowers,
Feels the soul within him climb
To the awful verge of manhood,
As the energy sublime
Of a century bursts full-blossomed
On the thorny stem of Time.

Through the walls of hut and palace
Shoots the instantaneous throe
When the travail of the ages
Wrings earth's systems to and fro;
At the birth of each new era,
With a recognising start,
Nation wildly looks at nation,
Standing with mute lips apart,
And Truth's mighty man-child
Leaps beneath the future's heart.

For mankind are one in spirit,
And an instinct bears along,
Round the earth's electric circle,
The swift flash of right or wrong.

Whether conscious or unconscious,
Yet Humanity's vast frame,
Through its ocean-sundered fibres
Feels the gush of joy or shame
In the gain or loss of one race
All the rest have equal claim.

James Russell Lowell (1819–1891)

THE DIVINE IMAGE

To Mercy, Pity, Peace and Love,
All pray in their distress,
And to these virtues of delight
Return their thankfulness.

For Mercy, Pity, Peace and Love,
Is God our Father dear;
And Mercy, Pity, Peace and Love,
Is Man, His child and care.

For Mercy has a human heart;

Pity, a human face;
And Love, the human form divine;
And Peace, the human dress.

Then every man, of every clime,
That prays in his distress,
Prays to the human form divine:
Love, Mercy, Pity, Peace.

And all must love the human form,
In heathen, Turk, or Jew,
Where Mercy, Love, and Pity dwell,
There God is dwelling too.

William Blake (1757–1827)

OF ONE HEART

Although a difference in opinions or modes of worship may prevent an entire external union, need it prevent our union in affection? Though we cannot think alike, may we not love alike? May we not be of one heart, though we are not of one opinion? Without all doubt we may. Herein all the children of God may unite, notwithstanding these small differences. These remaining as they are, they may forward one another in love and in good works. . . . I dare not presume to impose my mode of worship on any other. I believe it is truly primitive and apostolical. But my belief is no rule for another. I ask not therefore of him with whom I would unite in love, Are you of my Church? Of my congregation? Do you receive the same form of church government, and allow the same church officers with me? Do you join in the same form of prayer wherein I worship God? I inquire not, Do you receive the supper of the Lord, in the same manner and posture as I do? Nor, whether in the administration of baptism, you agree with me in admitting sureties for the baptised, in the manner of administering it, or the age of those to whom it should be administered. Nay, I ask not of you (as clear as I am in my own mind) whether you allow baptism and the Lord's supper at all. Let all these things stand by: we will talk of them if need be, at a more convenient season. My only question at present is, Is thine heart right as my heart is with thy heart? If it be, give me thy hand. I do not mean, Be of my opinion. You need not. I do not expect or desire it. Neither do I mean, I will be of your opinion. I cannot. It does not depend on my choice: I can no more think that I can see or hear as I will. Keep you your opinion, I mine: and that as steadily as ever. You need not even endeavour to come over to me, or bring me over to you. I do not desire to dispute those points, or to hear or speak one word concerning them. Let all opinions alone one one side and on the other. Only give me thy hand.

John Wesley (1703–1791) from a sermon

AT ONE WITH GOD

These things shall be: a loftier race
Than e'er the world hath known shall rise
With flame of freedom in their souls,
And light of knowledge in their eyes.

Nation with nation, land with land,
Unarmed shall live as comrades free;
In every heart and brain shall throb
The pulse of one fraternity.

Man shall love man with heart as pure
And fervent as the young-eyed throng,
Who chant their heavenly psalms before
God's face with undiscordant song.

New arts shall bloom of loftier mould,
And mightier music thrill the skies,
And every life shall be a song
When all the earth is paradise.

There shall be no more sin nor shame,
Though pain and passion may not die;
For man shall be at one with God
In bonds of firm necessity.

John Addington Symonds (1840–1893)

THE HEART OF MANKIND

Servants of God or sons
Shall I not call you? because
Not as servants ye knew

Your Father's innermost mind,
His, who unwilling sees
One of His little ones lost—
Yours is the praise, if mankind
Hath not as yet in its march
Fainted, and fallen, and died!

See! in the sands of the world
Marches the host of mankind,
A feeble wavering line.
Where are they tending?—A God
Marshalled them, gave them their goal.
Ah, but the way is so long!
Years they have been in the waste!
Sore thirst plagues them, the sands,
Spreading all round, overawe;
Factions divide them, their host
Threatens to break, to dissolve—
Ah, keep, keep them combined!
Else, of the myriad who fill
That army, not one shall arrive;
Sole shall they stray: in the sands
Flounder forever in vain,
Die one by one in the waste.

Then, in such hour of need
Of your fainting, dispirited race,
Ye like angels, appear,
Radiant with ardour divine!
Beacons of hope, ye appear!
Weakness not on your brow,
Ye alight in our van! at your voice,
Panic, despair, flee away.
Ye move through the ranks, recall
The stragglers, refresh the outworn,
Praise, re-inspire the brave.
Order, courage, return;
Eyes rekindling, and prayers,
Follow your steps as you go.
Ye fill up the gaps in our files,
Strengthen the wavering line,
Stablish, continue our march,

On, to the bound of the waste,
On, to the city of God.

Matthew Arnold (1822–1888) from Rugby Chapel

CHRISTIAN UNITY AND PROGRESS

Through the night of doubt and sorrow,
Onward goes the pilgrim band,
Singing songs of expectation,
Marching to the promised land.
And before us through the darkness
Gleameth clear the guiding light;
Brother clasps the hand of brother,
And steps fearless through the night.

One the light of God's dear presence,
Never in its work to fail,
Which illumines the wild rough places
Of this gloomy haunted vale.
One the object of our journey,
One the faith which never tires,
One the earnest looking forward,
One the hope our God inspires.

One the strain which mouths of thousands
Life as from the heart of one;
One the conflict, one the peril,
One the march in God begun;
One the gladness of rejoicing
On the Resurrection shore,
With one Father o'er us shining
In his love forevermore.

Go we onward, pilgrim brothers;
Visit first the cross and grave,
Where the cross its shadow flingeth,
Where the boughs of cypress wave.
Then a shaking as of earthquakes,
Then a rending of the tomb,
Then a scattering of all shadows.
And an end of toil and gloom.

Barnhardt S. Ingemann (1789–1862),
trans. by Rev. Sabine Baring-Gould (1834–1924)

6. Give Us Protection

IN THY LIGHT

How precious is thy loving kindness, O God!
And the children of men take refuge under the shadow of thy
wings.
They shall be abundantly satisfied with the fatness of thy
house;
And thou shalt make them drink of the river of thy
pleasures.
For with thee is the fountain of life:
In thy light shall we see light.

Psalms 36: 7–9

A SPIRIT OF WISDOM

Most merciful father, look graciously, we beseech Thee,
upon Thy Church in this land, that all things which be contrary
to her may be taken out of the way. Pour down upon her rulers
a spirit of wisdom and zeal, that in all things they may seek Thy
glory. And to all Thy people grant Thy protection, that, living
according to Thy will, they may be free to worship and serve
Thee with a quiet mind in the unity of the faith, and in the
knowledge and love of Thee, and of Thy Son Jesus Christ, Who
liveth and reigneth with Thee, in the unity of the Holy Ghost
ever one God, world without end. Amen.

Prayers in Use at Cuddesdon College (1904)

DESTROY US NOT

Look down, O Lord our God, from the throne of Thy
glorious Kingdom; look down upon us and destroy us not, yea,
rather deliver us from evil. From all evil and misfortune,
deliver us. As of old time Thou didst deliver our father, deliver

141

us. In all our straits, deliver us. From the evils of the world to come, deliver us. Spare us, O Lord. Have mercy upon us. Deliver us and let us never be confounded; for the sake of Jesus Christ, our Saviour and Redeemer. Amen.

Bishop Lancelot Andrewes (1555–1626)

LET THY RIGHT HAND GUARD US

Lord Jesus Christ, Keeper and Preserver of all things, let Thy right hand guard us by day and by night, when we sit at home, and when we walk abroad, when we lie down and when we rise up, that we may be kept from all evil, and have mercy upon us sinners. Amen.

St. Nerses of Clajes (4th century)

BE OUR SUPPORT

Eternal Light, shine into our hearts,
Eternal Goodness, deliver us from evil,
Eternal Power, be our support,
Eternal Wisdom, scatter the darkness of our ignorance,
Eternal Pity, have mercy upon us;
that with all our heart and mind and soul and strength we may seek thy face and be brought by thy infinite mercy to thy holy presence; through Jesus Christ our Lord.

Alcuin of York (735–804)

OUR THOUGHTS LIE OPEN

O Lord and Master of us all, whate'er our name or sign, we own thy sway, we hear thy call, we test our lives by thine.

Our thoughts lie open to thy sight, and naked to thy glance; our secret sins are in the light of thy pure countenance.

Our friend, our brother, and our Lord, what may thy service be? Nor name, nor sign, nor ritual word, but simply follow thee!

John Greenleaf Whittier (1807–1892)

A STUMBLING BLOCK

Grant, O Lord, that we may carefully watch over our tempers and every unholy feeling. Remove whatever in us may be a stumbling block in another's way; that, by conforming to thy will in small things, we may hope by thy protection and help to pass safely through the greater dangers and trials to which we may be exposed.

Christina Georgina Rossetti (1830–1894)

TILL ALL OUR WANDERINGS CEASE

O God of Bethel by whose hand thy people still are fed; who through this earthly pilgrimage hast all our fathers led—

Our vows, our prayers, we now present before thy throne of grace; God of our fathers, be the God of their succeeding race.

Through each perplexing path of life our wandering footsteps guide; give us each day our daily bread and raiment fit provide.

O spread thy covering wings around till all our wanderings cease, and at our Father's loved abode our souls arrive in peace.

Philip Doddridge (1702–1751)

DISPENSER OF JUSTICE

O Lord, O King, resplendent on the citadel of heaven, all hail continually; and of Thy clemency upon Thy people still do Thou have mercy.

Lord, Whom the hosts of cherubim in songs and hymns with praise continually proclaim, do Thou upon us eternally have mercy.

The armies aloft, O Lord, do sing high praise to Thee, even they to whom the Seraphim reply, 'Do Thou have mercy.'

O Christ, enthroned as King above, Whom the nine orders of angels in their beauty praise without ceasing, deign Thou upon us, Thy servants, ever to have mercy.

O Christ, Whom Thy one only Church throughout the world doth hymn, O Thou to whom the sun, and moon, and stars, the land and sea, do service ever, do Thou have mercy.

O Christ, those holy ones, the heirs of the eternal country,

143

one and all with utter joy proclaim Thee in a most worthy strain; do Thou have mercy upon us.

O Lord, O gentle Son of Mary free, O King of kings, Blessed Redeemer, upon those who have been ransomed from the power of death, by Thine own blood, have ever mercy.

O noblest unbegotten, yet Begotten Son, having no beginning of age, yet without effort (in the weakness of God) excelling all things, upon this Thy congregation in Thy pity, Lord have mercy.

O Sun of Righteousness, in all unclouded glory, supreme Dispenser of Justice, in that great day when Thou shalt strictly judge all nations, we earnestly beseech Thee, upon This Thy people, who here stand before Thy presence, in Thy pity, Lord, then have mercy upon us.

St. Dunstan (924–988)

MICHAEL MILITANT

O Michael Militant,
Thou king of the angels,
Shield thy people
With the power of thy sword,
Shield thy people
With the power of thy sword.

Spread thy wing
Over sea and land,
East and west,
And shield us from the foe,
East and west,
And shield us from the foe.

Brighten thy feast
From heaven above:
Be with us in the pilgrimage
And in the twistings of the fight;
Be with us in the pilgrimage
And in the twistings of the fight.

Thou chief of chiefs
Thou chief of the needy,
Be with us in the journey
And in the gleam of the river;

144

Be with us in the journey
And in the gleam of the river.

Thou chief of chiefs,
Thou chief of angels,
Spread thy wing
Over sea and land,
For thine is their fullness,
Thine is their fullness,
Thine own is their fullness,
Thine own is their fullness.

*From: The Sun Dances. Prayers and
Blessings from the Gaelic. Collected and
translated by Alexander Carmichael*

7. *For Equality among Men*

SON OF A KING

Grant us that we may never forget, O Lord, that every man is the son of a King.

Hasidic Prayer

SENTINEL OF THE POOR

A solitary Durwaish had taken up his abode in a corner of the desert. The king passed him, and the Durwaish, because retirement is the kingdom of contentment, did not lift up his head, nor show any signs of politeness. The monarch, conscious of his superior dignity, was chagrined, and said, 'This tribe of ragged mendicants resembles the brute beasts.' His vizier said to the Durwaish, 'When the monarch of the terrestrial globe passed by you, why did you not do him homage, nor behave even with common good manners?' He replied, 'Tell the monarch of the terrestrial earth to expect service from him who hopes to receive benefits; and let him know also that the monarch is for the protection of his subjects, and not the subjects for the service of the king. The king is the sentinel of the poor, although affluence, pomp and power are his portion. The sheep are not for the shepherd, but the shepherd is for their service.'

The Gulistan: Sadi of Shiraz (1184–1291)

ONE ARMY

Come, let us join our friends above,
Who have obtained the prize,
And on the eagle wings of love
To joy celestial rise.

146

Let saints below in concert sing
With these to glory gone,
For all the servants of our King
In earth and Heaven are one.

One family we dwell in Him,
One Church, above, beneath,
Though now divided by the stream,
The narrow stream of death.

One army of the living God,
To His command we bow;
Part of the host have crossed the flood,
And part are crossing now.

O Jesus, be our constant Guide!
Then, when the word is given,
Come, Lord of hosts, the waves divide,
And land us safe in Heaven.

Hymns of the Church of God:
selected by F. V. Mather (1866)

8. For Those who are Suffering

I AM INVOLVED

Any man's death diminishes me, because I am involved in mankind.

John Donne (1572–1631)

IN NEED OF THY MERCY

We beseech Thee, O Lord, remember all for good; have mercy upon all, O God. Remember every soul who, being in any affliction, trouble, or agony, stands in need of Thy mercy and help, all who are in necessity or distress, all who love or hate us.

Thou, O Lord, art the Helper of the helpless, the Hope of the hopeless, the Saviour of them who are tossed with tempests, the Haven of them who sail; be Thou All to all. The glorious majesty of the Lord our God be upon us; prosper Thou the work of our hands upon us, oh! prosper Thou our handiwork. Lord, be Thou within us, to strengthen us, without us, to keep us; above us, to protect us; beneath us, to uphold us; before us, to direct us; behind us, to keep us from straying; round about us, to defend us. Blessed be Thou, O Lord, our Father, for ever and ever. Amen.

Bishop Lancelot Andrewes (1555–1626)

PATIENCE, CONSTANCY AND HOPE

Be merciful, O Lord, to all our brethren and sisters that suffer any kind of persecution and affliction whether in mind or body, especially such as suffer for thy name and gospel; give them patience, constancy and steadfast hope, till thou send them full and good deliverance of all their troubles.

Christian Prayers (1566)

THE WOUNDED WORLD

O Thou Who are love, and seest all suffering, injustice, and misery which oppose Thy sway: have compassion, we beseech Thee, upon the work of Thine hands; look mercifully upon the wounded world and its inhabitants, laden with errors, labours and sorrows; fill our hearts with compassion for those who suffer; and bring near Thy kingdom of mercy and peace; for the sake of Jesus Christ our Lord.

after Eugène Bersier (1831–1889)

EVERY CRY OF PAIN

May my heart lend its ear to every cry of pain, like as the lotus bears its heart to drink the morning sun. Let not the fierce sun dry one tear of pain before I have wiped it from the sufferer's eye. But let each burning human ear drop on my heart and there remain, nor ever be brushed off until the pain that caused it is removed.

Buddhist Scriptures (5th century B.C.*)*

SINS OF CIVILISATION

Merciful Father, we come to Thee confessing the sins of our civilisation, in which we have all shared. We have been so bent upon our selfish ends that we would not stop to have mercy. When we have seen those whom the injustices of the world have bruised and beaten, we have passed by on the other side. We have built around ourselves the walls of privilege, within which we might not hear the passions of exploited men, the weeping of women, the bitter cry of children robbed of happy youth. O God of judgement, make us fit to ask for Thy forgiveness, before it is too late.

Anon.

MAKE OUR LAND FRUITFUL

O Bounteous God, pour out Thy blessing on all families, and on all the lawful occupations of men. Make our land fruitful, and suffer us to enjoy its fruits in health, peace and thankfulness. Especially we commend to Thy fatherly goodness all who are in any affliction, the sick and the sorrowful, the tempted and the destitute, the captive and those who are oppressed by war or tyranny. Comfort them by Thy Holy Spirit; let not their trials be too sore for them; give them patience and an inward assurance of Thy goodness. Let their sufferings work together for the purifying of their souls and the renewal of the inner man; and in outward things do unto them as seemeth best to Thy Fatherly wisdom; . . . through Jesus Christ our only Saviour, to whom with Thee and the Holy Spirit, be all praise and glory. Amen.

Philipp Jakob Spener (1635–1705)

MEAT TO THE HUNGRY

Thou, O Lord, providest enough for all men with Thy most liberal and bountiful hand; but whereas Thy gifts are, in respect of Thy goodness and free favour, made common to all men, we (through our naughtiness, niggardship, and distrust) do make them private and peculiar. Correct Thou the thing which our iniquity hath put out of order; let Thy goodness supply that which our niggardliness hath plucked away. Give Thou meat to the hungry and drink to the thirsty; comfort Thou to sorrowful; cheer up the dismayed; strengthen Thou the weak; deliver Thou them that are prisoners; and give Thou hope and courage to them that are out of heart.

Anon.

TO WORK IN SECURITY

O Lord, our heavenly Father, we commend to Thy protecting care and compassion the men and women of this and every land now suffering distress and anxiety through lack of work; prosper, we pray Thee, the councils of those who are engaged in the ordering of industrial life, that all people may be set free from want and fear, and may be enabled to work in security and peace, for the happiness of the common life and the well-being of their countries. Through Jesus Christ our Lord.

Anon.

COMPASSION FOR SUFFERERS

O Thou Who art love, and Who seest all the suffering, injustice and misery, which reign in this world; have pity, we implore Thee, on the work of Thy hands. Look mercifully upon the poor, the oppressed, and all who are heavy laden with error, labour and sorrow. Fill our hearts with deep compassion for those who suffer, and hasten the coming of Thy kingdom of justice and truth; for the sake of Jesus Christ our Lord.

Eugène Bersier (1831–1889)

THE CRY OF THE HOMELESS

Jesus, Son of man, look in mercy upon all who suffer the lack of livelihood and, like Thee, have nowhere to lay their head; let Thy pity and compassion move us to house the homeless and lighten the burdens of the needy and distressed: that in Thee all the families of the earth may be blessed.

O Lord Jesus Christ, born in a stable: hear the cry of the homeless and refugees; and so move our wills by Thy Spirit that we cease not until all have found home and livelihood, for Thy name's sake.

Frederick Brodie MacNutt (1873–1919)

FOR THOSE NEAREST DESPAIR

Though this kingdome were sometime called Scotia major, that is in Greek, darkenes, and now may justly recover the auncient title of Scotia major, (being in greater darkenes), yet that God that caused light to shine out of the darkenes in the beginning, caused also the beams of piety, learning and religion, to shine from hence unto other Nations, that sate in darkenes and in the shadow of death, for as there came many swarmes hither from forraine Countryes to be trayned up in learning and religion. . . . So this Beehive sent many swarms of learned Philosophers and religious Mounkes (much differing from the Mounkes of these days) into forrain Kingdomes. . . . Mee thinks our mercifull God, whose property is, then to show his mercies greatest when they are neerest to be despaired of, having caused in the depth of our discomfort and despaire, a

151

most glorious Starre to arise out of the North, doth in this great
mercy give full assurance of all other blessings whatsoever. . . .

Archbishop William O'Donnell (17th century)

COLD, OR IN SORROW

O Holy Spirit of God,
who with Thy holy breath doth cleanse the hearts and minds
of men.
comforting them when they be in sorrow,
leading them when they be out of the way,
kindling them when they be cold,
knitting them together when they be at variance,
and enriching them with manifold gifts;
by whose working all things live:
We beseech Thee to maintain and daily to increase
the gifts which Thou hast vouchsafed to us;
that with Thy light before us and within us
we may pass through this world
without stumbling and without straying;
who livest and reignest with the Father and the Son,
everlastingly.

A Booke of Christian Prayer: Erasmus (1466–1536)

9. Unity of All Things

THE KEYS OF HEAVEN

Glory be to God the Creator of all things.
He is the Guardian and disposer of all affairs.
To Him belong the keys of the heavens and the earth:
Praise be to God the Lord of the Worlds.

The Koran

WHEN THE BOOKS ARE OPEN

O Lord Jesus Christ, before whose Judgement seat we must appear and give good account of the things done in the body; grant, we beseech Thee, that, when the books are open in that day the faces of Thy servants may not be ashamed; through Thy merits, O blessed Saviour, One God, world without end.

The Altus: St. Columba (521–597)

MAN AND BEAST

Rejoice in God, O ye tongues: give the glory to the Lord and the Lamb.

Nations and languages and every creature, in which is the breath of life,

Let man and beast appear before him, and magnify his name together.

Christopher Smart (1722–1771)

STOREHOUSE OF DIVINE BOUNTY

We must recover reverence for the earth, and its resources, treating it no longer as a reservoir of potential wealth to be exploited, but as a storehouse of Divine bounty on which we utterly depend.

The Malvern Document: Archbishop William Temple's Malvern Conference (1941)

153

THE ONE FIRE

Truth is one: sages call it through various names.
It is the one Sun that reflects in all the ponds;
It is the one water which slakes the thirst of all;
It is the one air which sustains all life;
It is the one fire which shines in all houses;
Colours of the cows may be different, but milk is white;
Flowers and bees may be different, but honey is the same;
Systems of faith may be different, but God is one.

As the rain dropping from the sky
wends its way towards the ocean,
So the prostrations offered in all faiths reach the One God,
who is supreme. *Hindu Scriptures (Rig Veda)*

AS A MOTHER

Even as a mother at the risk of her life would watch over her only child, so let us with boundless mind and goodwill survey the whole world.

Buddhist Scriptures (Metta Sutta)

SPIRIT OF THE WHOLE

Prayer is the effort to live in the spirit of the whole.

Samuel Taylor Coleridge (1772–1834)

ALL SHOULD OBEY

The rain of his infinite mercy refresheth all places, and the table of his bounty is spread far and near.

O merciful God, who out of thine hidden treasures affordest daily sustenance to the Guebre and the infidel, how canst thou exclude thy friends, thou who deignest thus favourably to regard thine enemies? Clouds and wind, the moon, the sun, and the sky are all busied, that thou, O man, mayst obtain thy bread, and eat it not in neglect. For thy sake, all these revolve and are obedient: it is not therefore consistent with the rules of justice that thou only shouldst not obey.

The Gulistan: Sadi of Shiraz (1184–1291) (compilation)

THE INWARD EYE

The day of days . . . is the day on which the inward eye opens to the unity of things.

Ralph Waldo Emerson (1803–1882)

THE FLAME OF LAMPS

A Hindu girl named Kiságotamí gave birth to a son. When the boy was able to walk by himself, he died. The young girl carried the dead child clasped to her bosom, and went from house to house, asking if anyone would give her medicine for it. Some regarded her as mad; but a wise man said, 'My good girl, I cannot cure your son, but I know of a doctor who can attend to it. You must go to Pára Taken; he can give medicine.' Kiságotamí went to him, and said, 'Lord and Master, do you know of any medicine that will be good for my boy?' Pára Taken said, 'I know of some.' She asked, 'What medicine do you require?' The sage replied, 'I require a handful of mustard-seed taken from a house where no son, husband, parent, or servant has died.' The girl said, 'Very good,' and went about with her dead child, asking for the mustard-seed. The people said, 'Here is some mustard-seed, take it.' Then the girl asked, 'In my friend's house has there died a son, a husband, a parent, or a servant?' They replied, 'Lady what is this you say? The living are few but the dead are many.' Then she went to other houses; but one said, 'I have lost my son,' another, 'I have lost my parent,' until at last she said, 'This is a heavy task I have undertaken. I am not the only one whose son is dead. In the whole Sávatthi country children are dying, parents are dying.' She went and laid her child down in a forest, then came to Pára Taken. He said to her, 'Have you received the handful of mustard-seed?' She answered, 'I have not. The people of the village told me the living are few, but the dead are many.' Pára Taken said to her, 'You thought that you alone had lost a son; the law of death rules all, there is no permanence.' The Kiságotamí became a votary. Once when she was engaged in her devotions, she observed the lights in a house now shining, now extinguished, and reflected, 'My state is like those lamps.' Then in a vision the lord appeared to her, and said, 'All living beings resemble the flame of those lamps, one moment lighted,

155

the next extinguished; they only who have arrived at Nirvana are at rest.' Kiságotamí, on hearing this, became possessed of intuitive knowledge.

Parables (Buddhist Scriptures) (5th century B.C.*)*

NO DIFFERENCE OF CASTES

Mandhata said to Narada, 'I see persons of every colour, and we are all subject to love, anger, fear, thought, grief, hunger, and labour. Where then is the difference of castes?'

Narada replied, 'There is no difference of castes: all the universe is pervaded by the Supreme Being. The creatures of God have passed into classes by their actions.'

Learning should be rescued from every consideration of high rank or low, a consideration that cannot for a moment be compatible with instruction; and the heart should be kept free from all [such] infatuation.

He is a devotee and a wise man all of whose engagements are pursued through every instruction he may meet with; who is devoted, ignorant of cruelty, and lives as a friend of all the creatures; who, uninfluenced by favour, is directed only by infallible reason; and who is master of his senses.

Truth is God himself, and it is divine meditation; by it the world is caused, governed and preserved. Falsehood is darkness. Those two are the stations of heaven and hell.

There is no virtue in the world greater than that of doing good to others.

Without virtue everything would cease to be.

Hindu, Padma Purana, Swarga,
Khanda Scriptures (compilation)

FOR THIS WORLD

O God, we thank Thee for this universe, our great home; for its vastness and its riches, and for the manifoldness of the life which teems upon it and of which we are a part. We praise Thee for the arching sky and the blessed winds, for the driving clouds and the constellations on high. We praise Thee for the salt sea and the running water, for the everlasting hills, for the trees, and for the grass under our feet. We thank Thee for our senses by which we can see the splendour of the morning, and hear the jubilant songs of love, and smell the breath of the springtime. Grant us, we pray Thee, a heart wide open to all this joy and beauty, and save our souls from being so steeped in care or so darkened by passion that we pass heedless and unseeing when even the thornbush by the wayside is aflame with the glory of God.

Enlarge within us the sense of fellowship with all the living things, our little brothers, to whom Thou hast given this earth as their home in common with us. We remember with shame that in the past we have exercised the high dominion of man with ruthless cruelty, so that the voice of the earth, which should have gone up to Thee in song, has been a groan of travail. May we realise that they live, not for us alone, but for themselves and for Thee, and that they love the sweetness of life even as we, and serve Thee in their place better than we in ours.

When our use of this world is over and we make room for others, may we not leave anything ravished by our greed or spoiled by our ignorance, but may we hand on our common heritage fairer and sweeter through our use of it, undiminished in fertility and joy, so that our bodies may return in peace to the great mother who nourished them and our spirits may round the circle of a perfect life in Thee.

Hymns of the Social Awakening:
Walter Rauschenbusch (1861–1918)

THE EARTH IS OUR MOTHER

Truth which is mighty, righteousness which is strong, consecration and dedication to holiness, sustain the world: may the world, the mistress of the past and future, give us free room!

May the earth, the place of habitation, which containeth all things, which holdeth all treasure, which suffereth every creature that hath life to repose on its golden breast; may the earth, which holdeth fire whose presence is in all men, grant us the object of our desires!

The earth is our mother.

May thy hills and thy snow-clad mountains, may thy waste and the woodland, O world, be pleasant! Unwearied may I dwell on the many-coloured world.

And thou, O earth, do thou givest me sweetness of speech!

With the odour of thee which exists in humanity—loveliness and beauty in men and women, in the horse and the elephant—which is the glory of the maiden—fill us, too, with that: may no one hate us!

I praise the world which is continually renewed.

May clean waters flow for our body. I wash me thoroughly and am clean.

All the range of thee, O earth, which I look over by the help of the sun—may the sight of my eye lose none of it, till the latest years which are to come!

May thy summer, O earth, thy rains, thine autumn, thine early and late winter, thy spring—may thine appointed seasons, thy years, thy day and night, O world, yield us blessings as it were milk!

Thou hast many paths on which men go, a highway for the chariot and for the cart, paths on which the proud and the humble travel. The world which endureth the burden of the oppressor beareth up the abode of the lofty and of the lowly, suffereth the hog, and giveth entrance to the wild boar.

May fire, sun, and water give me wisdon. May I be a lord on the earth.

May I be full of force, pressing forward: may I scatter all them that are violent.

May the peaceful earth, whose fragrance is excellent, whose breasts contain the heavenly drink, bless me with her milk!

Thou art the capacious vessel of humanity, bestowing all desires and art not exhausted; that which thou lackest may the lord of creation fill up—the firstborn of righteousness!

Mother earth, do thou fix and establish me, that it may be well with me—thou that art the associate of heaven!

Hindu Scriptures (Atharva-Veda)

10. Prayers for Selflessness

THOU ART ENOUGH

Whatever share of this world Thou dost bestow on me, bestow it on Thine enemies, and whatever share of the next world thou dost give me, give it to Thy friends. Thou art enough for me!

Rabi'a of Basra

I SURRENDER MY ALL

All the Buddhas in all regions, I entreat with my hands folded,
May they light the lamp of Dharma, for those lost in suffering's wastes.

With folded hands now I petition the Jinas who are ready for Nirvana,
To stay here still for many ages, so that the world may not be struck with blindness.

Heedless of body, heedless of goods, of the merit I gained and will gain still,
I surrender my all to promote the welfare of others.

Sāntideva (circa 750) Bodhicarayávatára:
translation by Lionel David Barnett (1871–1960)
in The Path of Life *(1911)*

MEAT TO THE HUNGRY

O God our Father, in Whom we know that those ensnared in penury of things needful for the body cannot set their minds on Thee; have pity, we beseech Thee, on the poor, that by Thy removing of their misery they may rise up to Thee in praise; Thou, O Lord, providest enough for all men, and Thy Goodness is common to all; we, by our greediness, have disordered Thy world; give Thou meat to the hungry and drink to the thirsty, comfort the sorrowful, cheer the dismayed, strengthen the weak, and give Thou hope and courage to them that are out of heart; have compassion on so many great miseries, O Fountain of all good things and blessedness; for Thine Only Son, our Lord and Saviour Jesus Christ's sake. Amen.   *Elizabethan Prayer Book*

SIMPLICITY OF THY TRUTH

O God, the Saviour and protector of all them that trust in Thee, turn away from us all false gleams of selfish and worldly wisdom; that under the teaching of Thy spirit we may find pleasure in the simplicity of Thy truth, and have the wisdom which comes of Thy holy fear. So in guilelessness let us be children, but in understanding men. Amen.

Rowland Williams (1817–1870)

FOR ANOTHER

And lay down and offer up your lives for one another. Here is the love of, and unto the brethren manifest, to lay down their lives for one another.

Epistles: George Fox (1624–1691)

FOR THE GLORY OF THE LORD

Potent is He that promised to be with us in all such enterprises as we take in hand for the glory of the Lord.

John Knox (1505–1572)

THE COMMON WEAL

God weigheth more with how much love a man worketh than how much he doeth. He doeth much who doeth a thing well. He doeth well that rather serveth the common weal than his own will.

Thomas à Kempis (1380–1471)

THE MEANING OF CHARITY

Charity is the free gift of anything not injurious. If no benefit is intended, or the gift is harmful, it is not charity. There must be also the desire to assist, or to show gratitude. It is not charity when gifts are given from other considerations, as when animals are fed that they may be used, or presents given by lovers to bind affection, or to slaves to stimulate labour. It is found where man, seeking to diffuse happiness among all men—those he loves, and those he loves not—digs canals and pools, makes roads, bridges, and seats, and plants trees for shade. It is found where, from compassion for the miserable and the poor, who have none to help them, a man erects resting places for wanderers, and drinking-fountains, or provides food or raiment, medicine for the needy, not selecting one more than another. This is true charity, and bears much fruit.

Siamese, Buddhist, Kathá, Chari Scriptures

GRACE TO STAND UPRIGHT

Give us, O Lord, a humble spirit, that we may never presume upon thy mercy, but live always as those who have been much forgiven. Make us tender and compassionate toward those who are overtaken by temptation, considering ourselves, how we have fallen in times past and may fall yet again. Make us watchful and sober-minded, looking ever unto thee for grace to stand upright, and to persevere unto the end; through thy Son Jesus Christ our Lord.

Daily Prayer: Dean Charles John Vaughan (1816–1897)

NO SHOES

Have mercy on me, O Beneficent One—I was angered for I had no shoes; then I met a man who had no feet.

Chinese Saying

THINK OF DESTINY

Think of the totality of all Being, and what a mite of it is yours; think of all Time, and the brief fleeting instant of it that is allotted to yourself; think of Destiny, and how puny a part of it you are.

Marcus Aurelius (121–180)

RELIEF FOR THE DISTRESSED

Thou sayest, 'When I have enough I will relieve the distressed.' How I pity thee! Thou wilt never relieve them.

Albitis

PEACE AND RECONCILIATION

Destroy the spirit of self-seeking in individuals and nations. Give to the peoples and statesmen thoughts of peace and reconciliation. Thou canst find a way where men know not what to do.

Swedish Prayers, from The Message of the World-Wide Church: William Paton

INJURE NOT OTHERS

A good work performed with a pure heart, though small, is not trifling. How large is the seed of the banyan-tree?

Look closely at musk; its hue is dark, but it perfumes all things. Thus hidden are the virtues of men of weight.

Those who look after the faults of others are often ignorant of their own.

If you consider your possessions as your own, fools will agree with you.

That alone belongs to you which you have bestowed.

From buried wealth what is derived? Anxiety alone.

Be a man evildoer or unlettered, charity regards only his destitution.

To what end is liberality without love?

Injure not others, O men, and live for ever!

Hindu Scriptures (Vemana)

MOVEMENT OF THE HEART

It is not by a miracle, but by a movement of the heart that we are benefited, by a submissive spirit. Let us believe, let us trust, let us hope, and God will never reject our prayer.

François de Salignac de la Mothe Fénélon (1651–1715)

162

11. *Grant Us Freedom*

PRISON OF SELFISH DESIRE

O timeless and eternal Spirit, liberate us from the prison house of selfish desire, of worldly standards and of petty ambition into the spacious heaven of Thy love. May the peace of the eternal Father brood over us; may love of the eternal Son surround us; may the strength of the eternal Spirit dwell within us.

Anon.

THE CYPRESS TREE

They asked a wise man why, out of many trees which the Almighty hath created, lofty and fruit-bearing, the cypress alone is called *azad* or free, although it beareth not fruit? He replied, 'Every tree hath its appointed fruit and season, with which it is at one time flourishing, and at another time destitute and withering; to neither of which states is the cypress exposed, being always flourishing, as is the state of those who are free.' Place not your heart in that which is transitory; for the river Tigris will continue to flow through Bagdad after the Califs will have ceased to reign. If you are able, imitate the date tree in liberality; but if you have not the means of munificence, be an *azad* or free, like the cypress.

The Gulistan: Sadi of Shiraz (1184–1291)

CONQUER ONESELF

It is better by yielding to Truth to conquer Opinion, than by yielding to Opinion to be defeated by Truth.

No one is free who does not conquer himself.

Epictetus (1st century)

163

PERFECTION FROM THE BEGINNING

Singularly radiating is the wondrous light;
Free is it from the bondage of matter and the senses.
Not binding by words and letters,
The Essence is nakedly exposed in its pure eternity.
Never defiled is the wind-nature;
It exists in perfection from the very beginning.
By merely casting away your delusions
The Suchness of Buddhahood is realised.

The Practice of Zen:
translation by Chang Chen-Chi

DOMINION OF THE CONSCIENCE

Stephen, King of Poland, said to those who tried to persuade him to constrain some of his subjects who were of a different religion, to embrace his, 'I am a king of men, not of consciences. The dominion of the conscience belongs exclusively to God.'

Cope's Anecdotes: quoted by
Wilson Armistead (1819–1868)

GREAT REASON

'The spiritual body (*dharmakaya*), as to its substance (*hypostasis*), is like the vast expanse of Space. The Nature of Man and his Reason were originally one and undivided; simply by reason of covetous desire his True Nature was perverted, and the six modes of migrational existence and the four kinds of birth were introduced into the world.'

'(*Mâha* or *Prajña Pâramitâ*) signifies "vast" and "unbounded". The particular reference is to the boundless and infinite void known as "Great Reason".'

Confucius says, 'Look up at it, it is higher than you can see! Bore into it, it is deeper than you can penetrate! Look at it as it stands before you; suddenly it is behind you [i.e. it cannot be grasped].

When the *Prajñâ Pâramitâ* has been fully practised, then we clearly behold that the five skandha* are all empty, vain, and unreal. So it is we escape the possibility of sorrow or obstruction.

164

All these things around us (*ye dhammá*) being thus stript or devoid of qualities (*lakshana*), there can be no longer birth or death, defilement or purity, addition or destruction. In the midst then of this void (*sûnyatâ*), there can be neither *rúpa, vedaná, sanjná, sanskára,* or *vijnána**; nor yet organs or sense, whether the eye, or nose, ear, or tongue, body, or mind (*manas*); nor yet objects of sense, i.e., matter (*rúpa*), or sound, odour, or taste, or ideas (*dharma*); nor yet categories of sense (*dhátu*), such as the union of the object and subject in sight, in smell, in touch, in taste, in apprehension.

So there will be no such thing as ignorance (*avidyâ*), nor yet freedom from ignorance, and therefore there can be none of its consequences; and therefore no such thing as decay or death (*jará* or *marana*), nor yet freedom from decay and death. So neither can there be a method (or way) for destroying the concourse of sorrows. No such thing as wisdom, and no such thing as attaining [happiness or rest], as there will be not aught that can be attained.

The Bôdhisatwa resting on this *Prajná Páramitá,* no sorrow or obstruction can then affect his heart, for there will be no such thing as sorrow or obstruction. Therefore, having no fear or apprehension of evil, removing far from him all the distorting influences of illusive thought, he arrives at the goal of Nirvana.

Sin King or *Heart Sutra* or
Mâha-prajna-pâramitâ-hridaya Sutra (compilation)

* 1. *Rupa-skandha,* the organs of sense and objects of sense.
2. *Vijnána-skandha,* intelligence or consciousness of sensation.
3. *Vedana-skandha,* pleasure, pain or the absence of either.
4. *Sanjná-skandha,* the knowledge or belief arising from names and words such as ox, house, etc.
5. *Sanskára-skandha,* the passions, hatred, fear, etc.

MAN'S SPIRITUAL NATURE

Although a man may earnestly desire to enter the path to Nirvana and studiously pursue the directions of the various discourses (*Shasters*) on the subject, he may nevertheless miss altogether attaining his desired aim. Now the two laws contained in the idea of *chi-kwan* are simply these: that which is spoken of as *chi* (fixity) is the first mode (or, gate to Nirvana), and consists in overcoming all the entanglements of the mind;

that which is called *kwan* (meditation) is the Rest which follows or accompanies the separation of mind from all external influences. Once 'fixed,' a man will tenderly foster the good principles of knowledge (heart-knowledge). Possessed of true meditation, a man has gained the mysterious art of liberating his spiritual nature (his soul).

Now for the purpose of assisting those who wish to practise these two principles (*chi-kwan*), we have put together the following brief sections:

1. Accomplishment of external means. These are five:

(a) Observing the Precepts purely and perfectly (i.e., the Ten Commandments);

(b) Relates to food and clothing;

(c) Relates to the possession of a pure place of abode, e.g. where no business is transacted, and where there are no contentions or disputes;

(d) Relates to freedom from all worldly concerns and influences. There are four things to be avoided under this head: (1) to desist from all share in ruling or governing a people; (2) to desist from all wordly friendships, and all social or family connexions; (3) not to follow any trade or art, whether of medicine, sorcery, or other persuasion; (4) to desist from all professional engagements connected with wordly learning, discussion, instruction, and so on;

(e) Relates to the promotion of all virtuous knowledge, of which there are three divisions: (1) taking care of all religious books; (2) endeavouring to promote agreement among religious persons, so that there shall be no division or confusion; (3) endeavouring to transmit and inculcate, by every expedient of mind and action, the true principles of virtuous knowledge.

We have thus briefly glanced at the five sorts of preparatory observances requisite for the final acquisition of *chi-kwan*.

On Chiding the Evil Desires

These evil desires are five: every one who enters on the practice of meditation with a view to perfect himself in the system called *chi-kwan,* must overcome these desires. They are commonly known in the world as the lust after beauty, sound, smell, taste, touch.

These considerations respecting the forbidden desires are

166

taken from the discourses of the Great-conveyance (*Mahâ yana*) School; and in these also we find the following—Alas! for the miseries which all creatures endure constantly from these five desires! And still they seek after their indulgence, and are never satisfied! These five desires conduce to our continuance in misery, as fuel which revives and supports a fire.

Casting Away Hindrances

The hindrances spoken of are five: viz., covetousness, anger, sloth, restlessness, unbelief. In the previous section we spoke of desire for external gratification, the object being in one of the five categories of sense. But now we are speaking, in brief, of the desires which are originated in the mind itself.

The fourth hindrance is threefold: (1) restlessness of body; which cannot be still in any position; (2) restlessness of the vocal organs; (3) restlessness of mind.

There are three kinds of unbelief: (1) That sort of doubt about oneself that leads a man to think thus: 'All my faculties are dark and dull; the pollution of sin in my case is very great; I am unlike anyone else.' Thinking thus about himself, a man in the end will be unable to attain perfection, for whilst sojourning in the present world, it is difficult to ascertain what principles of virtue there may be within the heart. (2) That which relates to one's Religious Teacher, as if a man were to say: 'My teacher has no dignified way about him, or peculiar marks of excellency; he cannot, then, possess any great religious endowments; how then can he instruct me?' The disciple should argue even thus: 'My master, although he is not perfectly pure, is yet able to promote in my mind the love of religion.' (3) There is a third kind of belief which relates to the Law: for this is the argument, 'that the mind of man, which is naturally so taken up with worldly concerns, can never with faith and reverence undertake religious duties; and that there can be no sincerity in such profession.' But what then? [Such a] doubt is the very principle of failure.

Harmonising the Faculties

1. The first duty regards 'food'; and with respect to this the rule is that one's individual desires should be regulated according to Reason.

2. The second thing to be adjusted is 'sleep'. [As] the Sutra says, 'By not yielding to the influence of sloth, the life is cleansed and there is nothing further to attain.'

3. With respect to the body: care must be taken that no violent exertion be used previous to entering on the exercise of 'meditation', lest the breath be agitated, and the mind in consequence be unsettled. (There follows a description of the correct placing of the mat, one's clothing, hands and body, and of the cleansing of the mouth.)

4. Next, with respect to 'breathing'. There are four kinds of breathing. There are four kinds of respiration: (a) windy respiration; (b) a gasping respiration; (c) emotional breathing; (d) pure respiration. The first three modes are unharmonised conditions; the last is harmonised. [It is] when there is neither noise nor gasping nor uneven breathing, but when the respiration is calm and regular, the sign of an equable and well-balanced mind.

5. Lastly, with respect to 'harmonising' the mental faculties, there are several schemes for doing this: on entering, being fixed, and leaving the condition of absolute rest. On entering *Samâdhi*, all confused thoughts must be suppressed and harmonised so that they cannot get the upper hand. And, next, there must be some fixed object for the eye to gaze on when the mind is fickle or dead. When engaged in the actual enjoyment of *Samâdhi*, take care that neither body, breath, nor mind be allowed to relax from its state of discipline. On emerging from *Samâdhi*, a man ought first to scatter or dissipate the influences which bind his heart, by opening his mouth and letting go his breath. (There follows the remainder of this method of 'leaving the condition of absolute rest.')

Chi-kai, selected from his Sian-chi-kwan

A PREPARED STATE OF MIND

There is a serene dignity in the reprimand of silence, which brings over an offending spirit something of the holiness and majesty of God, who works all his glorious wonders, in nature and in grace, with the impressive solemnity of silence. In silence he meets the soul; in silence he penetrates the conscience; in silence he spreads before the guilty accumulated wrongs against him; and, with neither speech nor language, shakes the earth of man's fallen nature to its very centre. And hence it is that scarcely any species of correction or instruction is so totally repugnant to the carnal mind, as that which is accompanied with the down-breaking, flesh-crucifying power of silence; the felt consciousness of which repugnance occasions it to be but seldom resorted to in appealing to the hearts and consciences of those with whom we have to do, in the character of monitors or reprovers; and, therefore, it often happens, that the offended and offender, the teacher and the learner, are beclouded and bewildered in a multiplicity of words, wherein little is effected beyond the nourishing of self-complacency in those who speak, and a spirit of disputation in those who hear.

It is greatly to be desired that more attention were paid, on the part of religious instructors, to the value and importance of a prepared state of mind, before they proceed to the performance of their allotted duties. 'The preparation of the heart in man, and the answer of the tongue, is of the Lord.' Would you then be really influential as 'good stewards of the manifold grace of God,' seek, in the first place, by earnest prayer, and watching thereunto with all perseverance, to obtain from your heavenly Father the gift of his Holy Spirit, to clothe your own souls with that pure stillness in which (as in the 'glassy sea,' spoken of by the beloved apostle), the reflection of truth can alone be received.

Until an experimental acquaintance with Divine truth is in some measure wrought in ourselves, be assured we are in no condition to produce any deep and lasting effect upon others—for things will only act, and cause to act, according to their nature; and that which is merely the result of study, and which exists but in the mode of this or the other notion or opinion of our own mind, will do not more than produce its own likeness of opinions and notions in those we desire to influence, if it does not generate the alternative of wrangling and jangling, to prove how far it may be right or wrong.

If nothing can be acquired to any efficient purpose in human knowledge, except the mind be concentrated on the object before it, so neither can any valuable acquaintance with Divine truths be wrought out, but by the subjugation of every wandering imagination, and the 'bringing into captivity every thought to the obedience of Christ.' All this is the waiting upon, and watching for, and diligently obeying the smallest movements of the Holy Spirit of truth, who is promised and bestowed as our 'guide into all truth,' and to whom we are to hearken as the scholar listens to the directions of his master.

Select Miscellanies . . . of the Society of Friends (1851)

12. Action before Mere Words

LIFTING OUR EYES TO HEAVEN

Prayer doth not consist either in the bending of our knees, or the service of our lips, or the lifting up of our hands or eyes to heaven; but in the elevation of our souls towards God. These outward expressions of our inward thoughts are necessary in our public, and often expedient in our private, devotions; but they do not make up the essence of prayer, which may truly and acceptably be performed, where these are wanting.'

Bishop George Snalridge (1663–1719)

TO HONOUR ALL MEN

Teach us, O Lord, to see every question of foreign policy in the light of our creed; that we may check in ourselves and in others every temper which makes for war, all ungenerous judgements, all promptings of self-assertion, all presumptuous claims; that being ever ready to recognise the needs and aspirations of other nations, we may, with patience, do whatsoever in us lies to remove suspicions and misunderstandings; and to honour all men in Jesus Christ our Lord. Amen.

Bishop Brooke Foss Westcott (1825–1901)

SOCIAL JUSTICE

Where the rights of property conflict with the establishment of social justice or the general social welfare, those rights should be overriden, modified, or, if need be, abolished.

The Malvern Document (1941),
Archbishop William Temple's Malvern Conference

171

FOLLOW HIS WAY

The instruments God demands are those who constantly in prayer and worship verify their ideals before His august Will, verify and improve, and never cease to verify them. . . . The only hope for the world lies in those who at least attempt to know Him and to follow His Way.

Message to All Peoples: Madras Conference

THE BOOK OF FATE

Just Words do not the saint or sinner make, Action alone is written in the book of fate.

Sikh Scriptures

SERENITY OF MIND

Show us, O Blessed One, that though we can recite but little of the Teaching, yet put its Precepts into practice, ridding ourselves of craving and delusion, and possessed of knowledge and serenity of mind, cleaving to nothing in this or any other world, then we are true disciples of Thee, O Blessed One.

Thoughts on the Way, Buddhist Scriptures

THE ACTIVE DUTY

That is the active duty which is not for our bondage; that is knowledge which is for our liberation; all other duty is good only unto weariness; all other knowledge is only the cleverness of an artist.

Hindu Scriptures (Vishnu Parána)

WAIT FOR THE RIGHT TIME

There is nothing too difficult to be obtained by those who, before they act, reflect well themselves, and thoroughly consult with chosen friends.

There are failures even in acting well. The work not done by suitable methods will fail, although many stand up to protect it. The chariot is weak at sea, and the ship on land.

There will be an end to his life who, having climbed out to the end of the branch, ventures to go farther.

172

The crow will overcome an owl in the daytime. Is there anything difficult for him who acts with right instruments at the right time?

The self-restraint of the energetic is like the drawing back of the foot of the ram in order to butt.

If a rare opportunity come, let a man do that which is rarely done.

They may successfully meditate the conquest of the world who can think silently and wait for the right time.

Hindu Scriptures (Cural II)

IMPROVING MANKIND'S CONDITION

The best way of worshipping God is in allaying the distress of the times, and improving the conditions of mankind.

Persian Scriptures

ACCORDING TO HIS ACT

I call heaven and earth to witness that whether a person be Jew or Gentile, man or woman, manservant or maidservant, according to his act does the Divine Spirit rest upon him.

Seder Eliyahu Rabbah

MISERY TO COMFORT

Do not be content with showing friendship in words alone; let your heart burn with loving kindness for all who may cross your path.

The wrong in the world continues to exist just because people talk only of their ideals, and do not strive to put them into practice. If actions took the place of words, the world's misery would very soon be changed to comfort.

Abdu'l-Baha (1884–1921)

SHEEP OR DOG?

In the grove of Gotama lived a Brahman, who, having bought a sheep in another village, and carrying it home on his shoulder to sacrifice, was seen by three rogues, who resolved to take the animal from him by the following stratagem. Having separated, they agreed to encounter the Brahman on his road as if coming from different parts. One of them called out, 'O Brahman! why dost thou carry that dog on thy shoulder?'

'It is not a dog,' replied the Brahman; 'it is a sheep for sacrifice.' As he went on, the second knave met him, and put the same question; whereupon the Brahman, throwing the sheep on the ground, looked at it again and again. Having replaced it on his shoulder, the good man went with mind waving like a string. But when the third rogue met him and said, 'Father, where art thou taking the dog?' the Brahman, believing his eyes bewitched, threw down the sheep and hurried home, leaving the thieves to feast on that which he had provided for the gods.

Hindu Scriptures (Pilpay)

GREEN AND SWEET

If the very law of life is a law of change; if every blossom of beauty has its root in fallen leaves; if love and thought, and hope would faint beneath to constant light, and need for their refreshing the darkness and the dews; if it is in losing the transient that we gain the eternal; then let us shrink no more from sorrow, and sigh no more for rest; but have a genial welcome for vicissitude, and make quiet friends with loss and death. Through storm and calm, fresh be our courage, and quick our eye, for the various services that may await us. Nay, when God Himself turns us not hither and thither, when He sends us no changes for us to receive and consecrate, be it ours to create them for ourselves, by flinging ourselves into generous enterprises and worthy sacrifice; by the stirrings of sleepless aspiration, and all the spontaneous vicissitudes of holy and progressive souls; keeping always the moral spaces round us pure and fresh by constant thought of truth and the frequent deed of love. And then, when, for us, too, death closes the great series of mortal changes, the past will lie behind us green and sweet as Iden, and the future before us in the light of eternal peace. Tranquil and fearless we shall resign ourselves to God, to conduct us through that ancient and invisible way, which has been sanctified by the feet of all the faithful, and illumined by the man of griefs.

Hours of Thought: James Martineau (1805–1900)

13. *Joyfulness*

THE ROTTEN RAGS OF MEMORY

I come in Self-annihilation and the grandeur of Inspiration;
To cast off Rational Demonstration by Faith in the Saviour,
To cast off the rotten rags of Memory by Inspiration,
To cast off Bacon, Locke, and Newton from Albion's
covering,
To take off his filthy garments and clothe him with
Imagination.

The Tiger: William Blake (1757–1827)

THE HIGHEST GOOD

The highest good may be likened to water.
Water benefits all creatures yet does not strive or argue with
them.
It rests content in those lowly places which others despise.
Thus it is very near the Tao.

The Way of Acceptance, Tao Te Ching:
Lao Tse (604–517 B.C.)

LOVE IS THE LESSON

Most glorious Lord of life, that on this day
didst make thy triumph over death and sin:
and having harrowed hell, didst bring away
captivity thence captive us to win:
This joyous day, dear Lord, with joy begin,
and grant that we for whom Thou diddest die,
being with Thy dear blood clean washed from sin,
may live for ever in felicity.

And that Thy love we weighing worthily,
may likewise love Thee for the same again:
and for Thy sake that all like dear didst buy
with love may one another entertain.
So let us love, dear love, like as we ought,
love is the lesson which the Lord us taught.

Edmund Spenser (1552–1599)

WE MUST DARE TO BE HAPPY

Let us never be afraid of innocent joy; God is good, and what He does is well done; resign yourself to everything, even to happiness; ask for the spirit of sacrifice, of detachment, of remuneration, and, above all, for the spirit of joy and gratitude—that genuine and religious optimism which sees in God a Father, and asks no pardon for His benefits. We must dare to be happy, and dare to confess it, regarding ourselves always as the depositaries, not as the authors of our own joy.

Henri Frédéric Amiel (1821–1881)

UNITY AND CONCORD

O God, we long for the hour of love and union, the day of the spiritual harmony of all who love Thee. We strain our ears towards the East and towards the West, towards the North and towards the South, to hear the song of love and fellowship chanted in the meetings of the faithful. We yearn to see the friends united as a string of gleaming pearls, as the brilliant Pleiades, as the rays of the sun, as the gazelles of one meadow.

May it come soon, the joyful tidings that the believers are the very embodiment of sincerity and truthfulness, the incarnation of love and amity, the living symbols of unity and concord.

Abdu'l-Baha (1884–1921)

14. All Religions are the Same

SHAME FOR WRONGDOING

A gospel minister relates, that in the course of his travels in America, a cavilling physician denied that the Divine light and Spirit was in every one; and affirmed that it was not in the Indians, some of whom were present; whereupon, said the minister, I called an Indian to us, and asked him whether or no, when he did lie, or do wrong to any one, there was not something in him that did reprove him for it; and he said there was such a thing in him, that did so reprove him, and he was ashamed when he had done wrong, or spoken wrong.

Journal, Vol. II, George Fox (1624–1691)

THE LIGHT IS THE SAME

The lamps are different but the light is the same.

Jalaluddin Rumi

TILL THE UNIVERSE REJOICES

All nations and languages repeat the name of God, even infancy lisps it—Allah, Tangaí, Yezdán, Elohim. Yet cannot his praise be duly expressed by mortal till the dumb man shall be eloquent, and stocks and stones find a voice; till the silent universe rejoices in language.

The sun sinks down in the ocean, and azure-hued vapours arise; it is nature's incense of devotion perfuming the heavens.

Ride thou on for eternity through the glowing heavens, mounted on thy fantasy, thou shalt not stride beyond his threshold!

Soar thou beyond all limit to the roof of the universe, thou shalt behold one tile of his dwelling—one tile, no more.

Persian, Anwari, Plidonia Scriptures (compilation)

BEAMS OF WISDOM

O, under various sacred names adored!
Divinity supreme! All potent Lord!
Author of nature, whose unbounded sway
And legislative power all things obey.

Majestic God, all hail! To Thee belong
The suppliant prayer and tributary song:
To Thee from all Thy mortal offspring due:
From Thee we came, from Thee our being drew.

But, O Great Father, thunder-ruling God,
Who in thick darkness mak'st thy dread abode,
Thou, from whose bounty all good gifts descend,
Do Thou from ignorance mankind defend!
The clouds of vice and folly, O control
And shed the beams of wisdom on the soul!

Cleanthes (301–225 B.C.*)*

COMMON GROUND

Have the religions of mankind no common ground? Is there not everywhere the same enrapturing beauty beaming forth from many thousand hidden places? Broad indeed is the carpet God has spread, and beautiful the colours He has given it. . . . There is but one lamp in this house, in the rays of which, wherever I look, a bright assembly meets me. . . . O God! whatever road I take joins the highway that leads to Thee.

Sufi Scriptures

ALL GOD'S FAITHFUL SONS

One holy Church of God appears
Through every age and race,
Unwasted by the lapse of years,
Unchanged by changing place.

From oldest times, on furthest shores,

Beneath the pine or palm,
One Unseen Presence she adores,
With silence or with psalm.

Her priests are all God's faithful sons
To serve the world raised up;
The pure in heart her baptised ones,
Love, her communion cup.

The truth is her prophetic gift,
The soul her sacred page,
And feet on mercy's errand swift
Do make her pilgrimage.

O living Church, thine errand speed;
Fulfil thy task sublime;
With bread of life earth's hunger feed;
Redeem the evil time!

Samuel Longfellow (1819–1892)

MAN THE DELIVERER

East and west went my soul to find
Light, and the world was bare and blind,
And the soil herbless where she trod
And saw men laughing scourge mankind,
Unsmitten by the rod
Of any God.

Then, 'Where is God? and where is the aid?
Or what good end of these?' She said;
'Is there no God or end at all,
Nor reason with unreason weighed,
Nor force to disenthral
Weak feet that fall?'

O fool, that for brute cries of wrong
Heard not the grey glad Mother's song
Ring response from the hills and waves,
But heard harsh noises all day long
Of spirits that were slaves
And dwelt in graves.

With all her tongues of life and death,
With all her bloom and blood and breath,
From all years dead and all things done,
In th' ear of man the Mother saith,
'There is no God, O Son,
If thou be none.'

Algernon Charles Swinburne (1837–1909)

15. Prayers for Peace

ANXIOUS CRAVINGS

To thee, O God, we turn for peace . . . but grant us too the blessed assurance that nothing shall deprive us of that peace, neither ourselves nor our foolish earthly desires, nor my wild longings, nor the anxious cravings of my heart.

Journals of Sören Kierkegaard (1813–1855), edited by
Alexander Drew (Oxford University Press, 1938)

NATIONS OF CHRISTIANS

If Christian nations were nations of Christians, all war would be impossible, and unknown amongst them.

Soame Jenyns (1704–1787)

PEACE IN THE WORLD

O God and Father of all, whom the whole heavens adore: Let the whole earth also worship thee, all kingdoms obey thee, all tongues confess and bless thee, and the sons of men love thee and serve thee in peace: through Jesus Christ our Lord.

Prayers for Today: edited by John Elphinstone-Fyffe
(1958), B. T. Batsford Ltd. ©

PRAYER FOR PEACE

O God of love, O King of peace,
Make wars throughout the world to cease;
The wrath of sinful man restrain:
Give peace, O God, give peace again!

Remember, Lord, thy works of old,
The wonders that our fathers told;
Remember not our sin's dark stain:
Give peace, O God, give peace again!

Whom shall we trust but thee, O Lord?
Where rest but on thy faithful word?
None ever called on thee in vain;
Give peace, O God, give peace again!

Where saints and angels dwell above,
All hearts are knit in holy love:
Oh, bind us in that heavenly chain!
Give peace, O God, give peace again!

Sir Henry Williams Baker (1821–1877)

PEACE AND UNITY

O Lord Jesus Christ, who didst say to thine Apostles, 'Peace I leave with you, My peace I give unto you'; regard not our sins but the faith of thy Church, and grant it that peace and unity which is agreeable to thy will, who livest and reignest with the Father and the Holy Spirit, one God, world without end. Amen.

Roman Missal (c. 8th century)

PRAYER AT THE KISS OF PEACE

Almighty Lord, who lookest down from heaven on thy Church, save us thy unworthy servants and grant us thy peace, thy love, and thy assistance. Give us grace to love one another with pure hearts and clear consciences, without guile or falsehood, so that we who have been called in the same hope and are made partakers of the same holy Bread, may all remain united at heart in the bond of peace that is Christ: with whom and with the Holy Spirit thou art blessed for ever and ever. Amen.

The Manual of Catholic Prayer

THY WAYS OF PEACE

Summon, we beseech Thee, O God of Hosts, Thy people to the banner of our Lord, that aided by His might and girded with His power, they may scatter the designs of them that delight in war, and may seek to build Thy ways of peace upon the earth; through Jesus Christ our Lord.

The Kingdom of God Council of Clergy
and Ministers for Common Ownership (1946)

GRANT GOODWILL TO US

O God, to Whom glory is sung in the highest; while on earth peace is proclaimed among men of goodwill; grant that goodwill to us Thy servants; cleanse us from evil, and give peace to all Thy people; through Thy mercy, O blessed Lord God, Who dost live and govern all things, world without end.

Mozarabic Liturgy

THY COMMANDMENT IS BROAD

Come to us, O Lord! open the eyes of our souls, and show us the things which belong to our peace and the path of life; that we may see that, though all man's inventions and plans come to an end, yet Thy commandment is exceeding broad—broad enough for the rich and poor, for scholar, tradesman, and labourer, for our prosperity in this life and our salvation in the life to come.

Charles Kingsley (1819–1875)

PEACE BY ALL MEANS

The blessing of the Lord rest and remain upon all His people, in every land, of every tongue; the Lord meet in mercy all that seek Him; the Lord comfort all who suffer and mourn; the Lord hasten His coming, and give us, His people, peace by all means.

Bishop Handley Carr Glyn Moule (1841–1920)

PEACE TO OUR CONSCIENCES

O God, in Thee alone can our wearied spirits find full satisfaction and rest, and in Thy love is the highest joy. Lord, if we have Thee, we have enough, and we are happy if Thou wilt but give peace to our consciences, and make us know how gracious and merciful Thou art. Preserve in our hearts that peace which passeth all understanding, and make us better and holier in time to come. Strengthen those of us, and Thy people who are in any sorrow or perplexity, by the inward comfort of Thy Holy Spirit, and bid us all know that our light affliction, which is but for a moment, worketh for us a far more exceeding and eternal weight of glory: for there will come a time when Thou wilt bring us to the place of perfect rest, where we shall behold Thy face in righteousness, and be satisfied from Thy eternal fulness; through Jesus Christ our Lord. Amen.

Melchior Ritter (late 17th century)

THE AUTHOR OF PEACE

Lord God Almighty, Who art our true Peace and Love eternal, enlighten our souls with the brightness of Thy peace, and purify our consciences with the sweetness of Thy love, that we may with peaceful hearts wait for the Author of peace, and in the adversities of this world may ever have Thee for our Guardian and Protector; and so being fenced about by Thy care, may heartily give ourselves to the love of Thy peace. To Thy honour and glory. Amen.

Mozarabic Liturgy

PEACE IN OUR TIMES

Mercifully receive, O Lord, the prayers of Thy people, that all adversities and errors may be destroyed, and they may serve Thee in quiet freedom, and give Thy peace in our times; through Jesus Christ our Lord. Amen.

Leonine Sacramentary (5th century)

PEACE AND GOODWILL

Glory be to God in the highest, and on earth peace, goodwill towards men; for unto us is born this day a saviour, Who is Christ the Lord. We praise Thee, we glorify Thee, we give thanks unto Thee, for this greatest of Thy mercies. O Lord God, Heavenly King, God the Father almighty. O Lord, the only begotten Son Jesus Christ, O Lord God, Lamb of God, Son of the Father, Who wast made man to take away the sins of the world, have mercy upon us by turning us from our iniquities. Thou Who wast manifested to destroy the works of the devil, have mercy upon us by enabling us to renounce and forsake them. Thou Who art the great Advocate with the Father, receive our prayer, we humbly beseech Thee. Amen.

Bishop Thomas Ken (1637–1711)

REST FROM THE STORM

Almighty and merciful God, we beseech Thee to give us rest from the storm of war, for Thou wilt bestow on us all good things if Thou givest us peace both of soul and body; through Jesus Christ our Lord. Amen.

Leonine Sacramentary (5th century)

CONSOLER OF THE SORROWFUL

O God, the consolation of all such as be sorrowful, and the salvation of them that put their trust in Thee, grant unto us, in this dying life, that peace for which we humbly pray, and hereafter to attain unto everlasting joy in Thy presence; through our Lord Jesus Christ. Amen.

Roman Breviary

BLESS US AND KEEP US

The Lord bless us and keep us, the Lord make his face to shine upon us, and be gracious unto us, the Lord lift up his countenance upon us and give us peace, now and evermore.

The Jewish Temple Blessing (7th century B.C.)

DEFENDED FROM FEAR

O God, from whom all early desires, all good counsels and all just works do proceed, give unto thy servants that peace which the world cannot give, that our hearts may be set to obey thy commandments, and also that by thee we being defended from the fear of our enemies may pass our time in rest and quietness; through the merits of Jesus Christ our Saviour. Amen.

Gelasian Sacramentary (5th century)

CHILDREN OF QUIETNESS

O God, make us children of quietness, and heirs of peace.

St. Clement

INTO PERFECT PEACE

O God, the might of all them that put their trust in Thee; Grant that we may be conquerors over all that makes war upon our souls, and in the end may enter into perfect peace in Thy presence; through Jesus Christ our Lord.

Roman Breviary

HOSTILITY AT AN END

For he is our peace, who has made us both one, and has broken down the dividing wall of hostility, by abolishing in his flesh the law of commandments and ordinances, that he might create in himself one new man in place of the two, so making peace, and might reconcile us both to God in one body through the cross, thereby bringing the hostility to an end.

Ephesians 2: 14–16

THE WAY OF JUSTICE

Almighty God, our heavenly Father,
guide we beseech thee the nations of the world
into the way of justice and truth
and establish among them that peace
which is the fruit of righteousness.

Prayers in Time of War, S.C.M. Press (1939)

THAT WE MAY BE WORTHY

O peaceful King of Peace, Jesus Christ, give unto us Thy Peace, and confirm unto us Thy Peace, and forgive us our sins so that we may be worthy to come and go in Peace.

African Liturgy

LIVE IN PEACE

Live in peace with one another, and keep above that straightened spirit of strife which is below and out of the Power and Truth and Love of God.

Epistles: George Fox (1624–1691)

OM

Om* . . .
May God protect us,
May he guide us,
May he give us strength and right understanding,
May love and harmony be with us all,
Om . . . Peace—Peace—Peace.

Hindu Scriptures (Upanishads)

*The word for universal energy from which sound and speech developed; therefore a sacred word.

ALL IN PEACE

May there be peace in the higher regions; may there be peace in the firmament; may there be peace on earth.

May the waters flow peacefully; may the herbs and plants grow peacefully; may all the divine powers bring unto us peace. The supreme Lord is peace. May we be all in peace, peace, and only peace; and may that peace come unto each of us.
Shanti (Peace)—*Shanti*—Shanti!

Hindu Scriptures (Vedas)

THE CONTENTED MAN

He who does not know how to be content with what he has is poor, however rich he may be; but he who has learned to be content is rich even though he may have very little. ... Excessive wants are the seat of suffering; and the labour of weariness of this world of life and death arise from covetousness. He who wants little and so is above the concerns of this life is perfectly free both as to body and mind. ... Contentment is the domain of wealth and pleasure, of peace and rest. The contented man is happy even though his bed is the bare ground; while the man who knows not the secret of being content is not satisfied even when dwelling in heavenly places.

Buddhist Scriptures

PLENTY IN THY TOWERS

Lord give us peace in our days, for there is none that fighteth for us but Thou alone our God.

Lord, peace be made in Thy strength
And plenty in Thy towers.

God, of whom be holy desires, rightful counsels, and just deeds, give to Thy servants that peace that the world may not give, so that our hearts may be given to keep Thine hests and dread of our enemies may be taken from us, so that our times may be peaceable by Thy protection, by our Lord Jesus Christ Thy Son, that liveth with Thee and reigneth God, by all worlds of worlds.

M. S. Douce

PEACE AND LIGHT

May God bless youth! And I pray Thee, Lord, send peace and light to Thy people.

Feodor Mikhailovich Dostoevsky (1821–1881)

THE WAY OF PEACE

O Lord, vouchsafe to look mercifully upon us, and grant that we may ever choose the way of peace.

Sarum Missal

DESTROY WARS AND BATTLES

O Christ, the peace of the things that are on high, and the great rest of those that are below, establish O Lord in Thy peace and rest the four regions of the world. Destroy wars and battles from the ends of the earth, and disperse all those that delight in war; and by Thy divine mercy pacify the Church and the Kingdom, that we may have a safe habitation in all soberness and piety. And through Thy mercy and love forgive the debts and sins of them that are departed this life.

Liturgy of Malabar

SWEET TO US FOR EVER

O God, who art peace everlasting, whose chosen reward is the gift of peace, and who hast taught us that the peacemakers are Thy children; pour Thy peace into our souls, that everything discordant may utterly vanish, and all that makes for peace be sweet to us for ever.

Mozarabic Liturgy

THE TRUE AND LIVING WAY

Lead us, O Father, in the paths of peace;
Without Thy guiding hand we go astray,
And doubts appal, and sorrows still increase;
Lead us through Christ, the true and living way.

William Henry Burleigh (1812–1871)

GIVE PEACE AGAIN

O God of love, O King of peace,
Make wars throughout the world to cease;
The wrath of sinful man restrain:
Give peace, O God, give peace again.

Sir Herbert Williams Baker (1821–1877)

AGAINST WAR

O Lord, since the first blood of Abel cried to Thee from the ground that drank it, this earth of Thine has been defiled with the blood of man shed by his brother's hand, and the centuries

189

sob with the ceaseless horror of war. Ever the pride of kings, and the covetousness of the strong, has driven peaceful nations to slaughter. Ever the songs of the past and the pomp of armies have been used to inflame the passions of the people. Our spirit cries out to Thee in revolt against it, and we know that our righteous anger is answered by Thy holy wrath.

Break Thou the spell of the enchantments that make the nations drunk with the lust of battle and draw them on as willing tolls of death. Grant us a quiet and steadfast mind when our own nation clamours for vengeance or aggression. Strengthen our sense of justice and our regard for the equal worth of other peoples and races. Grant to the rulers of nations faith in the possibility of peace through justice, and grant to the common people a new and stern enthusiasm for the cause of peace. Bless our soldiers and sailors for their swift obedience and their willingness to answer to the call of duty, but inspire them nonetheless with a hatred of war, and may they never for private glory or advancement provoke its coming. May our young men still rejoice to die for their country with the valour of their fathers, but teach our age nobler methods of matching our strength and more effective ways of giving our life for the flag.

O Thou strong Father of all nations, draw all Thy great family together with an increasing sense of our common blood and destiny, that peace may come on earth at last, and Thy sun may shed its light rejoicing on a holy brotherhood of peoples.

Prayers for the Social Awakening:
Walter Rauschenbusch (1867–1918)

THE PEACE OF PARENTS

Moshi says, 'Benevolence is the heart of man; righteousness is the path of man. How lamentable a thing it is to leave the path and go astray, to cast away the heart and not to know where to seek for it! If a man lose a fowl or a dog, he knows how to reclaim it. If he lose his soul, he knows not how to reclaim it. The true path of learning has no other function than to teach us how to reclaim lost souls.'

Upon which text Kito relates this story. In a certain part of the country there was a well-to-do farmer, who had a son whom he indulged beyond all measure. So the child grew to be sly, selfish and undutiful. From an undutiful boyhood he grew to a reckless youth. He would fight and quarrel for a trifle, and spent his time in debauchery and riotous living. If his parents remonstrated with him, he would ask insolently, 'Who asked you to bring me into this world?' At length this young man became so great a scandal in the neighbourhood that the relatives and friends of the family urged his parents to disown and disinherit him. They threatened to do so, but he was an only child, and they postponed this last resort from time to time, until at last the relatives and friends declared that they must break off all intercourse with the parents unless this wicked son were disinherited. The parents, reflecting that to be so separated from their relatives would be a dishonour to their ancestors, agreed to disinherit the prodigal, and on a certain day all the relatives were gathered to their house that the act might formally be completed.

At that time the undutiful son was drinking and gambling with his evil associates, and one came and told him that his relatives and parents were convened to formally disown and disinherit him. 'What do I care?' said he. 'I am able to take care of myself; and if I choose to go to India or China, who is to prevent me? But I will swagger to this meeting, and make them all give me seventy ounces of silver to get rid of me.'

So taking a dagger, he went to the place where his parents and friends were assembled. But he resolved at first to listen from the veranda, and enjoy hearing their abuse of him. Peeping through a chink, he beheld his relatives one after another affixing their names to the petition of disinheritance, and this at last handed to his father. The father took a seal from a bag, and was about to affix it as the final act. 'Now is my time for leaping in among them,' thought the vagabond; but for a moment he held his breath. As the old man was about to seal the document, his wife clutched his hand and said, 'Pray wait a little. During fifty years that we have lived together, this has been the only favour I have ever asked of you—put a stop to this act of disinheritance. Though my son should beggar me, I cannot feel any resentment against him.' So speaking she sobbed aloud, and the old man, pushing the petition back to the relatives, said, 'Though we lose your countenance, and are renounced, we will not disown our son. He may indeed run through our means, but we shall not ask you for charity: we have but one life to lose, and we will die by the roadside seeking our one beloved child.'

The son hearing this, lay down on the road in silence: this love had burned away the self-will and baseness from him. In another moment he was kneeling before his parents, and said to his relatives, 'Entreat my parents for me that they shall delay disowning me for thirty days, and find if in that time I do not give proofs of repentance.' From that hour he became a loving and tender son, and an honour to his family. When at last, years afterwards, the venerable mother came to die, she said to her son, 'Had you not repented, I should have gone to hell, because of my foolish conduct towards you. But now I go to paradise.'

She spake truly. The troubled heart is hell, the heart at rest is paradise. The trouble or peace of parents depends upon their children. Let the young remember this, that they are daily consigning their parents to heaven or hell; and if they have lost their hearts, let them seek and find them, and bring them back again, that all may have joy.

Kit-5, compilation

LEAD US TO LIGHT

We intercede before thee for beloved Hindustan
and our prayer is the same
as that of ancient seekers after thee,
'From darkness lead us to light
and from shadows to reality.'
Mercifully grant that millions of this land
forever engaged in arduous pilgrimages
in search of peace and satisfaction
may at last lay down their weary burdens
at the feet of him who gives rest and peace
to all those who labour and are heavy laden.
May they come at last to the haven of peace,
even Jesus Christ,
and find in him thine own response
to their age-long quest.
To that end the frankincense of India's meditation,
the myrrh of its renunciation and sacrifice,
and the gold of its devotion

be laid at the feet of Jesus Christ
and may he be crowned Lord of all.

Augustine Ralla Ram

ALL THAT MAKES FOR PEACE

O God, who art Peace everlasting, whose chosen reward is the gift of peace and who hast taught us that the peacemakers are thy children, pour thy peace into our souls that everything discordant may utterly vanish and all that makes for peace be sweet to us for ever; through our Saviour Jesus Christ. Amen.

Mozarabic Sacramentary (600)

MORE THAN CONQUERORS

O God, the might of all them that put their trust in thee, grant that we may be more than conquerors over all things that make war upon our souls, that at the last we may enter into the perfect peace of thy presence through Jesus Christ our Lord. Amen.

Roman Breviary

16. Love of Our Fellow Man

WHAT IS THE PERFECTION OF LOVE?

To love our enemies; to love them to that extent, that they may become our brethren; to love thine enemies, that thou mayest wish them to become thy brethren; to love thine enemies, that they may be called into thy society; for thus did he love, who, as he hung upon the cross, exclaimed, 'Father, forgive them; they know not what they do!'

St. Augustine (354–430)

GREATER THAN ALL OTHERS

Ahuno Vairo: The man who conquers all by love is unconquerable. He is greater than all others and he can be such a man only by serving his brother-man, that is, sacrificing himself in the service of mankind.

Zoroastrian Credo: The Life and Teachings of Zoroaster, Mrs. Gool K. S. Shavaksha

VISIBLE UNITY

O God Who art one God, in Three persons, blessed for evermore, Who hast predestined us to glorify Thee in one body in Thy only-begotten Son, we earnestly pray Thee for the restoration of visible unity of worship and communion between the divided members of the Catholic Church in the East and in the West; and that all who confess Thy holy Name, and are called Christians, may be reunited, as at the beginning, in the Apostles' doctrine, and in the fellowship, and in the breaking of the bread, and in the prayers.

Remove, we beseech Thee, from us, and from all others,

whatever may hinder or delay this blessed reunion, all suspicions, prejudices, hard thoughts and judgements: and endue us with such ardent love toward Thee, and toward each other, that we may be one, even as Thou, Lord, art one with the Father, to whom in the unity of the Holy Ghost be all praise and glory and thanksgiving for ever. Amen.

Prayers in Use at Cuddesdon College (1904)

NO BITTERNESS

It were better to be of no church than to be bitter for any.

William Penn (1644–1718)

MERCY ON ALL MEN

The whole world before thee is as a grain in the balance.
And as a drop of dew that at morning cometh down upon the earth.
But thou hast mercy on all men, because thou hast power to do all things.
And thou overlookest the sins of men to the end they may repent.
For thou lovest all things that are.
And abhorrest none of the things which thou didst make;
For never wouldst thou have formed anything if thou didst hate it.
And how would anything have endured, except thou hadst willed it?
Or that which was not called by thee, how would it have been preserved?
But thou sparest all things, because they are thine,
O Sovereign Lord, thou lover of men's lives.

The Wisdom of Solomon 11: 22–26

FORGIVE OUR ENEMIES

O Lord Jesus Christ, we beseech Thee, forgive our enemies all their sins against Thee, and give us that measure of grace, that for their hatred we may love them, for their cursing we may bless them, for their injury we may do them good, for their persecution we may pray for them; after Thine example, Who

195

didst die for us sinners; Who livest and reignest with the Father in the unity of the Holy Ghost, world without end.

Archbishop William Laud (1573–1645)

FULL OF COMPASSION

I will extol thee, my God, O King;
And I will bless thy name for ever and ever.
Every day will I bless thee;
And I will praise thy name for ever and ever.
Great is the Lord and highly to be praised;
And his greatness is unsearchable.
Of the glorious majesty of thine honour,
And of thy wondrous works, will I meditate.
The Lord is gracious, and full of compassion;
Slow to anger, and of great mercy.
The Lord is good to all;
And his tender mercies are over all his works.
The Lord upholdeth all that fall,
And raiseth up all those that be bowed down.
The Lord is righteous in all his ways,
And gracious in all his works.
The Lord is nigh unto all them that call upon him,
To all that call upon him in truth.
He will fulfil the desire of them that fear him;
He will also hear their cry, and will save them.
The Lord preserveth all them that love him.

Psalm 145

GRACE TO FULFIL IT

Almighty and most merciful God, Who hast given us a new commandment that we should love one another, give us also grace that we may fulfil it. Make us gentle, courteous and forebearing. Direct our lives so that we may look to the good of others in word and deed. And hallow all our friendships by the blessing of Thy Spirit; for His sake Who loved us and gave Himself for us, Jesus Christ our Lord.

Bishop Brooke Foss Westcott (1825–1901)

PUT AWAY SUSPICION

Enable us, O Lord, to love Thee with all our heart and soul and mind and strength, and our neighbours as ourselves; that so the grace of Thy love may dwell in us for ever. Grant that all envy, jealousy and mistrust may die in us, and that suspicion and harsh judgements may be put away from us, while we live in continual fellowship with Thee; through Jesus Christ our Lord.

William Angus Knight (1836–1916)

FORGETFUL OF PAST ILL-WILL

O God of love, Who through Thy Son hast given us a new commandment that we should love one another, even as Thou didst love us, the unworthy and the wandering, and gavest Him up for our redemption: we pray Thee, Lord, to give us Thy servants, in all time of our life on earth, a mind forgetful of past ill-will, and a single heart to love our brethren; for the sake of Thy Son, Jesus Christ our Lord.

From the Coptic

AFTER THINE OWN EXAMPLE

O God, we have known and believed the love that Thou hast for us, may we by dwelling in love dwell in Thee, and Thou in us. May we learn to love Thee Whom we have not seen by loving our brethren whom we have seen. Teach us, O heavenly Father, the love wherewith Thou hast loved us. Fashion us, O blessed Lord, after Thine own example of love. Shed abroad, O Holy Spirit of love, the love of God and man in our hearts for Thy Name's sake. Amen.

Dean Henry Alford (1810–1871)

LOVE TOWARD ALL MEN

Our God and Father himself, and our Lord Jesus Christ, direct our ways; and the Lord make us to increase and abound in love toward one another, and toward all men, to the end that He may establish our hearts unblameable in holiness before

God, even our Father, at the coming of our Lord Jesus Christ
with all His saints. Amen.

1 Thessalonians 3:11–13, St. Paul (1st century)

FORGET PAST ILL-WILL

O God of Love, who hast given us a commandment that we
should love one another, even as thou didst love us and give thy
beloved Son for our life and salvation; we pray thee to give to
us thy servants, in all times of our life on earth, a mind forgetful
of past ill-will and a heart to love our brethren; for the sake of
Jesus Christ, our Lord and only Saviour. Amen.

Coptic Liturgy of St. Cyril (5th century)

LIGHT TO THE EARTH

All shall extol Thee, Thou creator of all: O God,
Who openest every day the doors of the gates to the East.
And cleavest the windows of the firmament,
Bringing forth the sun from his place,
And the moon from her dwelling:
Giving light to the whole world and the inhabitants thereof,
Whom Thou createdst by the attribute of mercy.

In mercy Thou givest light to the earth
And to them that dwell thereon,
And in Thy goodness renewest the creation every day
continually.
O King, Thou alone hast been exalted of yore;
Praised, glorified and extolled from days of old.

*Service of the Jewish Orthodox Synagogue
for the Festival of Tabernacles*

A PSALM OF LOVE

If I speak in the tongues of men and of angels, but have not
love, I am a noisy gong or a clanging cymbal. And if I have
prophetic powers, and understand all mysteries and all
knowledge, and if I have faith, so as to remove mountains, but
have not love, I am nothing. If I give away all I have, and if I
deliver my body to be burned, but have not love, I gain
nothing.

Love is patient and kind; love is not jealous or boastful; it is not arrogant or rude. Love does not insist on its own way; it is not irritable or resentful; it does not rejoice at wrong, but rejoices in the right. Love bears all things, believes all things, hopes all things, endures all things. . . .

So faith, hope, love abide, these three; but the greatest of these is love.

1 Corinthians 13, St. Paul (1st century)

LOVE THY NEIGHBOUR

You shall love the Lord your God with all your heart, and with all your soul, and with all your mind, and with all your strength.

The second is this, You shall love your neighbour as yourself. There is no other commandment greater than these.

Mark 12:30–31

LOVE ONE ANOTHER

A new commandment I give to you, that you love one another; even as I have loved you, that you also love one another.

John 13:34

ALWAYS HOPEFUL

Love is very patient, very kind. Love knows no jealousy; love makes no parade, gives itself no airs, is never rude, never selfish, never irritated, never resentful; love is never glad when others go wrong, love is gladdened by goodness, always slow to expose, always eager to believe the best, always hopeful, always patient.

Love never disappears.

Anon.

DEEDS THAT WIN THY LOVE

O Lord, grant us to love thee:
grant that we may love those that love thee;
grant that we may do the deeds that win thy love.

Mohammed (570–632)

A PASTURE FOR GAZELLES

My heart is capable of every form; it is a pasture for gazelles and a convent for Christian monks, the pilgrim's *Kaaba,* the tables of the Torah and the book of the Koran. I follow the religion of Love, whichever way his camels take.

Sufi Scriptures

PROTECTION TO ALL

An old man having embraced the religion of Sugata, his son reviled him. 'Why do you abuse me?' said the father. The son replied, 'You have abandoned the law of the Vedas, and followed a new law, which is no law.'

The father answered, 'There are different forms of religion: one looks to another world, the other is intended for the people. You should not abuse my religion, which grants protection to all beings. For surely there is no doubt that to be kind cannot be unlawful, and I know no other kindness than to give protection to all living beings. Therefore if I am too much attached to my religion, whose chief object is love, and whose end is deliverance, what sin is there in me, O child?'

But the son continued his abuse, and the father laid the matter before the king, who ordered the son to be executed. When the day for his execution arrived, the youth was brought before the king, who asked why he was so pale and thin. The youth replied, 'Seeing the day of death approaching, I could not eat.' The monarch said, 'Live then, and learn to respect a religion which enforces compassion for all beings.'

Buddhist Scriptures (Somadeva)—compilation

UNMARRED BY HATE

When peace is won, the adept in welfare needs to prove
An able, upright man, of gracious speech and kindly mood.

His wants are few; gentle, sense-disciplined, quick-witted, bluster-free,
He never stoops to conduct mean or low.

May creatures all abound in weal and peace;

May all be blessed with peace always; all creatures weak or
strong.

All creatures unseen or seen, dwelling afar or near,
Born or waiting birth—may all be blessed with peace!

Let none despise or flout his fellows anywhere;
Let none resentment bear; let none in anger live or hate.

Just as a mother shields from hurt her only child,
Let all-embracing love for all that lives be thine.

An all-embracing love for all the universe;
Unstinted love, unmarred by hate, not rousing enmity.

So, as you stand or walk, or sit, or lie, reflect
With all your mind on this; 'tis deemed a state divine.

Buddhist Scriptures (Metta Sutta)

BE LOVING-KIND

Do not deceive, do not despise
Each other anywhere.
Do not be angry, nor should ye
Secret resentments bear;

For as a mother risks her life
And watches o'er her child,
So boundless be your love for all,
So tender, kind and mild.

Yea, cherish goodwill right and left,
All round, early and late,
And without hindrance, without stint,
From envy free and hate.

While standing, walking, sitting down,
Whate'er you have in mind,
The rule of life that's always best
Is to be loving-kind.

Buddhist Scriptures

201

LOVE OF THY KNOWLEDGE

Adoring thy goodness, we make this our only prayer . . . that thou wouldst be willing to keep us alive all our lives in the love of thy knowledge.

Attributed to Apuleius (126–173), the prayer is addressed to Asklepios, God of Healing

NO HATRED IN OUR HEARTS

May it be Thy will, O Lord, that no man foster hatred against us in his heart, and that we foster no hatred in our hearts against any man; that no man foster envy of us in his heart, and that we foster no envy in our hearts of any man.

The Talmud

HAPPINESS

He who injures animals that are not injurious, from a wish to give himself pleasure, adds nothing to his own happiness, living or dead; while he who gives to creatures willingly the good of all sentient beings, enjoys bliss without end.

Hindu Scriptures (Manu)

OVERFLOWING STREAMS

Make channels for the streams of love,
Where they may broadly run;
And love has overflowing streams
To fill them everyone.
For we must share if we would keep
That blessing from above;
Ceasing to give, we cease to have—
Such is the law of love.

Archbishop Richard Chenevix Trench (1805–1886)

LOVE WHICH NEVER CEASES

O Lord, give us, we beseech Thee, in the name of Jesus Christ Thy Son, that love which can never cease, that will kindle our lamps but not extinguish them that they may burn in us and enlighten others. Do Thou, O Christ, our dearest Saviour, Thyself kindle our lamps, that they may evermore shine in Thy temple, that they may receive unquenchable light from Thee that will enlighten our darkness and lessen the darkness of the world. Lord Jesus, we pray Thee give Thy light to our lamps, that in its light the most holy place may be revealed to us in which Thou dwellest as the eternal priest, that we may always behold Thee, desire Thee, look upon Thee in love and long after Thee, for Thy sake. Amen.

St. Columba (521–597)

SEEK LOVE THERE

Seek love in the pity of another's woe,
In the gentle relief of another's care,
In the darkness of night, and the winter's snow
In the naked and outcast, seek love there!

William Blake (1757–1827)

THE HOLIER WORSHIP

O brother man! Fold to the heart thy brother;
Where pity dwells, the peace of God is there;
To worship rightly is to love each other,
Each smile a hymn, each kindly deed a prayer.

He whom the Master loved has truly spoken:
The holier worship which God deigns to bless
Restores the loss, and binds the spirit broken,
And feeds the widow and the fatherless!

Follow with reverent steps the great example
Of him whose holy work was 'doing good,'
So shall the wide earth seem our Father's temple,
Each loving life a psalm of gratitude.

Then shall all shackles fall; the stormy clangour

Of wild war music o'er the earth shall cease;
Love shall tread out the baleful fire of anger,
And in its ashes plant the tree of peace.

John Greenleaf Whittier (1807–1892)

FOR THE LOVE OF MAN

Blessed Lord, Who hast given us a new commandment, that
we love one another, and hast taught us that where envying and
strife is, there is confusion and every evil work; give us grace to
be kindly affectioned, and to love one another with a pure
heart; put far from us all anger and evil speaking, and grant
that we may obtain the blessing of the peacemakers, walking in
love, even as Thou, Lord, hast loved us, and given Thyself to
die for us. Amen.

*Daily Services for Christian Households:
compiled by the Rev. H. Stobart (circa 1867)*

LOVE THINGS HEAVENLY

Grant us, O Lord, not to mind earthly things, but to love
things heavenly; and even now, while we are placed among
things that are passing away, to cleave to those that shall abide;
through Jesus Christ our Lord.

Leonine Sacramentary (5th century)

TO COME TO OUR GLORY

O God, who by love alone art great and glorious, that art
present and livest within us by love alone: Grant us likewise by
love to attain another self, by love to live in others, and by love
to come to our glory, to see and accompany Thy love
throughout all eternity.

Thomas Traherne (1637–1674)

MAKE US SAVED SOULS TOGETHER

Almighty God, have mercy on all that bear me evil will, and
would me harm, and their faults and mine together, by such
easy tender, merciful means as Thine infinite wisdom best can
divine, vouchsafe to amend and redress, and make us saved

souls in heaven together where we may live and love together
with thee and thy blessed saints, O glorious Trinity, for the
bitter passion of our sweet saviour Christ. Amen.

Ascribed to Sir Thomas More (1478–1535)

PEACE IS THE FRUIT OF LOVE

You have only a day to pass on earth; so act as to pass that
day in peace.

Peace is the fruit of love; for to live in peace, we must learn to
suffer many things.

No one is perfect, all have their faults; every one is a burden
to others, and love alone makes the burden light.

If you cannot bear with your brothers, how will your
brothers bear with you?

It is written of the Son of Mary that he loved his own who
were in the world, and loved them even unto the end.

Love then your brothers who are in the world, and love them
unto the end.

Love is indefatigable; it never tires. Love is inexhaustible; it
lives and is born again of itself, and the more it pours itself
forth, the more it abounds.

I tell you of a truth that the heart of him who loves is a
paradise upon earth: God is within him, for God is love.

Love rests in the depths of pure souls, like a drop of dew in
the cup of a flower.

Oh! if you only knew what it is to love!

You say you love, and many of your brothers lack bread to
sustain their life, clothing to cover their naked limbs, a roof to
shelter them, a handful of straw to sleep upon, while you have
all things in abundance.

You say you love, and the sick in great numbers, languish
untended on their wretched bed; the unfortunate weep with no
one to weep with them; the little children, shivering with cold,
go from door, begging crumbs from the tables of the rich, and
receive them not.

You say that you love your brothers; what would you do
then if you hated them?

Félicité Robert de Lamennais (1782–1854)
from Words of a Believer

CHRISTIAN LOVE

O Lord, how joyful 'tis to see
The brethren join in love to thee!
On thee alone their heart relies;
Their only strength thy grace supplies.

How sweet, within thy holy place,
With one accord to sing thy grace,
Besieging thine attentive ear
With all the force of fervent prayer.

Oh, may we love the house of God,
Of peace and joy the blest abode;
Oh, may no angry strife destroy
That sacred peace, that holy joy!

The world within may rage, but we
Will only cling more close to thee,
With hearts to thee more wholly given,
More weaned from earth, more fixed on heaven.

Lord, shower us from above
The sacred gift of mutual love;
Each other's wants may we supply,
And reign together in the sky.

Jean Baptiste de Santeul, called Santolius Victorinus
(1630–1697), translation by John Chandler (1806–1876)

17. Towards Salvation

LOVE WHICH PASSETH KNOWLEDGE

I bow my knees unto the Father of our Lord Jesus Christ, of whom the whole family in heaven and earth is named, that he would grant you, according to the riches of his glory, to be strengthened with might by his Spirit in the inner man; that Christ may dwell in your hearts by faith; that ye, being rooted and grounded in love, may be able to comprehend with all the saints what is the breadth, and length, and depth, and height; and to know the love of Christ which passeth knowledge, that ye might be filled with all the fulness of God.

Ephesians 3: 14–19

THE CROWN OF GLORY

Almighty God, Who by Thy Son Jesus Christ didst give to Thy Holy Apostles many excellent gifts, and didst charge them to feed Thy flock; give grace, we beseech Thee, to all Bishops, the pastors of Thy Church, that they may diligently preach Thy Word, and duly administer the godly discipline thereof; and grant to the people that they may obediently follow the same; that all may receive the crown of everlasting glory; through Jesus Christ our Lord. Amen.

English Ordinal

SAVE OUR SOULS

Heavenly King, Holy Ghost, Spirit of truth, who art everywhere present, and fillest all things; the treasury of good things, and the bestower of life; come and dwell in us, and

207

purify us from every stain, and save our souls in thy goodness; through Jesus Christ our Lord. Amen.

Eastern Church Liturgy (3rd century)

HASTEN THE TIME

O God our heavenly Father, who didst manifest thy love by sending thine only begotten Son into the world that all might live through him, pour thy Spirit upon thy Church that it may fulfil thy command to preach the Gospel to every creature; send forth, we beseech thee, labourers into the harvest; and hasten the time when all shall be saved; through the same Jesus Christ our Lord. Amen.

The Splendour of God (1960)

GRACE TO TRUST THEE

Look in compassion, O heavenly Father, upon this troubled and divided world. Though we cannot trace Thy footsteps or understand Thy working, give us grace to trust Thee with an undoubting faith; and when Thine own time is come, reveal, O Lord, that new heaven and new earth wherein dwelleth righteousness, where the Prince of peace ruleth, Thy Son our Saviour Jesus Christ.

Dean Charles John Vaughan (1816–1897)

THE ENLIGHTENING WORD

O God, Who by Thine almighty Word dost enlighten every man that cometh into the world: enlighten, we beseech Thee, the hearts of us Thy servants by the glory of Thy grace, that we may ever think such things as are worthy and well-pleasing to Thy majesty, and love Thee with a perfect heart; through Jesus Christ our Lord.

Alcuin of York (735–804)

SELF-DENIAL

Blessed Lord, Who for our sakes wast content to bear sorrow, and want, and death, grant unto us such a measure of Thy Spirit that we may follow Thee in all self-denial and tenderness of soul. Help us, by Thy great love, to succour the afflicted, to relieve the needy and destitute, to comfort the feeble-minded, to share the burdens of the heavy-laden, and ever to see Thee in all that are poor and desolate.

Bishop Brooke Foss Westcott (1825–1901)

THY PROVIDENCE

And now, O God, we turn our thoughts wholly from the world and all worldly objects to look up to Thee. Thou hast dealt hitherto with us so preciously, that we cannot mistrust Thy Providence, but cast ourselves wholly upon Thee. We dedicate ourselves afresh to Thee. Give us the joys of Thy salvation. Let us find that whatever trials Thou dost put us to Thou art with us. Lead us, if Thou wilt, through the valley of the shadow of death, for even there Thou art with us. Bring us at last where Thou art, O our God, and our All. We are Thine, O our God, do with us what seems good in Thy sight—our God and our Portion for ever.

Bishop Gilbert Burnet (1643–1715)

THY KINGDOM IS NOW AT HAND

Vouchsafe to us, though unworthy, a plenteous outpouring of Thy Spirit to refresh Thy heritage, for Thy Kingdom is now at hand, and Thou art standing at the door. Hear us, we beseech Thee, O Lord. Amen.

John Milton (1608–1674)

KNOWLEDGE OF THY TRUTH

O Lord God, Who hast taught us to pray all together, and hast promised to hear the united voices of two or three invoking Thy Name; hear now, O Lord, the prayers of Thy servants unto their salvation, and give us in this world knowledge of Thy Truth, and in the world to come life everlasting; for the sake of Jesus Christ our Lord. Amen.

Armenian Liturgy

TEACH US THY WAY

Give ear, O Lord, unto our prayer, and attend unto the voice of our supplications. Teach us Thy way, O Lord. We will walk in Thy Truth. Unite our hearts to fear Thy Name. We will praise Thee, O Lord our God, with all our heart, and we will glorify Thy name for evermore; for great is Thy mercy towards us. Amen.

Psalm 86: 6–13

RULE OUR HEARTS

O God, forasmuch as without thee we are not able to please thee; mercifully grant that thy Holy Spirit may in all things direct and rule our hearts; through Jesus Christ our Lord. Amen.

Gelasian Sacramentary (5th century)

ONE EQUAL LIGHT

Bring us, O Lord God, at the last awakening into the house and gate of heaven, to enter into that gate and dwell in that house where there shall be no darkness nor dazzling, but one equal light; no noise nor silence, but one equal music; no fears nor hopes, but an equal possession; no ends or beginnings, but one equal eternity; in the habitations of Thy majesty and Thy glory, world without end.

John Donne (1573–1631)

A WEARY LAND

O Lord Jesus Christ, who art as the Shadow of a great rock in a weary land, who beholdest Thy weak creatures weary of labour, weary of pleasure, weary of hope deferred, weary of self; in Thine abundant compassion, and fellow feeling with us, and unutterable tenderness, bring us, we pray Thee, unto Thy rest.

Christina Georgina Rossetti (1830–1894)

TO TRUST THEE NOW

Look in compassion, O Heavenly Father, upon this troubled
and divided world. Though we cannot trace Thy footsteps or
understand Thy working, give us grace to trust Thee now with
an understanding faith, and when Thine own time is come,
reveal, O Lord, Thy new heaven and new earth, wherein
dwelleth righteousness, and where the Prince of Peace ruleth,
Thy Son our Saviour Jesus Christ.

Dean Charles John Vaughan (1816–1897)

AS CHICKENS UNDER THE HEN

With floods and storms thus we be tossed,
    Awake, good Lord, to Thee we cry.
    Our ship is almost sunk and lost.
    Thy mercy help our misery.
Man's strength is weak: man's wit is dull:
Man's reason blind. These things t'amend,
    Thy hand, O Lord, of might is full;
    Awake betime, and help us send.
    In Thee we trust, and in no wight:
    Save us as chickens under the hen.
Our crookedness Thou canst make right,
    Glory to Thee for aye. Amen.

Anon.

GUIDE OUR FEET

Blessed be the Lord God of Israel
for he hath visited and redeemed his people. . . .
to give knowledge of salvation unto his people
for the remission of their sins,
through the tender mercy of our God
whereby the dayspring from on high
hath visited us,
to give light to them that sit in darkness,
and in the shadow of death,
and to guide our feet into the way of peace.

Luke 1: 68, 77–79

NOT A JUDGEMENT

O Lord Jesus, let not Thy word become a judgement upon us, that we hear it and do it not, that we believe it and obey it not; Thou who with the Father and the Holy Spirit livest and reignest world without end.

Thomas à Kempis (1380–1471)

THE NAP

A poor man watched a thousand years before the gate of Paradise. Then, while he snatched one little nap—it opened and shut.

Persian Scriptures

HEAVENLY HEALING

O Christ, our Lord, Who art the physician of salvation, grant unto all who are sick the aid of heavenly healing. Amen.

Mozarabic Liturgy

TRIUMPHS OF MERCY

Arm of the Lord, 'awake, awake!'
Put on Thy strength, the nations shake,
And let the world adoring see
Triumphs of mercy wrought by Thee.

Say to the heathen, from Thy Throne,
'I am Jehovah, God alone!'
Thy voice their idols shall confound,
And cast their altars to the ground.

Let Zion's time of favour come;
O bring the tribes of Israel home;
And let our wondering eyes behold
Gentiles and Jews in Jesus' fold.

Almighty God, Thy grace proclaim,
Exalt the Saviour's glorious Name,

Let every foe before Him fall,
Confessed, adored, the Lord of all.

Hymns of the Church of God:
selected by F. V. Mather (1866)

HAIL THE DAY OF PENTECOST

Let songs of praises fill the sky;
Christ, our ascended Lord,
Sends down His Spirit from on high,
According to His word.
All hail the day of Pentecost,
The coming of the Holy Ghost!

The Spirit, by His heavenly breath,
New life creates within:
He quickens sinners from the death
Of trespasses and sin.
All hail the day of Pentecost,
The coming of the Holy Ghost!

The things of Christ the Spirit takes,
And shows them unto men;
The fallen soul His temple makes,
God's image stamps again.
All hail the day of Pentecost,
The coming of the Holy Ghost!

Hymns of the Church of God:
selected by F. V. Mather (1866)

HELP US WHEN WE CRY

O Most merciful!
O most bountiful!
God the Father Almighty!
By the Reemer's
Sweet intercession
Hear us, help us when we cry.

Bishop Richard Heber (1783–1826)

ENDLESS JOYS

Now may we find salvation nigh,
While we both fear and trust the Lord!
May grace descending from on high,
The pledge of endless joys afford!

We see how Truth and Mercy meet,
Since Christ the Lord came down from heav'n,
By whose obedience, so complete,
Justice is pleas'd, and Peace is giv'n.

Through Him let Righteousness abound,
And Virtue dwell on earth again;
May heav'nly influence bless the ground,
And glorious be Emmanuel's reign!

And art thou, Saviour, gone before,
To give us free access to God?
O keep us, that we stray no more,
But follow in the heav'nly road!

Hymns Original and Select: John Bulmer (1835)

WRITE SALVATION IN EACH HEART

Long have we sat beneath the sound
Of thy salvation, Lord;
But still how weak our faith is found
And knowledge of thy word!

Our righteous Ruler, and our God,
How little art thou known
By all the judgements of thy rod,
And blessings of thy throne!

How cold and feeble is our love!
How negligent our fear!
How low our hopes of joys above!
How few affections there!

Great God, thy sov'reign pow'r impart
To give thy word success;
Write thy salvation in each heart,
And make us learn thy grace.

Show our forgetful feet the way
That leads to joys on high,
Where knowledge grows without decay,
And love shall never die!

Hymns Original and Select: John Bulmer (1835)

SAVE OUR SOULS

Heavenly King, Paraclete, Spirit of Truth, present in all places and filling all things, Treasury of good and Choirmaster of life: come and dwell within us, cleanse us from all stains and save our souls.

Liturgy of St. John Chrysostom (345–407)

ONLY ONE WAY

There is but one possible way for man to attain this salvation, or life of God in the soul. There is not one for the Jew, another for the Christian, and a third for the Heathen. No; God is One, human nature is one, salvation is one, and the way to it is one; and that is, the desire of the soul turned to God. When this desire is alive, and breaks forth in any creature under heaven, then the lost sheep is found, and the Shepherd hath it upon His shoulders. Through this desire the poor prodigal son leaves his husks and swine, and hastes to his father; it is because of this desire that the father sees the son, yet while far off, that he runs out to meet him, falls on his neck, and kisses him. See here how plainly we are taught that no sooner is this desire arisen and in motion towards God, but the operation of God's spirit answers to it, cherishes and welcomes its first beginnings, signified by the father's seeing and having compassion on his son, whilst yet far off—that is, in the first beginnings of his desire. Thus does this desire do all: it brings the soul to God, and God into the soul; it cooperates with God, and is one life with God. Suppose this desire not to be alive, not in motion either in a Jew or a Christian, and then all the sacrifices, the service, either of the Law or the Gospels, are but dead works, that bring no life into the soul, nor beget any union between God and it. Suppose this desire to be awakened, and fixed upon God, though in souls that never heard either of the Law or of the Gospel, and then Divine Life, or operation of

215

God, enters into them, and the new birth in Christ is formed in those that never heard of his name. And these are they 'that shall come from the east, and from the west, and sit down with Abraham, and Isaac in the Kingdom of God.'

William Law (1636–1761) from The Spirit of Prayer

MANSION WITH THE BLEST

Brief life is here our portion;
Brief sorrow, short-lived care;
The life that knows no ending,
The tearless life is there.

O happy retribution!
Short toil, eternal rest;
For mortals, and for sinners
A mansion with the blest!

There grief is turned to pleasure;
Such pleasure, as below
No human voice can utter,
No human heart can know.

Yes! God, our King and Portion,
In fulness of His grace,
We then shall see for ever,
And worship face to face.

Strive, man, to win that glory;
Toil, man, to gain that light;
Send hope before to grasp it,
Till hope be lost in sight.

Exult, O dust and ashes,
The Lord shall be Thy part,
His only, His for ever,
Thou shalt be, and thou art.

Hymns of the Church of God:
selected by F. V. Mather (1866)

THE JOYFUL SOUND

From Greenland's icy mountains,
From India's coral strand,
Where Africa's sunny fountains

Roll down their golden sand;
From many an ancient river,
From many a palmy plain,
They call us to deliver
Their land from error's chain.

What though the spicy breezes
Blow soft o'er Ceylon's isle;
Though every prospect pleases,
And only man is vile;
In vain with lavish kindness
The gifts of God are strown;
The heathen in his blindness
Bows down to wood and stone.

Can we, whose souls are lighted
With wisdom from on high,
Can we to men benighted
The lamp of life deny?
Salvation! O Salvation!
The joyful sound proclaim,
Till each remotest nation
Has learnt Messiah's name!

Waft, waft, ye winds, His story,
And you, ye waters, roll,
Till like a sea of glory
It spreads from pole to pole;
Till, o'er our ransomed nature,
The Lamb for sinners slain,
Redeemer, King, Creator,
In bliss returns to reign.

Hymns of the Church of God:
selected by F. V. Mather (1866)

18. Prayers for Today

VAST, VOID AND CLEAR

Chao Chou asked Nan Chuan, 'What is the Tao?' Nan Chuan answered, 'The ordinary mind is Tao.' Chao Chou then asked, 'How can one approach it?' Nan Chuan replied, 'If you want to approach it, you will certainly miss it.' 'If you do not approach it, how do you know it is the Tao?' 'The Tao is not a matter of knowing, nor a matter of not knowing. To know is a delusory way of thinking, and not to know is a matter of insensibility. If one can realise the Tao unmistakably, his mind will be like the great space—vast, void, and clear. How, then, can one regard this as right and that as wrong?' Upon hearing this remark, Chao Chou was immediately awakened.

*Zen Buddhist koan or story, quoted in
The Practice of Zen, Chang Chen-Chi*

MADE BY US NOW

We are what we have made and our future is made by us now.

Mahavira (6th century B.C.)

DREAM OF HAPPINESS

Look to this day!
For it is life, the very life of life.
In its brief course lie all the varieties
And realities of your existence;
The bliss of growth,
The glory of action, the splendour of beauty.
For yesterday is but a dream,

218

And tomorrow is only a vision,
But today well-lived makes every yesterday a dream of happiness
And every tomorrow a vision of hope.

From the Sanskrit

FINAL HAPPINESS

Without purity of mind, to what end is the worship of God? Though we roam the wilds, sanctity is not in them; nor is it in the sky; nor on the earth at the confluence of holy streams. Make thy body pure and thou shalt behold the King.

The devout man by the gradual progress of his soul shall attain his desire. He who is converted into pure mind knows the great secret.

Convert thy body into a temple, and restrain thyself: give up evil thoughts, and see God with thy internal eye. When we know him we shall know ourselves.

Without personal experience, the mere savour of the scripture will not remove the fears of the aspirant; as darkness is never dispelled by a painted flame.

Though he roam to sacred Concan, no dog will turn into a lion; going to holy Benares will make no pig an elephant; and no pilgrimage will make a saint of one whose nature is different.

Be thy creed or thy prayers what they may, unless thou hast a little truth thou shalt not attain the path to happiness. He who possesses the truth is the twice-born.

The source of final happiness is inherent in the heart; he is a fool who seeks it elsewhere; he is like the shepherd who searched for the sheep which was in his bosom.

Why should you collect stones from the hills, and build fine temples? Why torment yourself so, while the God as a living being dwells within you?

Better the house-dog than the inanimate household goddess; and better than all demigods is the Lord of the universe.

That light, like the morning star, that dwells in the inmost heart of every man, is our refuge.

Hindu Scriptures (Vemana, 17th century)

PATHS LEADING TO DEATH

Sanyasis acquaint themselves with particular words and vests; they wear a brick-red garb, and shaven pates; in these they pride themselves; their heads look very pure, but are their hearts so?

Religion which consists in postures of the limbs is just a little inferior to the exercises of the wrestler.

In the absence of inward vision boast not of oral divinity.

All acts performed under a false guise are paths leading to death.

No man in the world considers truly who he is; alas! he cannot know his whole nature. How shall man learn to know himself?

False is the creed of those who hold that it is profitable to renounce the present life: cannot ye see that eternal existence commences in this life?

The man that has attained perfection draws no distinctions between night and day, the mind and universal nature, or himself and another man.

He among the sons of men merits the title of Yogi (saint) who knows the god is his heart: know thyself, and thou shalt become a deity.

Ignorant that the living principle exists in your own body, why do ye search, imagining that it is to be found elsewhere? Ye are like one who while the sun shines shall search with a lamp.

Hindu Scriptures (Vemana)

19. For Unity among Nations

A PERFECT HARMONY

Overrule, we pray thee, O God, the passions and designs of men. Let thy strong hand control the nations and bring out of the present discord a harmony more perfect than we can conceive: a new humility, a new understanding, a new hunger and thirst for thy love to rule the earth; through Jesus Christ our Saviour.

Anon.

UNTO ALL NATIONS

Almighty and everlasting God, the brightness of faithful souls, who didst bring the Gentiles to thy light, and madest known unto them him who is the true Light, and the bright and morning star; fill, we beseech thee, the world with thy glory, and show thyself by the radiance of thy light unto all nations; through Jesus Christ our Lord. Amen.

Gregorian Sacramentary

LET THY NAME BE GREAT

O Thou Who didst command Thy Apostles to go into all the world and to preach the Gospel to every creature: let Thy Name be great among the nations, from the rising up of the sun unto the going down of the same, O Lord our light and our salvation.

Anon.

THAT ALL MAY FIND THEE

O God, Who hast made of one blood all nations of men for to dwell on the face of the earth, and didst send Thy blessed Son, Jesus Christ, to preach peace to them that are afar off, and to them that are nigh: grant that all the peoples of the world may feel after Thee and find Thee; and hasten, O heavenly Father, the fulfilment of Thy promise to pour out Thy Spirit upon all flesh; through Jesus Christ our Saviour.

Bishop George Edward Lynch Cotton (1813–1886)

SHOW THYSELF TO ALL NATIONS

O Father everlasting, the light of faithful souls, Who didst bring the nations to Thy light and kings to the brightness of Thy rising: fill the world with Thy glory, we beseech Thee, and show Thyself unto all the nations; through Him Who is the true light and the bright and morning star, Jesus Christ, Thy Son our Lord.

Gothic Missal

THAT ALL MAY GLORIFY THEE

Almighty and everlasting God, that hast wrought the redemption of man after a miraculous manner, in sending Thy only Son to fulfil the promises made unto our fathers: Open up more and more the knowledge of that salvation, that in all the places of the earth, Thy truth and power may be made known, to the intent that all nations may praise, honour, and glorify Thee; through the selfsame Son, Jesus Christ. So be it.

Scottish Psalter (1595)

THE RADIANCE OF THY LIGHT

Almighty and everlasting God, the brightness of faithful souls, who didst bring the Gentiles to thy light and make known unto them him who is the true Light, and the bright and morning star.

Fill, we beseech thee, the world with thy glory, and show thyself by the radiance of thy light unto all nations; through Jesus Christ our Lord.

Gregorian Sacramentary (590)

THE KINGDOM IS THE LORD'S

All the ends of the earth shall remember and turn unto the Lord, and all the kindreds of the nations shall worship before thee. For the kingdom is the Lord's: and he is the ruler over the nations. Amen.

Psalm 22: 27–28

MOUNTAIN OF THE LORD

It shall come to pass in the latter days
that the mountain of the house of the Lord
shall be established as the highest of the mountains,
and shall be raised up above the hills;
and peoples shall flow to it,
and many nations shall come, and say:
'Come, let us go up to the mountain of the Lord,
to the house of the God of Jacob;
that he may teach us his ways
and we may walk in his paths.'
For out of Zion shall go forth the law,
and the word of the Lord from Jerusalem.
He shall judge between many peoples,
and shall decide for strong nations afar off;
and they shall beat their swords into ploughshares,
and their spears into pruning hooks;
nation shall not lift up sword against nation,
neither shall they learn war any more.

Micah 4: 1–3 (RSV)

SURE FOUNDATIONS

O heavenly Father, we thank thee for those who out of the bitter memories of strife and loss are seeking a more excellent way for the nations of the world, whereby justice and order may be maintained and the differences of peoples be resolved in equity. We pray thee to establish their purpose on sure foundations and to prosper their labours, that thy will may be done; for the sake of Jesus Christ our Lord.

Anon.

EVERLASTING DOMINION

I saw in the night visions,
and behold, with the clouds of heaven
there came one like the son of man,
and he came to the Ancient of Days
and was presented before him.
And to him was given dominion
and glory and kingdom,
that all peoples, nations and languages should serve him;
his dominion is an everlasting dominion,
which shall not pass away,
and his kingdom one
that shall not be destroyed.

Daniel 7: 13, 14 (RSV)

OF ONE BLOOD

One is your Father and ye are all brethren. . . . God is no respecter of persons, but in every nation he that revereth him is accepted of him. . . . He hath made of one blood all the nations of the earth.

New Testament

HASTEN THY PROMISE

O God, who hast made of one blood
all nations of men
for to dwell on the face of the earth,
and didst send thy blessed Son Jesus Christ
to preach peace to them that are afar off,
and to them that are nigh:
Grant that all the peoples of the world
may feel after thee and find thee;
and hasten, O Lord,
the fulfilment of thy promise
to pour out thy Spirit
upon all flesh;
through Jesus Christ our Lord.

Bishop George Edward Lynch Cotton (1813–1886)

EVERY NATION KNEELING

Men have rent their great concern, one among another, into sects, every party rejoicing in that which is their own. Wherefore leave them till a certain time. . . . One day God will call to them and say, 'Where are my companions?'. . . . And we will bring up a witness out of every nation and say, 'Bring your proofs.' And they shall know that the Truth is with God alone. . . . To its own book shall every nation be called. . . . And thou shalt see every nation kneeling.

The Koran

LET THE EARTH BE TAUGHT

Spirit of mercy, truth, and love,
O shed Thine influence from above;
And still from age to age convey
The wonders of this sacred day.

In every clime, by every tongue,
Be God's surpassing glory sung:
Let all the listening earth be taught
The wonders by our Saviour wrought.

Unfailing comfort, heavenly Guide,
Still o'er Thy holy Church preside;
Still let mankind Thy blessings prove;
Spirit of mercy, truth and love.

O Holy Father, Holy Son,
And Holy Spirit, Three in One;
Thy grave devoutly we implore,
Thy name be praise for evermore.

Hymns of the Church of God:
selected by F. V. Mather (1866)

BRING THE NATIONS NEAR

Arise, O God, and shine
In all Thy saving might,
And prosper each design
To spread Thy glorious light;
Let healing streams of mercy flow,
That all the earth Thy truth may know.

225

O bring the nations near,
That they may sing Thy praise;
Let all the people hear,
And learn Thy holy ways:
Reign, mighty God, assert Thy cause,
And govern by Thy righteous laws.

Exert Thy glorious power,
The nations then shall see,
And earth present her store,
In converts born of Thee:
God, our own God, His Church will bless,
And earth shall yield her full increase.

Hymns of the Church of God:
selected by F. V. Mather (1866)

A LITANY FOR ALL NATIONS

Eternal God, who hast made one of all nations who dwell upon earth, we confess that we have been led astray from Thy design by false guides and confused statesmen; so that we have foolishly striven for nation and race, and grown contemptuous of others. We thank Thee that our faces are now set towards the dawn of a better day; but because we cannot conquer our pride and uproot our hate, because we cannot establish righteousness and maintain peace without Thy aid, we wait upon Thee. Guide us, we beseech Thee, so that our world-wide brotherhood may have its roots in Thy universal Fatherhood, and graciously hear us as we pray.
That we may check in ourselves malicious feelings and ungenerous judgements:
Graciously hear us, O Christ.
That we may strive to remove the barriers that separate, and the suspicions that engender strife:
Graciously hear us, O Christ.

That we may learn to settle our international differences by wiser ways than war:
Graciously hear us, O Christ.
That we may understand the needs, and sympathise with the legitimate aspirations of other nations:

226

Graciously hear us, O Christ.

That we may respect their customs and traditions, and appreciate their teachers and prophets:

Graciously hear us, O Christ.

That we may be filled with a spirit of goodwill towards all men, and live together in peace:

Graciously hear us, O Christ.

That the nations whose glory has departed may learn by their past failure so to purge themselves from iniquity, that they may rise again to be more perfect instruments of Thy will:

Graciously hear us, O Christ.

That the nations which are foremost in knowledge and dominion may understand their responsibility, and devote their resources to the enrichment of those who are less favoured.

Graciously hear us, O Christ.

That the nations who are beginning their history may be blessed with wise counsellors and true leaders, that avoiding the mistakes which have darkened the past they may build themselves up into worthy peoples:

Graciously hear us, O Christ.

That the child races of the world may be respected, protected, and directed by all, that they may bear fruit after their kind, and take their places in the great world-family:

Graciously hear us, O Christ.

O God, the King of kings and Lord of lords, who dost by Thy providence rule the nations for the furtherance of Thy blessed purpose, we thank Thee for the abundant grace which Thou hast poured upon men, and for the gifts which we have received from others, and have been able to bestow upon them. Continue to lead us in the way of mutual help, that through diversity in unity we may come to fulness of life, to the joy of all mankind, and to the glory of Thy holy name; through Jesus Christ our Lord. Amen.

Now may our God and Father Himself, and our Lord Jesus, make you to increase and abound in love one toward another, and toward all men; to the end He may establish your hearts unblamable in holiness before our God and Father, at the coming of our Lord Jesus; to whom be the glory for ever and ever. Amen.

Public Worship: W. J. Tunbridge (circa 1920)

20. *Relationship with Other People*

MUTUAL KINDNESS

Dear ties of mutual succour bind
The children of our feeble race,
And, if our brethren were not kind,
This earth were but a weary place.
We lean on others as we walk
Life's twilight path with pitfalls strewn;
And 't were an idle boast to talk
Of treading that dim path alone.

Amid the snares misfortune lays
Unseen, beneath the steps of all,
Blest is the Love that seeks to raise
And stay and strengthen those who fall;
Till, taught by him who, for our sake,
Bore every form of Life's distress,
With every passing year we make
The sum of human sorrows less.

William Cullen Bryant (1794–1878)

SINGLE BROTHERHOOD

The believers are but a single Brotherhood: So make peace
and reconciliation between your brethren and fear God, that ye
may obtain mercy.

The Koran

CHARITY AND LOVE

Grant, O Lord, that this mind may be in us, which was also in Christ Jesus, Who left the heaven of Thy holiness and of Thy glory that He might take upon Him our sins and our sorrows, and seek and save that which was lost. Stir the hearts of Thy people that they may multiply their labours in the cause of charity and love, that they may minister to the wants of others, and by their good works lead many to glorify our Father Who is in heaven; through Jesus Christ our Lord.

Dean Charles John Vaughan (1816–1897)

PRESERVE US FROM ENVY

O God, who givest to all thy children liberally and upbraidest not, preserve us from all envy of the good of others, and from every kind of jealousy. Teach us to be thankful for what they have and we have not, and to delight in what they can achieve and we cannot, being generous of praise and slow to criticise, that we may fulfil the command of him who has taught us how to love our neighbour as ourself, even Jesus Christ our Lord. Amen.

Anon.

IN THE TIME OF TRIAL

O Thou God of peace, unite our hearts in Thy bond of peace, that we may live with one another continually in gentleness and humility, in peace and unity. O Thou God of patience, give us patience in the time of trial, and steadfastness to endure to the end. O Thou Spirit of prayer, awaken our hearts, that we may lift up holy hands to God, and cry unto Him in all our distresses. Be our Defence and Shade in the time of need, our Help in trial, our Consolation when all things are against us. Come, O Thou eternal Light, Salvation and Comfort, be our Light in darkness, our Salvation in life, our Comfort in death, and lead us in the strait way to everlasting life, that we may praise Thee for ever; through Jesus Christ our Lord. Amen.

Rev. Bernhard Albrecht (16th century)

I WILL EAT WITH HIM

Behold, I stand at the door and knock; if any one hears my voice and opens the door, I will come in to him and eat with him, and he with me.

Revelation 3: 20

JOY IN EACH OTHER

O God, our heavenly Father, who hast commanded us to love one another as Thy children, and hast ordained the highest friendship in the bond of Thy Spirit, we beseech Thee to maintain and preserve us always in the same bond, to Thy glory, and our mutual comfort, with all those to whom we are bound by any special tie, either of nature or of choice; that we may be perfected together in that love which is from above, and which never faileth when all other things shall fail. Send down the dew of Thy heavenly grace upon us, that we may have joy in each other that passeth not away; and having lived together in love here according to Thy commandment, may live for ever together with them, being made one in Thee, in Thy glorious kingdom hereafter, through Jesus Christ our Lord.

Devotions, George Hickes (1642–1715)

COMMON INTELLIGENCE

You are forgetting, too, the closeness of man's brotherhood with his kind; a brotherhood not of blood or human seed, but of a common intelligence; and that this intelligence in every man is God, an emanation from the deity.

Men exist for each other. Then either improve them or put up with them.

Marcus Aurelius (121–180)

SPEAKING AGREEMENT

Come together, O ye kinsmen all . . . to the glory of the mighty Guardian. . . . May your minds and your purposes be united. . . .

May we be in harmony with our kinsfolk, in harmony with strangers. . . .

230

Like friends we shall associate. . . . Harmonious, devoted to the same purpose, speak ye words in kindly spirit. . . .

Do not hold yourselves apart. ... Do ye come here, cooperating, going along the same wagon-pole, speaking agreement to one another.

Hindu Scriptures, Atharva-Veda

THE BROTHERHOOD OF MAN

O God, who art the Father of all mankind, we beseech Thee to give us a fuller realisation of our brotherhood, man with man, in Thee; and to raise up among us a deeper sense of truth and equity in all our dealings one with another; for the sake of Jesus Christ our Lord. Amen.

Anon.

THE COMMON GOOD

O God, we thank Thee for the abundance of our blessings, but we pray that our plenty may not involve want for others. Do Thou satisfy the desire of every child of Thine. Grant that the strength which we shall draw from this food may be put forth again for the common good, and that our life may return to humanity a full equivalent in useful work for the nourishment which we receive from the common store.

Prayers of the Social Awakening:
Walter Rauschenbusch (1861–1918)

BAPTISE OUR HEARTS

O Lord, baptise our hearts into a sense of the needs and conditions of all men. Amen.

George Fox (1624–1691)

EQUAL PARDON

I offer up unto Thee my prayers and intercessions, for those especially who have in any matter hurt, grieved, or found fault with me, or who have done me any damage or displeasure.

For all those also whom, at any time, I have vexed, troubled, burdened, and scandalised, by words or deeds, knowingly or in

231

ignorance: that Thou wouldst grant us all equally pardon for our sins, and for our offences against each other.

Take away from our hearts, O Lord, all suspiciousness, indignation, wrath and contention, and whatsoever may hurt charity and lessen brotherly love. Have mercy, O Lord, have mercy on those that crave Thy mercy, give grace unto them that stand in need thereof, and make us such that we may be worthy to enjoy Thy grace, and go forward to life eternal. Amen.

Thomas à Kempis (1380–1471)

KNOT THEM TO US

Most merciful and loving Father,
We beseech Thee most humbly, even with our hearts,
To pour out upon our enemies with bountiful hands
    whatsoever things Thou knowest may do them good.
And chiefly a sound and uncorrupt mind,
Where-through they may know Thee and love Thee in true
    charity and with their whole heart,
And love us, Thy children, for Thy sake.
Let not their first hating of us turn to their harm,
Seeing that we cannot do them good for want of ability.
Lord, we desire their amendment and our own.
Separate them not from us by punishing them,
But join and knot them to us by Thy favourable dealings with
    them.
And, seeing we be all ordained to be citizens of the one
    everlasting city,
Let us begin to enter into that way here already by mutual love,
Which may bring us right forth thither.

Elizabethan Prayer Book

WE HAVE FELLOWSHIP

This is the message which we have heard from him, and announce to you, that God is light, and in him is no darkness at all. If we say that we have fellowship with him and walk in darkness, we speak not and do not know the truth; but if we walk in the light, as he is in the light, we have fellowship one with another. He that saith he is in the light, and hateth his brother, is in the darkness until now. He that loveth his brother abideth in the light.

I John 1: 5–7; 2: 9–11

EVERY HEART HATH NEEDS

He prayeth best who leaves unguessed
The mystery of another's breast.
Why cheeks grow pale, why eyes o'erflow,
Or heads are white, thou need'st not know
Enough to note by many a sign
That every heart hath needs like thine.
Pray for us!

John Greenleaf Whittier (1807–1892),
The Prayer Seeker

NEVER JUDGE ANOTHER

Oh, Great Spirit, help me never to judge another until I have walked two weeks in his moccasins.

Sioux Indian prayer

THE GOLDEN RULE

May we take the word of reciprocity to serve as our rule of life—what we do not wish others to do to us, may we not do unto them.

Confucian

Do not approve for another what you do not like for yourself.

Gospel of Zarathustra

Do not do unto others that which you would not have them do unto you.

Hillel (60? B.C.–8 A.D.)

O God!
May I treat others
As I would be treated.

What I like not for myself
May I dispense not to others.

Abdullah Ansari (1005–1090)

Do unto all men as you would wish to have done unto you.

Mohammed (570–632)

Do nothing unto others which you would not have done unto
yourself.

Buddhist Scriptures.

Do unto others as you would they should do unto you.

Jesus of Nazareth (1st century)

PSALM 133

If there be one whose delight to wander
In pleasure's fields, where love's bright streams meander,
If there be one who longs to find
Where all the purer blisses are enshrined—
A happy resting-place of virtuous worth—
A blessed paradise on earth:

Let him survey the joy-conferring union
Of brothers who are bound in fond communion,
And not by force of blood alone,
But by their mutual sympathies are known,
And every heart and every mind relies
Upon fraternal, kindred ties.

O blest abode, where love is ever vernal,
Where tranquil peace and concord are eternal,
Where none usurp the highest claim,
But each with pride asserts the other's fame!
Oh, what are all the earthly joys, compared to thee,
Fraternal unanimity?

E'en as the ointment, whose sweet odours blended,
From Aaron's head upon his beard descended,
Which hung awhile in fragrance there,
Bedewing every individual hair,

234

And falling thence, with rich perfume ran o'er
　　The holy garb the prophet wore:

So doth the unity that lives with brothers
Share its best blessings and its joys with others,
　　And makes them seem as if one frame
Contained their minds, and they were formed the same,
　　And spread its sweetest breath o'er every part,
　　　　Until it penetrates the heart.

Gerbrand Brederode (1585–1618)
trans. by Sir John Bowring (1792–1872)

THEY WHO PRACTISE GOOD

E'en as the dew, that, at the break of morning,
　　All nature with its beauty is adorning,
　　And flows from Hermon calm and still,
　　And bathes the tender grass on Zion's hill,
　　And to the young and withering herb resigns
　　　　The drops for which it pines:

So are fraternal peace and concord ever
The cherishers, without whose guidance never
　　Would sainted quiet seek the breast—
　　The life, the soul of unmolested rest—
　　The antidote to sorrow and distress,
　　　　And prop of human happiness.
Ah! happy they whom genial concord blesses!
Pleasure for them reserves her fond caresses,
　　And joys to mark the fabric rare,
On virtue founded, stand unshaken there;
Whence vanish all the passions that destroy
　　　　Tranquility and inward joy.

Who practices good are in themselves rewarded,
For their own deeds lie in their hearts recorded;
　　And thus fraternal love, when bound
　　By virtue, is with its own blisses crowned,
And tastes, in sweetness that itself bestows,
What use, what power, from concord flows.

God in his boundless mercy joys to meet it;
　　His promises of future blessings greet it,

235

And fixed prosperity, which brings
Long life and ease beneath its shadowing wings,
And joy and fortune, that remain sublime
Beyond all distance, change, and time.

Gerbrand Brederode (1585–1619),
translated by Sir John Bowring (1792–1872)

CHRISTIAN BROTHERHOOD

The clouds that wrap the setting sun
When autumn's softest gleams are ending,
Where all bright hues together run
In sweet confusion blending:—
Why, as we watch their floating wreath,
Seem they the breath of life to breathe?
To Fancy's eye their motions prove
They mantle round the Sun for love.

When up some woodland dale we catch
The many-twinkled smile of ocean,
Or with pleased ear bewildered watch
His chime of restless motion;
Still as the surging waves retire
They seem to gasp with strong desire,
Such signs of love old Ocean gives,
We cannot choose but think he lives.

Wouldst thou the life of souls discern?
Nor human wisdom nor divine
Helps thee by aught beside to learn;
Love is life's only sign.
The spring of the regenerate heart,
The pulse, the glow of every part,
Is the true love of Christ our Lord,
As man embraced, as God adored.

But he, whose heart will bound to mark
The full bright burst of summer morn,
Loves too each little dewy spark
By leaf or floweret worn:
Cheap forms and common hues, 'tis true,
Through the bright shower-drop meet his view:

236

The colouring may be of this earth;
The lustre comes of heavenly birth.

Even so, who loves the Lord aright,
No soul of man can worthless find;
   All will be precious in his sight,
   Since Christ on all hath shined:
But chiefly Christian souls; for they,
Though worn and soiled with sinful clay,
   Are yet, to eyes that see them true,
   All glistening with baptismal dew.

   Then marvel not, if such as bask
      Inpurest light of innocence.
Hope against hope, in love's dear task,
      Spite of all dark offence.
   If they who hate the trespass most,
   Yet, when all other love is lost,
Love the poor sinner, marvel not;
Christ's mark outwears the rankest blot.

   No distance breaks the tie of blood;
      Brothers are brothers evermore;
Nor wrong, nor wrath of deadliest mood,
      That magic may o'erpower;
Oft, ere the common source be known,
The kindred drops will claim their own,
   And throbbing pulses silently
Move heart towards heart by sympathy.

   So it is with true Christian hearts;
      Their mutual share in Jesus' blood
      An everlasting bond imparts
         Of holiest brotherhood:
Oh, might we all our lineage prove,
Give and forgive, do good and love,
   By soft endearments in kind strife
   Lightening the load of daily life!

There is much need; for not as yet
      Are we in shelter or repose,
      The holy house is still beset
         With leaguer of stern foes;

Wild thoughts within, bad men without,
All evil spirits round about,
Are banded in unblest device,
To spoil love's earthly paradise.

Then draw we nearer day by day,
Each to his brethren, all to God;
Let the world take us as she may,
We must not change our road;
Not wondering, though in grief to find
The martyr's foe still keep her mind;
But fixed to hold love's banner fast,
And by submission win at last.

John Keble (1792–1866)

21. Help Us despite Ourselves

KEEP EVIL FROM US

King Zeus, grant us the good whether we pray for it or not, but evil keep from us though we pray for it.

Alcibiades, Plato (427–347 B.C.*)*

WELCOME ALL TRUTH

O Grant, O God, that we may wait patiently, as servants standing before their Lord, to know Thy will; that we may welcome all truth, under whatever outward form it may be uttered; that we may bless every good deed, by whomsoever it may be done; that we may rise above all strife to the contemplation of Thy Eternal Truth and Goodness; through Jesus Christ our Saviour. Amen.

Charles Kingsley (1819–1875)

THAT WE MAY PLEASE THEE

Lord Jesus, All-pure, purify us that we may behold Thee. All-holy, sanctify us that we may stand before Thee. All-gracious, mould us that we may please Thee. Very love, suffer us not to set at naught Thy love; suffer not devil, world, flesh, to destroy us; suffer not ourselves to destroy ourselves; us with whom Thou strivest, whom Thou desirest, whom Thou lovest.

Christina Georgina Rossetti (1830–1894)

LOVING PENITENCE

O God, though our sins be seven, though our sins be seventy times seven, though our sins be more in number than the hairs of our head, yet give us grace in loving penitence to cast ourselves down into the depths of Thy Compassion.

Christina Georgina Rossetti (1830–1894)

OUR DEPRAVED NATURE

Almighty God, as we cease not, though favoured with many blessings, to provoke thee by our misdeeds, as though we avowedly carried on war against thee, O grant that we, being at length warned by those examples by which thou invitest us to repentance, may restrain our depraved nature and in due time repent, and so devote ourselves to thy service, that thy name through us may be glorified. May we strive to bring into the way of salvation those who seem to be now lost, so that thy mercy may extend far and wide. Thus may thy salvation, obtained through Christ thine only-begotten Son, be known and embraced by all nations. Amen.

John Calvin (1509–1564)

ALWAYS RIGHT

Grant, O God, that we may always be right, for Thou knowest we will never change our minds.

Old Scottish Prayer

THE COVETOUS

What a rich man gives, and what he consumes, is his real wealth. Whose is the remainder which thou hoardest? Other covetous men will sport with that.

Hindu Scriptures (Hitopadesa)

WHEAT AND PEARLS

I saw an Arab sitting in a circle of jewellers of Basrah, and relating as follows: 'Once on a time, having missed my way in the desert, and having no provisions left, I gave myself up for lost: when I happened to find a bag of pearls. I shall never forget the relish and delight that I felt on supposing it to be fried wheat; nor the bitterness and despair which I suffered on discovering that the bag contained pearls.'

The Gulistan, Sadi of Shiraz (1184?–1291)

I DO NOT KNOW HOW

Lord of Creation! I do not know how to pray; I do not know what to say—I give Thee the entire prayer book.

Hasidic

FOR WHAT IS GOOD FOR US

Lord, we know not what is good for us. Thou knowest what it is. For it we pray.

Prayer of the Khond tribe who live in the Orissa and the Ganjam district of Madras in India

THE WORLD'S WORK

Every man can help on the world's work more than he knows of. What we want is the single eye, that we may see what our work is, the humility to accept it, however lowly, the faith to do it for God, the perseverence to go on till death.

Norman MacLeod (1812–1872)

THE SOUL OF MAN

Eternal and most gracious God, who hast stamped the soul of man with thine image, receive it into Thy revenue and make it a part of Thy treasure, suffer us not to undervalue ourselves, nor so to impoverish Thee as to give away these souls for nothing, and all the world is nothing if the soul must be given for it. Do this, O God, for His sake Who knows our natural infirmities, for He had them, and knows the weight of our sins,

for He paid a dear price for them, Thy Son our Saviour Jesus
Christ. Amen.

John Donne (1573–1631)

EVER FAITHFUL, EVER SURE

Let us, with a gladsome mind,
Praise the Lord, for He is kind;
For His mercies shall endure,
Ever faithful, ever sure.

He, with all-commanding might,
Filled the new-made world with light:
For His mercies shall endure,
Ever faithful, ever sure.

All things living He doth feed,
His full hand supplies their need:
For his mercies shall endure,
Ever faithful, ever sure.

He His chosen race did bless,
In the wasteful wilderness:
For His mercies shall endure,
Ever faithful, ever sure.

He hath with a piteous eye
Looked upon our misery:
For His mercies shall endure,
Ever faithful, ever sure.

Let us then, with gladsome mind,
Praise the Lord, for He is kind:
For His mercies shall endure,
Ever faithful, ever sure.

*Hymns of the Church of God:
selected by F. V. Mather (1866)*

22. Give Us Strength

NOTHING CAN HURT US

O God, animate us to cheerfulness. May we have a joyful sense of our blessings, learn to look on the bright circumstances of our lot, and maintain a perpetual contentedness under Thy allotments. Fortify our minds against disappointments and calamity. Preserve us from despondency, from yielding to dejection. Teach us that no evil is intolerable but a guilty conscience; and that nothing can hurt us, if, with true loyalty of affection, we keep Thy commandments, and take refuge in Thee. Amen.

Complete Works: William Ellery Channing (1780–1842)

FOR OUR LOVE BE LOVED

Lord Jesus Christ now give us grace, so to honour God, and to love other Christians, and ourselves to be lowly of heart, that we may for our honouring be honoured, for our love be loved, and for our meekness be lifted up into the high bliss of heaven, where with the Father and the Holy Spirit thou reignest God for ever and ever. Amen.

St. Edmund Rich (1170–1240)

WE ARE FRAIL

O God, our Father, we are exceedingly frail, and indisposed to every virtuous and gallant undertaking. Strengthen our weakness, we beseech thee, O God, that we may do valiantly in this spiritual war; help us against our own negligence and cowardice, and defend us from the treachery of our unfaithful hearts; for Jesus Christ's sake.

St. Augustine (354–436)

243

DRAW US WITH CORDS

O Lord Jesus Christ, take us to Thyself, draw us with cords to the foot of Thy Cross; for we have not strength to come, and we know not the way. Thou art mighty to save, and none can separate us from Thy love: bring us home to Thyself; for we are gone astray. We have wandered; do Thou seek us. Under the shadow of Thy Cross let us live all the rest of our lives, and there we shall be safe. Amen.

Archbishop Frederick Temple (1821–1902)

A LIVING FAITH

Almighty God, who, of Thy great love to man, didst give Thy dearly beloved Son to die for us upon the Cross as at this time, grant us grace ever to bear in mind His most precious suffering and death, and to deny ourselves and to take up our Cross and follow Him. May we die unto sin, and crucify the flesh with the affections and lusts thereof. Give unto us a living faith in our Redeemer and a thankful remembrance of His death. Help us to love Him better for His exceeding love to us, and grant that our sins may be put away, and nailed to the Cross, and buried in His grave, that they may be remembered no more against us; Through the same, Thy Son, Jesus Christ our Lord. Amen.

Bishop William Walsham How (1823–1897)

THY SPIRIT AND LOVE

Lord, we pray not for tranquillity, nor that our tribulations may cease; we pray for Thy Spirit and Thy Love, that Thou grant us strength and grace to overcome our adversary; through Jesus Christ our Lord. Amen.

Girolamo Savonarola (1452–1498)

YIELDING TODAY

Eternal God, who committest to us the swift and solemn trust of life; since we know not what a day may bring forth, but only that the hour for serving Thee is always present, may we wake to the instant claims of Thy holy will; not waiting for tomorrow, but yielding today.

Lay to rest by the persuasion of Thy spirit, the resistance of our passion, indolence or fear. Consecrate with Thy presence the way our feet may go; and the humblest work will shine, and the roughest places be made plain.

Lift us above unrighteous anger and mistrust into faith and hope and charity, by a simple and steadfast reliance on Thy sure will. In all things draw us to the mind of Christ, that Thy lost image may be traced again, and Thou mayest own us as at one with Him and Thee.

James Martineau (1805–1900)

SAFE LODGING

O Lord, support us all the day long of this troublous life, until the shadows lengthen and the evening comes, and the busy world is hushed, and the fever of life is over and our work is done. Then, Lord, in Thy mercy, grant us a safe lodging, a holy rest, and peace at last.

Anon. (16th century)

THROUGH CLOUDS OF MISERY

Lord God, look upon those to whom this world is dark; pity the lonely and sad-hearted, the forsaken and forgotten, the penitent and remorseful, the sinful and the miserable: teach them that the light of Thy countenance can find its way through prison bars and pierce through the thick black clouds of misery. Show them of little hope, the bow in the cloud, how it is made by the light of God shining upon the darkness of earth. So shine upon our steps and so shed the light of Thy countenance upon our tears that we may see the bow of Hope glorious in the clouds, giving us hope that above and beyond this world of trial and change there may be days of happy rest, that we through our changing lot may have the shining light of Thy countenance upon us, and the blessing of Almighty God.

George Dawson (1821–1876)

WHEN SUFFERING SHALL CLOSE

The day of rest once more comes round,
The day to all believers dear;
The silver trumpets seem to sound,
That called the tribes of Israel near;
Ye people, all, obey the call,
And in Jehovah's courts appear.

Obedient to Thy summons, Lord,
We to the sanctuary come;
Thy gracious presence here afford,
And send Thy people joyful home;
Of Thee our King O may we sing,
And none with such a theme be dumb.

O hasten, Lord, the day when those
Who love Thee here shall see Thy face;
When suffering shall for ever close,
And they shall reach their destined place;
Then shall they rest, supremely blest,
Eternal debtors to Thy grace.

Hymns of the Church of God:
selected by F. V. Mather (1866)

23. *For Working People*

THY RADIANCE

O Christ, Our Lord, the Guide of all and each, and Bearer of the burdens of the world; encompass with Thy love the workers in field and farm, in factory and mine, on roads and rail and in the air, in offices and shops, in entertaining and refreshment, in maintenance of law; into Thy care, O Lord, we commit all travellers, and workers in the docks and on the seas, all those who plan and build and teach and have responsibility; bless women everywhere; bless all who tend and cook and clean; and shed Thy radiance on all who know, and those who do not know, that in labour they serve Thy people and our people, Thy Father and our Father; and this we pray in Thy Name, Who art with the Father and the Holy Ghost, God for evermore. Amen.

*The Kingdom of God, Council of
Clergy and Ministers for Common Ownership (1946)*

MERCY ON ALL WHO LABOUR

O Christ, who camest not to be ministered unto but to minister, have mercy upon all who labour faithfully to serve the common good. O Christ, who didst feed the hungry multitude with loaves and fishes, have mercy upon all who labour to earn their daily bread. O Christ, who didst call unto Thyself all them that labour and are heavy laden, have mercy upon all whose work is beyond their strength. And to Thee, with the Father and the Holy Spirit, be all the glory and the praise.

A Diary of Private Prayer: John Baillie (1741–1806)

FOR ALL WHO TOIL

O God, Father of all men, we pray for all who toil in mill or mine; for all by whose labour we are clothed and fed; for all who work in the darkness of the earth; for those who build and adorn our houses; for those who trade in shop or market; and for those who go down to the sea in ships and do business in great waters. May our service and our merchandise be holy unto the Lord. May we do justly and love mercy and walk humbly with thee, for thy Name's sake.

Anon.

FOR WORKING MEN

O God, Thou mightiest worker of the universe, source of all strength and author of all unity, we pray Thee for our brothers, the industrial workers of the nation. As their work binds them together in common toil and danger, may their hearts be knit together in a strong sense of their common interests and destiny. Help them to realise that the injury of one is the concern of all, and that the welfare of all must be the aim of every one. If any of them is tempted to sell the birthright of his class for a mess of pottage for himself, give him a wider outlook and a nobler sympathy with his fellows. Teach them to keep step in a steady onward march, and in their own way to fulfil the law of Christ by bearing the common burdens.

Grant the organisations of labour quiet patience and prudence in all disputes, and fairness to see the other side. Save them from malice and bitterness. Save them from the headlong folly which ruins a fair cause, and give them wisdom resolutely to put aside the two-edged sword of violence that turns on those who seize it. Raise up for them still more leaders of able mind and large heart, and give them grace to follow the wiser counsel.

When they strive for leisure and health and a better wage, do Thou grant their cause success, but teach them not to waste their gain on fleeting passions, but to use it in building fairer homes and a nobler manhood. Grant all classes of our nation a larger comprehension for the aspirations of labour and for the courage and worth of these our brothers, that we may cheer them in their struggles and understand them even in their sins.

And may the upward climb of Labour, its defeats and its victories, in the further reaches bless all classes of our nation, and build up for the republic of the future a great body of workers, strong of limb, clear of mind, fair in temper, glad to labour, conscious of their worth, and striving together for the final brotherhood of all men.

Prayers of the Social Awakening:
Walter Rauschenbusch (1861–1918)

24. *Lord Forgive Us*

FORGIVE THAT IS PAST

Lord, for Thy tender mercy's sake, lay not our sins to our charge, but forgive that is past, and give us grace to amend our lives; to decline from sin and incline to virtue, that we may walk with a perfect heart before Thee, now and evermore.

John Lydney

HEAR OUR SUPPLICATIONS

Lord God of Israel, there is no God like Thee in heaven above or on earth beneath, Who keepest covenant and mercy with Thy servants and to their supplications, O Lord our God, and hearken unto the cry and the prayer which Thy servants pray before Thee this day. Forgive all that have sinned against Thee and all that have transgressed against Thee. Hear Thou our prayer and our supplications in heaven Thy dwelling-place, and when Thou hearest, forgive. Amen.

King Solomon (10th century B.C.*)*

THOSE WE HAVE WRONGED

Lord, let it be thy good pleasure to bless all those whom we have in any way wronged, and to forgive all those who have wronged us; and to comfort those who are sad, to give health to the sick, ease to those who are in pain, patience to the afflicted, food to the hungry, clothes to the naked, and liberty to the captives. . . . Bless all our relations, friends and neighbours. . . . Through Jesus Christ our Lord.

Bishop Thomas Ken (1637–1711)

250

CLEANSE US

Almighty and merciful God, the fountain of all goodness, who knowest the thoughts of our hearts, we confess that we have sinned against thee and done evil in thy sight. Forgive us, O Lord, we beseech thee, and cleanse us from the stains of our former offences. Give us grace and power to put away all hurtful things; so that being delivered from the bondage of sin we may bring forth fruits worthy of repentance. O eternal light, O eternal goodness, deliver us from evil; O eternal power, be our support; O eternal wisdom, scatter the darkness of our ignorance. Grant that with all our heart, and mind, and strength we may evermore seek thy face; and finally bring us in thine infinite mercy to thy holy presence; through Jesus Christ our Lord.

Alcuin of York (735–804)

FORGIVE THEM

Father, forgive them; for they know not what they do.

St. Luke 23: 34

FORGIVING ANOTHER

Humanity is never so beautiful as when praying for forgiveness, or else forgiving another.

J. R. F. Richter

MANIFOLD SINS

Almighty God, Father of our Lord Jesus Christ, Maker of all things, Judge of all men; we acknowledge and bewail our manifold sins and wickedness, which we, from time to time, most grievously have committed, by thought, word and deed, against Thy Divine Majesty, provoking most justly Thy wrath and indignation against us. We do earnestly repent, and are heartily sorry for our misdoings; the remembrance of them if grievous upon us; the burden of them is intolerable. Have mercy upon us, have mercy upon us most merciful Father; for Thy Son our Lord Jesus Christ's sake. Forgive us all that is past; and grant that we may ever serve and please Thee in newness of life, to the honour and glory of Thy name: through Jesus Christ our Lord. Amen.

Archbishop Thomas Cranmer (1489–1556)

PARDON OUR SINS

O God the Father Almighty, Creator and Governor of all things; O God the Son Eternal, our Redeemer, Intercessor and Judge; O God the Holy Ghost, the Sanctifier, Who with the Father and the Son together art worshipped and glorified, have mercy upon us. Pardon, O Lord, the sins and offences of our past lives, for Thy mercy's sake; from pride and vanity, from selfishness and envy, from love of the world and forgetfulness of Thee, good Lord, deliver us. O Lord, we beseech Thee mercifully to hear our prayers and supplications for all mankind, and especially for Thy Holy Church throughout the land. For the Queen and all who are in authority, that they may rule in righteousness and minister true judgement to the people. For all bishops and ministers, that they may be guided by Thy Holy Spirit to a knowledge of the Truth, and may be both teachers and patterns to their flocks. We beseech Thee to hear us, O Lord, for all who are in trouble, suffering and distress; for the needy and them that have no helper; for the sick, the dying and the mourners. For our relations, friends and benefactors; for our enemies, persecutors and slanderers; for all with whom we live or have to do. Hear us, O Lord, we humbly beseech Thee, for the sake of Jesus Christ, the Son of God. Amen.

An Ancient Litany, adapted 1489

25. *Personal Prayers*

FINDING GOD

O Lord our God, grant us grace to desire thee with our whole heart; that, so desiring, we may seek, and, seeking, find thee; and so finding thee, may love thee; and loving thee, may hate those sins from which thou hast redeemed. Amen.

St. Anselm (1033–1109)

BE TRANSFORMED

Do not be conformed to this world but be transformed by the renewal of your mind, that you may prove what is the will of God, what is good and acceptable and perfect.

Romans 12: 2

MĄKE US GENTLE

Almighty and most merciful Father, who hast given us a new commandment that we should love one another, give us also grace that we may fulfil it. Make us gentle, courteous and forebearing. Direct our lives so that we may look each to the good of the other in word and deed. And hallow all our friendships by the blessing of thy Spirit; for his sake who loved us, and gave himself for us, Jesus Christ our Lord.

Bishop Brooke Foss Westcott (1825–1901)

SHOWERS OF BLESSINGS

He who sets his heart, concentrates his mind, and sits absorbed in silent meditation shall not be a prey to evil even though living in this world of passions, and in the future world he shall receive showers of blessings. . . . He who with a steady heart raises his voice and without ceasing prays shall be freed from his sins and shall obtain birth into Paradise.

Buddhist Scriptures

ALL IS CONQUERED

O God, help me to victory over myself, for difficult to conquer is oneself, though when that is conquered, all is conquered.

Jain Scriptures

FELLOWSHIP

Give me a heart that beats
In all its pulses with the common heart
Of human kind, which the same things make glad,
The same make sorry! Give me grace enough
Even in their first beginnings to detect
The endeavours which the proud heart still is making
To cut itself from off the common root,
To set itself upon a private base,
To have wherein to glory of the kind!
Each such attempt in all its hateful pride
And meanness, give me to detect and loathe—
A man, and claiming fellowship with men!

Archbishop Richard Chenevix Trench (1807–1886)

I ASK PARDON

O Lord, be gracious unto us! In all that we hear or see, in all that we say or do, be gracious unto us. I ask pardon of the Great God. I ask pardon at the sunset, when every sinner turns to Him. Now and for ever I ask pardon of God. O Lord, cover us from our sins, guard our children and protect our weaker friends.

Bedouin camel-driver's prayer

AWAIT THE OUTCOME

Some pray: Let me sleep with that woman! Do thou, Marcus, pray: Let me not lust to sleep with her! Others pray: Let me be done with that man! Thou: Let me not wish to be done with him! Others: Let me not lose my little child! Thou: Let me not fear to lose him! In short, pray in this spirit, and await the outcome.

Marcus Aurelius (121–180 A.D.*)*

TEACH ME WISDOM

I confess I can see, but I cannot moderate, nor love as I ought. I pray thee for thy loving kindness sake supply my want in this particular. And so make me love all, that I may be a blessing to all: and well-pleasing to thee in all. Teach me wisdom, how to expend my blood, estate, life, and time in thy service for the good of all, and make all them that are round about me wise and holy as Thou art. That we may all be knit together in Godly Love, and united in Thy service to Thy honour and Glory.

Centuries of Meditation: Thomas Traherne (1908)

THE WONDERFUL LOVE

Give us, O Lord God, a deep sense of Thy holiness; how Thou art of purer eyes than to behold iniquity, and canst not overlook or pass by that which is evil.

Give us no less, O Lord, a deep sense of Thy wonderful love towards us; how Thou wouldst not let us alone in our ruin, but didst come after us, in the Person of Thy Son Jesus Christ, to bring us back to our true home with Thee.

Quicken in us, O Lord, a Spirit of gratitude, of loyalty and of sacrifice, that we may seek in all things to please Him who humbled Himself for us, even to the death of the Cross, by dying unto sin and living unto righteousness; through the same Jesus Christ our Lord.

Dean Charles John Vaughan (1816–1897)

I WILL DEFEND THY PURPOSE

Do with me henceforth as Thou wilt. I am of one mind with Thee, I am Thine. I decline nothing that seems good to Thee. Send me whither Thou wilt. Clothe me as Thou wilt. Will Thou that I take office or live a private life, remain at home or go into exile, be poor or rich, I will defend Thy purpose with me in respect of all these.

Epictetus (1st century)

I MUST FOLLOW

Lead me, O God, and I will follow, willingly if I am wise, but if not willingly I still must follow.

Early Stoic

THE GRASS MUST BEND

Ke K'ang, distressed about the number of thieves in his kingdom, inquired of Confucius how he might do away with them. The sage said, 'If you, sir, were not covetous, the people would not steal, though you should pay them for it.'

Ke K'ang asked, 'What do you say about killing the unprincipled for the good of the principled?' Confucius said, 'In carrying on your government why use killing at all? Let the rulers desire what is good, and the people will be good. The grass must bend when the wind blows across it.'

How can men who cannot rectify themselves, rectify others?

Analects: Confucius (551–478 B.C.)

EXAMINE FIRST YOURSELF

Four things should always be kept in mind, namely: examine first yourself and then others; examine first your own troubles and then the troubles of others; examine first your own will and then the wills of others; examine first your own principles and then the principles of others.

Advice to a Layman: Buddhist

INFINITE GOODNESS

Cultivating an unbounded friendly mind,
Continually strenuous night and day,
One will spread infinite goodness through all the regions.

Buddhist Scriptures (Sutta Nipata)

PROFOUND MEDITATION

May that soul of mine, which mounts aloft in my waking and my sleeping hours, an ethereal spark from the light of lights, be united by devout meditation with the spirit supremely blest and supremely intelligent!

May that soul of mine, the guide by which the lowly perform their menial work and the wise versed in science, worship that soul which is the primal oblation within all creatures, be united by devout meditation with the Spirit supremely blest and supremely intelligent!

May that soul of mine, which is the ray of perfect wisdom, pure intellect, and permanent existence, the indistinguishable light set in mortal bodies, without which no good act is performed, be united by devout meditation with the Spirit supremely blest and supremely intelligent!

May that soul of mine, in whose eternal essence is comprised whatever has past, is present, or will be hereafter, be united by devout meditation with the Spirit supremely blest and supremely intelligent!

May that soul of mine, which contains all sacred scriptures and texts, as spokes held in the axle of the chariot-wheel, and into which the essence of all created forms is interwoven, be united by devout meditation with the Spirit supremely blest and supremely intelligent!

May that soul of mine, which, distributed also through others, guides mankind as the charioteer guides his steeds—the soul fixed in my breast, except from old age, swift in its course—be united by profound meditation with the Spirit supremely blest and supremely intelligent!

Hindu Scriptures

A LIGHT IN THE HEART

When the heart of men has been revivified and illumined by the Primal Spirit, he has arrived at intelligence; for intelligence is a light in the heart distinguishing between truth and vanity. Until he has been so revivified and illumed, it is impossible for him to attain to intelligence at all. But having attained to intelligence, then, and not until then, is the time for the attainment of knowledge, for becoming wise. Intelligence is a primal element, and knowledge the attribute thereof. When from knowledge he has successively proceeded to the attainment of divine light, and acquaintance with the mysteries of nature, his last step will be perfection, with which his upward progress concludes.

'Arise and look around, for every atom that has birth
Shines forth a lustrous beacon to illumine all the earth.'

The instinctive spirit should feed and supply the spirit of humanity, as the oil feeds and supplies the flame in a lamp. The traveller must aim at completing this lamp, so that his heart may be illumined, and he may see things as they really are.

Sufi Compilation

THE RULE

Praise to the Lord, the perfectly enlightened Buddha, the
All-Enlightened One.
Praise to the Lord, the perfectly enlightened Buddha, the
All-Enlightened One.
Praise to the Lord, the perfectly enlightened Buddha, the
All-Enlightened One.

I go to the Buddha for Refuge,
I go to the Doctrine for Refuge,
I go to the Order for Refuge.
Again I go to the Buddha for Refuge,
Again I go to the Doctrine for Refuge,
Again I go to the Order for Refuge.
A third time I go to the Buddha for Refuge,
A third time I go to the Doctrine for Refuge,
A third time I go to the Order for Refuge.

I undertake the rule of training to refrain from killing or
harming living things.

I undertake the rule of training to refrain from taking that
which is not given.
I undertake the rule of training to refrain from licentiousness
in sensual pleasures.
I undertake the rule of training to refrain from falsehood.
I undertake the rule of training to refrain from liquors which
engender slothfulness.

'Pansil' (said in Buddhist devotions)

LEAD US HEAVENLY FATHER

Lead us, Heavenly Father, lead us,
O'er the world's tempestuous sea;
Guard us, guide us, keep us, feed us,
For we have no help but Thee;
Yet possessing
Every blessing,
If our God our Father be.

Saviour, breathe forgiveness o'er us;
All our weakness Thou dost know;
Thou didst tread this earth before us,
Thou didst feel its keenest woe:
Lone and dreary,
Faint and weary,
Through the desert Thou didst go.

Spirit of our God, descending,
Fill our hearts with heavenly joy,
Love with every passion blending,
Pleasure that can never cloy:
Thus provided,
Pardoned, guided,
Nothing can our peace destroy.

Hymns of the Church of God:
selected by F. V. Mather (1866)

GUARD THY SHEEP

Jesus, the Shepherd of the sheep,
Thy little flock in safety keep,
The flock for which Thou camest from Heaven,
The flock for which Thy life was given.

Thou sawest them wandering far from Thee,
Secure, as if from danger free;
Thy love did all their wanderings trace,
And bring them to a wealthy place.

O guard Thy sheep from beasts of prey,
And guide them that they never stray;
Cherish the young, sustain the old;
Let none be feeble in Thy fold.

Secure them from the scorching beam,
And lead them to the living stream;
In verdant pastures let them lie,
And watch them with a Shepherd's eye.

O may Thy sheep discern Thy voice,
And in its sacred sound rejoice;
From strangers may they ever flee,
And know no other guide but Thee.

Lord, bring Thy sheep that wander yet,
And let the number be complete;
Then let Thy flock from earth remove,
And occupy the field above.

Hymns of the Church of God:
selected by F. V. Mather (1866)

26. Prayers for the Present Life

THOU SPAREST ALL

For thou lovest all the things that are,
and abhorrest nothing which thou hast made:
for never wouldst thou have made any thing
if thou hadst hated it.
And how could anything have endured,
if it had not been thy will?
or been preserved, if not called by thee?
But thou sparest all: for they are thine,
O Lord, thou lover of souls.

Wisdom of Solomon 11: 24–26

REVERENCE FOR LIFE

There flashed through my mind, unforeseen and unsought,
the phrase, Reverence for Life.

*Out of My Life and Thought:
Albert Schweitzer (1875–1965)*

SWEET PROMISE OF SPRING

O Lord, we thank Thee that again we have seen the glory of the changing year, the sweet promise of the Spring, the glow of Summer, and the wealth of Autumn, the warmth and tenderness of Winter's home. We bless Thee for quiet hours, when the soul in solitude has been filled full with Thee; for sweet thoughts which none but ourselves have known; for songs in the night, when Thou hast held our eyes waking. And now we stand upon the threshold of another year, and we know not what may be the end thereof unto us. But, knowing surely

261

that all things work together for good to them that love Thee, may we wait patiently and toil quietly, though the waiting be long and the toil hard, for Thou art our Guide, and heaven is our Home.

George Dawson (1821–1876)

LEADERS OF PEOPLE

Almighty God of Justice, confound, we beseech Thee, the works of those who use the resources of their countries, the labour of men, women, and children, and the blood of armed forces, to the furthering of evil purpose and neglect of common good; raise up, we pray Thee, leaders of people who shall maintain in sacred trust that which is committed to their care, for the happiness of men, and for Thy glory; through Jesus Christ our Lord.

The Kingdom of God: Council of Clergy and Ministers for Common Ownership (1946)

THE HOPE OF GLORY

Almighty God, Father of all mercies, we thine unworthy servants do give thee most humble and hearty thanks for all thy goodness and loving kindness to us and to all men. We bless thee for our creation, preservation, and all the blessings of this life; but above all for thine inestimable love in the redemption of the world by our Lord Jesus Christ; for the means of grace and for the hope of glory. And we beseech thee, give us that due sense of all thy mercies, that our hearts may be unfeignedly thankful, and that we may show forth thy praise, not only with our lips but in our lives; by giving up ourselves to thy service and by walking before thee in holiness and righteousness all our days; through Jesus Christ our Lord, to whom with thee and the Holy Ghost be all honour and glory, world without end.

Bishop Edward Reynolds (1599–1676)

UNSHAKEN STAFF

Our God, may we lay hold of Thy Cross, as of a staff that can stand unshaken when the floods run high. It is this world and not another, this world with all its miseries—its ruin and sin—that Thou hast entered to redeem by Thine agony and bloody sweat. Amen.

Canon H. Scott Holland (1847–1918)

CLOSE TO HEAVEN

Of all those who have taken the long journey, who has returned of whom I can ask tidings? O friend! take care to lose nothing in sight for hope of something in that close-barred seraglio—for, rest assured, thou shalt not rest here!

Since from the beginning of life to its end there is for thee only this earth, live at least as one who is on the earth, and not like one buried beneath it.

Wherever I cast my eyes I see the sward of paradise, and its crystal stream. One would say that this meadow, issuing from fires beneath, is transformed to a celestial abode. Repose thyself in this abode, close to the heavenly beauty!

Thou, man, who art the universe in little! Cease for a moment from thy absorption in loss and gain: take one draught at the hand of him who presses creation's cut to thy lips, and so free thyself at once from the cares of this world, and those about another!

Rubaiyat: Omar Khayam

OUR DWELLING PLACE

The Creator, Lord of light, praise we.
The Teacher, Lord of Purity, praise we.
The day-times praise we.
The pure water praise we.
The stars, the moon, the sun, the trees, praise we.
The mountains, the pastures, dwellings and fountains, praise we. . . .
The well-created animals praise we.
We praise all good men; we praise all good women.
We praise thee, our dwelling-place, O Earth.

263

We praise thee, O God, Lord of the dwelling-place.

Zend-Avesta (Zoroastrian)

A SWEET EXISTENCE

Justice is the soul of the universe. The universe is a body; the senses are its angels; the heavens, the elements, and all beings, its limbs; behold the eternal unity—the rest is only illusion.

Why should a man who possesses a bit of bread securing life for two days, and who has a cup of fresh water—why should such a man be commanded by another who is not his superior, and why should he serve one who is only his equal?

In this world he who possesses a morsel of bread, and some nest in which to shelter himself, who is master or slave of no man, tell that man to live content; he possesses a very sweet existence.

Rubaiyat: Omar Khayam

EARTH IS THE MOTHER

Truth, greatness, universal order, strength, consecration . . . support the Earth.

Thy snowy mountain heights, and thy forests, O Earth, shall be kind to us! The brown, the black, the red, the multicoloured, the firm Earth . . . we have settled upon, not suppressed, not slain, not wounded.

Into thy middle set us, O Earth . . . into the nourishing strength that has grown up from thy body. . . . The Earth is the Mother and we the Children of the Earth. . . .

A great gathering-place, thou great Earth, hast become. . . .

The fragrance, O Earth, that has risen from thee, which the plants and flowers hold . . . with that make us fragrant; not any one shall hate us!

That fragrance of thine which has entered into the lotus . . . with that make us fragrant; not any one shall hate us!

That fragrance of thine which is in men, the loveliness and charm that is in male and female . . . with that do thou blend us; not any one shall hate us! Amen.

Vedic Hymn

ALL EXISTING THINGS

God loves all existing things.

St. Thomas Aquinas (1227–1274)

27. At Eventime

ABIDE WITH US

Abide with us, Lord, for it is towards evening and the day is far spent. Abide with us and with thy whole Church. Abide with us in the end of the day, in the end of our life, in the end of the world. Abide with us with thy grace and bounty, with thy holy word and sacrament, with thy comfort and thy blessing. Abide with us when over us cometh the night of affliction and fear, the night of doubt and temptation, the night of bitter death. Abide with us and with thy faithful, through time and eternity.

Johann Konrad Wilhelm Löhe (1808–1872)

SAVE ME THROUGH THE COMING NIGHT

The day is past and over;
All thanks, O Lord, to Thee!
I pray Thee now, that sinless
The hours of dark may be.
O Jesu! keep me in Thy sight,
And save me through the coming night.

The joys of day are over;
I lift my heart to Thee,
And ask Thee that offenceless
The hours of dark may be.
O Jesu! make their darkness light,
And save me through the coming night.

The toils of day are over;
I raise the hymn to Thee,
And ask, that free from peril

266

The hours of dark may be.
O Jesu! keep me in Thy sight,
And guard me through the coming night.

Be Thou my soul's Preserver.
O God! for Thou dost know
How many are the perils
Through which I have to go:
Lover of men, O hear my call,
And guard and save me from them all.

Hymns of the Church of God:
selected by F. V. Mather (1866)

28. Guidance

PERPLEXITIES OF MODERN LIFE

Guide us, O Christ, in all the perplexities of our modern social life, and in Thine own good time bring us together in love and unity, making the kingdoms of this world Thy kingdom as Thou willest. Amen.

James Adderley (19th century)

TO IMPROVE TO PERFECTION

O almighty God, inspire us with this divine Principle; kill in us all the Seeds of Envy and Ill-will; and help us, by cultivating within ourselves the Love of our Neighbour, to improve in the love of Thee. Thou hast placed us in various Kindreds, Friendships, and Relations, as the School of Disciples for our Affections: Help us, by the due exercise of them, to improve to Perfection; till all partial Affection be lost in that entire universal one, and Thou, O God, shalt be all in all. Amen.

Bishop Joseph Butler (1692–1752)

WISDOM TO REDEEM THE TIME

O God of time and eternity, who makest us creatures of time, to the end that when time is over we may attain Thy blessed eternity. With time which is Thy gift, give us also wisdom to redeem the time lest our day of grace be lost, for the sake of Jesus Christ our Lord. Amen.

Christina Georgina Rossetti (1830–1894)

MAY ALL MEN PROSPER

O kind Father, loving Father, through Thy mercy we have spent our day in peace and happiness; grant that we may, according to Thy will, do what is right.

Give us light, give us understanding, so that we may know what pleases Thee.

We offer this prayer in Thy presence, O wonderful Lord:

Forgive us our sins. Help us in keeping ourselves pure. Bring us into the fellowship of those in whose company we may remember Thy name.

[Through Nanak] may Thy Name forever be on the increase, and may all men prosper by Thy grace.

Guru Gobind Singh (1666–1708)

LET US NOT STRAY

O Lord Jesus Christ, Who art the Way, the Truth, and the Life, we pray Thee suffer us not to stray from Thee, who art the Way, nor to distrust Thee, who art the Truth, nor to rest in any other thing than Thee, who art the Life.

Teach us by Thy Holy Spirit what to believe, what to do, and wherein to take our rest. Amen.

Erasmus (1466–1536)

LASTING ETERNITY

Lord we believe, but would believe more firmly. We hope, but would hope more securely. We love, but would love more warmly. By thy wisdom do thou direct us, by thy righteousness do thou keep us, by thy sweet mercy comfort and protect us.

Let pride never corrupt us, nor flattery move us, not evil entice us from thee.

Grant us grace to cleanse our memories, to check our tongues, to restrain our senses.

Let us overcome love of pleasure by self-denial, love of money by freely giving, heat of temper by gentleness.

Make us prudent in counsel, steadfast in danger, patient in adversity, humble in prosperity, temperate in meat and drink, diligent in duty, careful for others.

Let us learn from thee, O God, how little is all that is earthly, how great all that is heavenly; how short all that is of time, how lasting all that is of eternity.

Treasury of Devotions

THAT WHICH IS WORTH KNOWING

Grant to us, O Lord, to know that which is worth knowing, to love that which is worth loving, to praise that which pleaseth thee most, to esteem that which is most precious unto thee, and to dislike whatsoever is evil in thy eyes. Grant us with true judgment to distinguish things that differ, and above all to search out and to do what is well pleasing unto thee, through Jesus Christ our Lord. Amen.

Thomas à Kempis (1380–1471)

GOD PILOT US

May the strength of God pilot us.
May the power of God preserve us.
May the wisdom of God instruct us.
May the hand of God protect us.
May the way of God direct us.
May the shield of God defend us.
May the host of God guard us against the snares of evil
    and the temptations of the world.
May Christ be with us.
Christ before us.
Christ in us.
Christ over us.
May Thy salvation, O Lord, be always ours this day and
    forever more.

St. Patrick (389?–4610

WITH THY RIGHT HAND

Give of Thy peace to our troubled hearts, and let the Comforter brood over us this day. Give us true understanding of all our duties, and strength for their faithful performance; make us to be faithful servants, day by day, till such happy time as Thou shalt put away the work, and close the gates, and shut us in, to the quietness of the grave. Guide us with Thy right hand along this weary, dusty road of life, and receive us at last into Thine Eternal City. Amen.

George Dawson (1821–1876)

WE MAY HEAR THY VOICE

Lord of the harvest, the nations are waiting for Thy message, and asking for messengers, and there are few who go, and few who give, and few who pray. O grant that we may hear Thy voice, and help in whatever way we can, by prayer, by gifts, and by service, to make Thy gospel known to all the world. Amen.

W. Pakenham Walsh (1820–1902)

THINK THOSE THINGS THAT ARE GOOD

O Lord, from whom all good things do come, grant to us, Thy humble servants, that by Thy holy inspiration we may think those things that are good, and by Thy merciful guiding may perform the same, through Jesus Christ our Lord. Amen.

Pope Gelasius (492–496)

TOUCH OUR CHILLED HEARTS

Open our eyes, Thou son of life and gladness,
That we may see that glorious world of Thine:
It shines for us in vain while drooping sadness
Enfolds us here like mist; come power benign,
Touch our chilled hearts with vernal smile,
Our wintry course do Thou beguile,
Nor by the wayside ruins let us mourn,
Who have the eternal towers for our appointed bourne.

John Keble (1792–1866)

TILL ALL OUR WANDERINGS CEASE

O God of Bethel, by whose hand
Thy people still are fed,
Who through this weary pilgrimage
Hast all our fathers led;

Our vows, our prayers, we now present

271

Before Thy throne of grace:
God of our fathers, be the God
Of their succeeding race.

Through each perplexing path of life
Our wandering footsteps guide;
Give us each day our daily bread,
And raiment fit provide.

O spread Thy covering wings around,
Till all our wanderings cease,
And at our Father's loved abode
Our souls arrive in peace!

Such blessings from Thy gracious hand
Our humble prayers implore;
And Thou shalt be our chosen God
And portion evermore.

Hymns of the Church of God:
selected by F. V. Mather (1866)

LIGHT EVERY DARK RECESS

Holy Spirit, from on high,
Bend on us a pitying eye;
Animate the drooping heart,
Bid the power of sin depart.

Light up every dark recess
Of our heart's ungodliness;
Show us every devious way,
Where our steps have gone astray.

Teach us, with repentant grief,
Humbly to implore relief;
Then the Saviour's blood reveal,
All our deep disease to heal.

Other groundwork should we lay,
Sweep those empty hopes away;
Make us feel that Christ alone
Can for human guilt atone.

May we daily grow in grace,

And pursue the heavenly race,
Trained in wisdom, led by love,
Till we reach our rest above.

*Hymns of the Church of God:
selected by F. V. Mather (1866)*

GUIDE US

In the name of the merciful and compassionate God. Praise belongs to God, the Lord of the worlds, The merciful, the compassionate! Thee we serve and thee we ask for aid. Guide us in the right path.

The Koran (opening chapter)

29. *For the Unity of All Religions*

CITY OF OUR GOD

God, in his earthly temple, lays
Foundations for his heavenly praise;
Where saints with joy his wonders tell,
Jehovah still delights to dwell.

What glories were describ'd of old!
What wonders are of Zion told!
The city of our God below
Each heathen nation yet must know.

Here let the Gentile and the Jew,
Through grace begin their lives anew;
While ransom'd spirits join to sing,
The source whence all our blessings spring.

Lord, number us in thine account,
With natives of thy holy mount;
That we, at length, may all appear,
With those who found salvation here!

Hymns, Original and Select:
John Bulmer (1835)

ONE HOPE

Grant, O Lord, that as there is one Spirit, one Lord, one
Faith, and one hope of our calling; so Thy Church as one
Body, may draw all nations into peace and unity; through Him
in Whom all men are one, our Saviour Jesus Christ.

Anon.

ONE TRUE CHURCH

Thou hast quieted those who were in confusion. Praise to Thy calmness! O Lord, make quiet in Thy Churches; and blend and unite, O Lord, the contentious sects; and still and rule also the conflicting parties, and may there be at every time one true Church, and may her righteous children gather themselves together to confess Thy graciousness. Praise to Thy reconciliation, O Lord God. Amen.

St. Ephraim the Syrian (306–373)

GOD IS ONE

Altar flowers are of many species, but all worship is one. Systems of faith are different, but God is one.

Hindu Scriptures

JESUS SHALL REIGN

Jesus shall reign where'er the sun
Doth his successive journeys run;
His kingdom stretch from shore to shore,
Till moons shall wax and wane no more.

To Him shall endless prayer be made,
And praises throng to crown His head;
His Name, like sweet perfume, shall rise
With every morning sacrifice.

People and realms of every tongue
Dwell on His love with sweetest song,
And infant voices shall proclaim
Their early blessings on His Name.

Blessings abound where'er He reigns;
The prisoner leaps to lose his chains;
The weary find eternal rest,
And all the sons of want are blest.

Let every creature rise and bring
Peculiar honours to our King;

Angels descend with songs again,
And earth repeat the loud Amen.

Hymns of the Church of God:
selected by F. V. Mather (1866)

COMING TOGETHER

The Beloved of the Gods honours men of all sects with gift and manifold honour. But the Beloved of the Gods does not think so much of a gift and honour as that there should be a growth of the essential among men of all sects. . . .

Coming together of the sects is therefore commendable in order that they may hear and desire to hear one another's Teaching. For this is the desire of the Beloved of the Gods, that all sects shall be well informed and conducive of good.

And those who are favourably disposed towards this or that sect shall be informed: the Beloved of the Gods does not so much think of gift or honour as that there may be a growth of the essential among all sects and also mutual appreciation.

Asoka (Rock Edict XII, 3rd century)

DO NOT WORRY

God is our Great Parent; do not worry but believe in him.

Bunjiro (1814–1883)

Index

compiled by Dennis J. Nisbet, Member, Society of Indexers

279

280